Hitchhiking through Asperger Syndrome

Lise Pyles

Foreword by Tony Attwood

Jessica Kingsley Publishers
London and Philadelphia

First published in the United Kingdom in 2002 by
Jessica Kingsley Publishers Ltd,
116 Pentonville Road,
London N1 9JB, England
and
325 Chestnut Street,
Philadelphia, PA 19106, USA.

www.jkp.com

Library of Congress Cataloging in Publication Data
A CIP catalog record for this book is available from the Library of Congress

British Library Cataloguing in Publication Data
A CIP catalogue record for this book is available from the British Library

ISBN 1 85302 937 8

Printed and Bound in Great Britain by
Athenaeum Press, Gateshead, Tyne and Wear

Contents

Foreword

I first met Lise and her son at my diagnostic clinic in Brisbane, Australia in October 1998. During the assessment I asked her son to describe himself and he said, 'I like to be alone a lot, solitary, don't really like people that much.' His difficulty understanding and relating to other people was quite conspicuous and typical of a 14-year-old boy with Asperger Syndrome. His description of his mother was remarkably perceptive: 'The type that doesn't get angry easily, has feelings for other people, willing to help people out.' Lise's book is an expression of her feelings for people, especially those with Asperger Syndrome, and thereby provides sound advice for fellow parents. Her story is typical of many parents who have a son or daughter who shares the same profile of abilities as her son. Her own story has a happy ending and Lise recounts her experiences of what has helped or hindered his progress. She states, 'He still has Asperger Syndrome but it doesn't have *him*.' Other parents will want to know the secrets of their success.

Although the book is primarily written for parents, I read the manuscript with my text liner in constant use, highlighting her descriptions and advice and gaining much insight to aid me in my professional role. She provides an explanation of the syndrome in terms that are clear and accurate. Her chapter on coming to terms and moving forward examines many issues that are extremely important for parents. One of the more sensitive issues is that some parents may recognise characteristics of Asperger Syndrome in themselves or other family members.

There are several chapters on schools and educational services. She reviews appropriate services from resources and programs in conventional schools to homeschooling. She also helps parents negotiate the bureaucratic systems from an international perspective, having experience of schools in the United States, United Kingdom and Australia. The strategies to facilitate inclusion will be especially valuable to educators. Parents will also benefit from ideas to resolve conflict with school authorities. She describes the problems the child can encounter such as bullying, social exclusion, and coping with sensory aspects of the classroom environment and difficulties with particular school subjects. Many parents contemplate the option of homeschooling and a whole chapter is devoted to providing an explanation of the benefits and costs of homeschooling. There are two contentious treatments for children with Asperger Syndrome, namely medication and changing diet. Lise provides advice from her personal experiences and further information to help parents make their own decisions. One of the purposes in writing the book was to encourage parents to trust their instincts. She writes as a mentor, companion and navigator, providing information and options, and generates a positive attitude in the reader. A positive attitude and mutual understanding are essential ingredients for success.

Lise answers parents' questions and raises issues they may not have considered, such as the financial costs of services and adjustments to the family budget. Potential hazards are identified with solutions or detours using humorous examples and quotations. One I will remember is when her son was asked 'What is your definition of Hell?' He replied, 'Surprises.' His answer is a surprise for those who have yet to understand the nature of Asperger Syndrome. This book will help parents achieve that understanding and become not only more knowledgeable, but empowered in their ability to achieve real progress.

Tony Attwood
Brisbane 2001

Acknowledgements

A major thrust of this book is that a great deal can be accomplished to improve the circumstances of a child with Asperger Syndrome without a lot of help from outside agencies or a great deal of financial outlay. For that reason, in writing this book I have specifically tried to go 'within' our family's experience to show how it can be done, rather than reaching out to many other organizations, books, experts, or resources. Still, no one lives in a vacuum nor accomplishes much in life without help along the way. The same can be said for the writing of this book. Therefore, I would like to acknowledge several people for their contributions in encouragement, morale boosting, thoughtful comments, and practical assistance.

Liane Holliday Willey has been a considerable force behind this project, prodding me into undertaking it in the first place and giving me the courage to say what I want to say. I would like to thank my father for helping me believe I could be a writer, and my mother, who gave me great footing on the parenting path. I owe my husband Bill deep gratitude for his support over all of our years together. And I would like to thank my younger son Jay for putting up with my many hours at the keyboard. He gave up a lot of Monopoly games for this. I would especially like to thank my older son John for allowing me to tell his story. It takes a lot of courage and kindness to open one's life up to help the lives of others.

Finally, I'm indebted to many other people for being an inspiration to me and for making our road easier in so many ways. I would especially like to thank Bonnie Grimaldi, Paul Shattock, Tony Attwood, Barb Kirby, Cafi Cohen, Laurie Peckham, Deb Reynolds, Steve Zucker, Kerry Haynes, Holly Woodhouse, Allison Kelly, Kathleen Bigham, and the Dave Cooper family. I would also like to acknowledge the profound impact made on my life by two people who are now deceased – educator John Holt, and my dear friend, Lana Hayward.

Preface

I wrote this book for three reasons. First, there are many books on the subject of Asperger Syndrome but few with a mom or dad's day-to-day viewpoint – the straight scoop, so to speak. When I discussed my book plans two years ago with Dr. Tony Attwood, a world-renowned expert on Asperger Syndrome who also diagnosed my son, he said, 'This is what parents need. If you've been down the path, you can then, almost as a scout, come back and say what it was like and what helped and what didn't help. I think that's what parents find so useful.' In that vein, I hope you, the reader, find this book useful.

The second reason for writing this book is because too many parents of children with Asperger Syndrome (or parents who suspect their child may have it) still feel panicked and helpless. Asperger Syndrome is becoming well known, and various therapies, learning programs, books, schools, and clinics, are out there. The problem is, *where* out there? Parents too often find them to be fragmented, scattered geographically, expensive, or filled up. Many families play some frustrating waiting games trying to find or qualify for services.

Parents need to find ways to work with their special needs child right now, here, today, even when support systems in the community are not in place. Our kids need help in many areas, including communication, sensory issues, motor skills, behavior, and social skills, and it's often tricky to keep outside services going in all these areas for your child. I can almost guarantee that there will be at least some period of time during your long stretch of parenting when your child will be left in the lurch with some or even all of these issues going unaddressed. At those times, you as

11

a parent will feel, 'No one is going to help. It's all up to me.' And you will be correct.

Raising a child with Asperger Syndrome is a rewarding journey, but it can be long and lonely and you will be the navigator. Every child with Asperger Syndrome is different, and each family must chart its own path, mile by mile. It's akin to hitchhiking – you will get lots of rides along the way in the form of help from others, but you will also wear out a lot of your own shoe leather. At least, you should.

Your child will have the brightest future, then, if you think like a hitchhiker. You will want to be on the lookout for 'rides', which will come to you in the form of therapies, tests, assessments, classes, special services, aides, medications, etc., to help address the many issues of Asperger Syndrome. But a good hitchhiker is wary and discriminating. Some rides come at a price, move too fast or slow, take detours, or dump you out on the shoulder just when you start to doze. So don't doze. Keep focused on your child and where you want to head, and then be prepared to get out and walk long distances on foot.

There are other authors and agencies that can tell you about the various outside services that may be available to you. My aim, the third reason for writing this book, is to talk about those long distances between rides. I called this book *Hitchhiking Through Asperger Syndrome* because hitchhiking is exactly how our family endured. When our son was young and facing so many challenges, not only were there no books on Asperger Syndrome, it hadn't been coined as a term. There were no tailored therapies, support groups, or websites. Nevertheless, our son made terrific improvements over the years and is today doing beautifully, as you will see in Chapter 1.

We tried many things – special education, mainstream, homeschool, public school, private school, medication, diet, and vitamins. As if life weren't interesting enough, we also lived in three different countries during this time (US, UK, and Australia). That taught us that location was not nearly so important as our attitude; we could make progress anywhere; and in most cases the quality of help we received had less to do with money spent or diplomas of people involved, and more to do with the good hearts of regular folks. For us, the things that helped the most were the things that we did ourselves. Most of them were free or cheap. The best things we did were to not wait for others to come to our rescue, and to refuse to believe people who spoke bleakly about our son's future. A positive attitude and persistence can do a lot.

Even though this entire book may be as homely and unsophisticated as your grandma's recipe box, it has ideas that work and that you can use now. When I hear of families in distress today as they wait months for services, pay huge sums of money for private therapies, move house just to access programs, or have to take school districts to court for services not rendered, I think that the roll-up-your-sleeves-and-do-it-yourself method may be worth a mention. I'm only sorry that many parents today feel at the mercy of the experts about every little thing. Basic knowledge about Asperger Syndrome can be learned for the price of a book or two, and after that you are the true expert, because you know your child.

The last thing that I want to mention here is Time. You have a finite amount of it. American humorist Will Rogers once said, 'You can be on the right track but if you don't move you're going to get run over.' This day must count. Put that message on your mirror, in your wallet, on the inside of your coffee cup – wherever you will see it. I'll say it again. This day must count. It is fatally easy to become convinced that only experts know what to do and if you just wait long enough for the experts (to call you back, to fit you into their schedule, to write their report, to start the program they promised) all will be well. I'm here to tell you that you cannot afford the time. Your child will be another day older tomorrow, but how has waiting for a phone call helped him?

If you know or suspect that your child has Asperger Syndrome and you are not getting enough support from outside sources, do not panic but start reading. There are things that you can do, today, with no money, to understand your Asperger child and help him, no matter where in the world you live. You may find my opinions blunt and low tech (not to mention devoid of technical jargon that seems designed to make parents feel stupid), but my homespun suggestions might just work. At least they are in your hands at this very second and ready to go.

In the words of Teddy Roosevelt, 'Do what you can, with what you have, where you are.' Exactly.

Chapter 1

Our Story

In 1984, John was born exactly on his due day. That should have been a sign that this child would defy the norm. According to my doctor, babies born on their due dates are a statistical oddity.

John was an easy baby. He rarely cried, rarely needed to be comforted, and kept himself amused by the hour. I've since learned that babies who have autistic tendencies seem to come in one of two varieties – rarely crying or always crying. The only thing that upset John – *really* upset him – was when we uncovered his legs to change his diapers or undress him for a bath. For those few minutes you'd have thought we were abusing him, and nothing would comfort him but covering him up again as quickly as possible.

John's infancy seemed as happy as any child's and, new parents that we were, we didn't guess anything was amiss. He got his vaccinations and his 'well baby checks' on time, had a good appetite, was in the ninetieth percentile for height and weight, and met most of the normal milestones.

We did notice that he never really crawled. He seemed to go from creeping inchworm style to walking. We also noticed that he was a bit late in talking. I remember worrying about this, and I specifically recall counting the number of words he could say by age two and being relieved that he just made the magic number that my pediatrician had given us. John didn't seem much interested in doing the two-word sort of talking. Similar to walking, he seemed to skip a stage, going from single words to talking full sentences. I do remember his first word. It was 'yee-ite' (light).

John was fascinated with lights. When he was only a month or two old and sitting in a baby carrier on the kitchen table, his dad Bill gently swung the light above him, letting it twirl a little. John was entranced. His whole body went rigid, his face contorted, and one arm twisted in an odd little posture. He held his breath for a second, then would let it out and relax, before doing it all again. His whole body was electric with delight.

Anything that thrilled our new baby thrilled us. Babies are rather tame to watch when they spend the lion's share of their days eating and sleeping, so a genuine expression of excitement was a lot of fun.

I think it is rather ironic now. I look back on those days when we saw that funny little posture in infancy, that fixation on something that was neither human nor the typical toy, his absorbing interest to the exclusion of almost everything else. Today researchers are more skilled at recognizing autistic disorders in quite young infants, and I have to think that the signs were there. We just didn't know it.

Lights continued to fascinate our young son. We have videos of John in T-shirt and diaper, standing on the third step of our split-level house, the only stair step from which he could reach the wall light switch. On. Off. On. Off. Every few clicks he would stop and do his spasmodic body language. We thought it charming. Again, it may have been a sign. Looking back, I can see many, many signs of autistic tendencies, but of course at that time we'd never heard of autism or Asperger Syndrome and thought our baby was just unique and wonderful. He was, of course.

Sensory anomalies often (not always) accompany Asperger Syndrome. The flickering of lights had an allure to John that bordered on the obsessive. Spinning objects also held his interest – ceiling fans, spinning toys, rotary lawn sprinklers. And water – not the wetness of it but the play of sunshine in it (which we only learned after years and years).

Not all children on the autistic spectrum are attracted to lights and fans, of course. Other items which may fascinate could be vacuum cleaners, vents, heating ducts, license plates, drains, bumpers, tires, sticks, door knobs, coat hangers or any number of other things. The list is long and varied. What is typical though is that the item of choice is often something utilitarian instead of a toy. If the child does play with toys, he may play with them somewhat unusually, perhaps lining them up or playing with just one part (perhaps the wheel or the handle of a toy) rather than using the toys in imaginary play. In any case, once an interest begins (whether Thomas the Tank Engine or Hoover the vacuum cleaner), it can often dominate the child's attention to an unusual degree.

I didn't spend a whole lot of time focusing on these little oddities though. This was just a personality quirk, I thought, and all kids have their idiosyncrasies, don't they?

Throughout most of this, I'd been working in an office job. I'd gone back to work as soon as John had turned six weeks old in fact (John didn't seem to mind), and Bill was ably in charge at home. This suited everyone until around the time that John was two and a half, when Bill also went to work outside the home and John began daycare.

The daycare manager gave us our first wake-up call about John's differences. She complained that he'd bitten other kids and his talking was antisocial – a lot of talk about pumpkins and witches. The biting seemed like typical kid stuff to me, and the talk we attributed to Halloween and a recent viewing of *Wizard of Oz* on TV. The thing was, though, John couldn't switch topics. In fact, at Christmas these were still his favorite topics.

Daycare was not satisfied with my explanations and referred us to a federally mandated (but state-run) program for assessment. Its purpose was to identify 'at risk children' and get them into early intervention programs. And so it was that, at age three, my John ignored, rebelled, and occasionally cooperated his way through several assessment tests. I have repressed most of that from my memory at this point (it was an awful day), but I know there were tests of motor skills, language comprehension, identifying pictures, sequencing, and several other things.

I remember crying by the end of the day. Surely my child should have been able to do these things! At home, when just he and I were together, he could say his colors; he could answer questions and follow simple directions. Couldn't he? I honestly wasn't sure what he could and couldn't do by this point, but I felt like we were being blindsided. I kept thinking to myself, if I'd *known* a certain thing was going to be on the test, I'd have made sure to teach him that! But as much as I wanted to blame my parenting, there were oddities that were difficult to explain. Once when the tester pointed to a picture of a teacup, John said calmly, 'spider'. Why would he do that? (The tester explained that instead of looking at the whole teacup, he had focused on a tiny pattern on the cup that was a spidery-looking flower.)

Because my bright and curious boy got low marks on every test, he was given a place in an early intervention preschool funded by the state. As the therapist expressed it, even if John did know some of this stuff, the fact that he wouldn't answer (and ultimately barked, growled, giggled, and crawled under furniture) was a flag something was going on with him. We agreed to the special class.

It was a good environment for him. He remained there for two years. It was here that I learned about sensory integration disorder. This had to do with difficulties John had with sounds, lights, smells, and tactile sensations (taste seemed to present less of a problem, although he was and is finicky about creamy textured foods). Sensory integration disorder explained many idiosyncrasies – why he liked to have his legs covered as a baby, and why as a youngster he chose to wear long soft clothing even on hot days, even having his hood up unless I fussed at him to pull it down. His tactile defensiveness also explained why he panicked to feel his hands messy with anything gooey. It explained why he complained about the smell of the school bus, why walking into a grocery store brought out the worst in him. Perhaps it even explained his fascination with lights and fans, fireworks, and water fountains. He complained about sunlight but seemed to crave the visual input of flashing light and dark. Sensory integration was only one of the problems John was having, but it seemed to touch every aspect of his day.

John went to the special preschool in the mornings and was bused to an after-school daycare program in the afternoons. Daycare was tough on him. This didn't make sense to me. Daycare was loose and unstructured so it should be easier, I thought! I now know that less structured times are overwhelming for kids with Asperger Syndrome. Rather than playing with other kids, each afternoon he would be found in self-imposed (or sometimes teacher-imposed) exile, facing away from the kids. He often had a blanket draped over his head.

It was not long before the daycare staff suggested that John 'did not really fit in with their program' and would need to find another daycare. That was the first of four we were asked to leave over the next couple of years. Each time, I cried my eyes out. They had rejected this little person that I loved, and my bottom-of-the-barrel inadequacy as a mom was now confirmed. Each new daycare meant another anxiety-producing period of adjustment for John.

Preschool went well. Besides sensory integration disorder, testing had surfaced motor issues, language issues, visual and auditory processing deficits, and an IQ score on the border of mental retardation. I felt that last one was wrong and told the psychologist so, but I had no answers for anything else. After two years of the special preschool, we were invited to a meeting and told that John should go to kindergarten in a self-contained class somewhere else in the district. John never did go to his local neighborhood school.

There were just four or five kids in the new class, which was in a very small trailer behind the grade school. It was quiet and clean and very structured and it had its own private bathroom. John was there for kindergarten and also first grade. Throughout this timeframe, the plan was that John would gradually work toward attending a regular mainstream kindergarten, staying for increasingly long periods. This never worked. Each day, the teacher's aide guided him down to the regular classroom. Each day, John made noises, crawled under desks, disrupted the class with giggles or growls or conversely had a tantrum. Defeated, John and the aide would retreat back to the little classroom, where John would try to pull himself back together again.

I'm ashamed to say how long this went on. The teachers, geared to dealing with children with behavioral or emotional delays, were sure John was manipulating them. I assumed they knew what they were doing – wrong! John's behavior and emotions were out of control, but we know that this stemmed from sensory, social, and communication delays. It was not about willful behaviour. John simply couldn't – *couldn't* – cope with the larger classroom. Trying to force it was as hopeless as trying to force someone into speaking Swahili. Whether you try to coerce, bribe, use smiley face behavior charts, token systems, or withhold privileges – if that person doesn't know Swahili, he can't speak it! For John, fitting into a classroom was as foreign as speaking Swahili. It couldn't just happen.

Of course, at that point, no one knew what Asperger Syndrome was. We didn't understand the social deficits John was experiencing, and so we spent all that time trying to force our agenda on him, looking *at* him rather than through his eyes. We did our best in our ignorance, but now that I have the advantage of hindsight and knowledge of Asperger Syndrome, I realize it wasn't even close to being what he needed.

Besides the school assessments, we also tried to get him diagnosed medically, hoping some sort of medication would help. We went to the Children's Hospital in Denver for a comprehensive session with a pediatric neurologist. They also did a blood work-up (looking for Fragile X or metabolic disorders) and an electroencephalogram (EEG, looking for epilepsy). Eventually we saw a psychiatrist too.

The neurologist gave us the diagnosis 'Attention Deficit Disorder with mild autistic features.' Now, I was willing to believe the Attention Deficit Disorder (ADD) part, because John would get fixated on his own projects and had great difficulty transitioning to anything the teacher wanted him to do, but when I read a pamphlet on autism, it talked only about totally unreachable kids who were lost in their own worlds and who didn't communicate. Balderdash! John talked and liked being with us. I threw out the possibility that there was any autism going on (in spite of seeing a few of the signs on the checklist) and forgot about it. If only the neurologist had taken the time to explain things better.

At that time, we were getting disgusted with assessments in general. I was glad to have the test results, but we, especially my husband, soon got the idea that we were living out the old adage, 'when all you have is a hammer, everything looks like a nail.' It seemed to us that every specialist found something wrong that was always conveniently right in his area of expertise. The physical therapist found motor problems. The language therapist uncovered language deficits. Nobody ever said, 'no problem here.' Between the school and the doctor, John had received the following labels: gross motor deficits, fine motor deficits, expressive language problems, sensory integration problems, poor muscle tone, mid-line problems, mild Tourette Syndrome, ADD with autistic traits, minimal brain disorder, and borderline mental retardation. How could all of this get packed into one kid?

It was all very discouraging. The chaotic mix of so many different labels was not only hard on morale, it didn't seem to make sense. We were looking for a single problem to explain John's difficulties, but instead of zeroing in on anything specific, we were pointed in a dozen different directions.

At least the neurologist put John on Ritalin. It had an immediate and positive effect. John was more manageable, the teachers were thrilled, and we finally felt like we were making some progress. It was unfortunate that John did not like the way that he felt physically when he was on Ritalin – he had insomnia, loss of appetite, afternoon headaches, and also a number of nose-bleeds that may or may not have been related. Still, it seemed a small price to pay.

And so, we limped along. At least we solved one problem in John's favor. After getting dumped out of the fourth daycare, Bill and I finally realized that going to school *and* after-school daycare were clearly too much for him to cope with. I tendered my resignation from a thirteen-year career and became a stay-at-home mom. By this time we had another son who was just over a year old, and I wanted to be home for him too, so that made the decision even easier. It was a huge step financially, though. At the time I quit work my paycheck was larger than my husband's, but it was a great investment in our family and one that we have never regretted.

John continued to have good days and bad days at school. He had fewer tantrums while medicated, but by second grade he still couldn't handle a mainstream classroom and hated school as much as ever. He was developing tics (facial grimacing, eye-blinking) and was becoming increasingly aware of his lack of success at school. The kids at school made sure he knew it. He asked me what a 'retard' was after he'd been told he rode the 'retard bus'. Because he was in a special classroom that combined kids of various ages, John was also the youngest child in his class. He concluded he was not only dumb, but 'the dumbest kid in the dumb class.' I cannot tell you how heartbreaking hearing that was, but as terrible as I felt, how must John have felt?

It's to his credit that he even got out of bed every day and went off to school like a soldier doing battle. I don't know if he felt there was no option, but he never used guile to fake an illness like some kids do. He was told he had to go, just like his dad went off to work. Off he went.

And then one day he met two neighbor girls that didn't go to school. This fascinated him so much that he talked about it daily and one day boldly asked them about it. He found out that they were homeschoolers and at that moment he had a new obsessive topic. 'Can we homeschool too? Why can't we homeschool too?'

Although it's common now, I had never heard of homeschooling. It was a subject John wouldn't let drop, however. Eventually I chatted with the girls' mom and she answered my many questions. Was it legal? Did I have to have a teaching degree? Could I handle it? She assured me that I could legally teach my child, but since she had a teaching degree herself, I still came away feeling that this was an option for other people, not us.

Soon after that John's teacher informed me that John's special education class would soon be getting larger and including more serious behavior problems. She worried about John in that environment. She knew it didn't fit him (since he was not behaviorally or emotionally delayed, at least not in the typical sense), but there was nothing else in the school district that came close to filling his needs. She had no answers, but I was grateful for the heads-up. Coincidentally, my husband was in line for a possible new job in England, and the thought of trying to start over in a new school district, in a new *country*, scared me silly. Suddenly homeschooling was worth a second look. At least it was portable.

The fog really lifted, though, during a conversation with the school psychologist one day. I was lamenting that John's academic progress seemed stalled and he was falling further and further behind. The psychologist said, 'John just seems like a puppy learning to stay. Every ounce of concentration is wrapped up in just *being* in the classroom, in staying put when his instincts are telling him to run away. There is nothing left in him for academics.'

It was an 'Aha!' moment. Things crystallized. That was it exactly. Bill and I talked it over and decided that teaching him at home might be better. We reasoned it couldn't do any worse. We felt the school system had had nearly five years (two years of preschool, then kindergarten through most of second grade) to figure how to make things work for John and now it was our turn.

We informed the school that John would be withdrawn from school and set the date, March 4, 1992 (March forth! I told myself) for our first day of homeschool. Oh gosh, it was scary.

By starting just a couple of months before the end of the school year, I left myself an escape hatch. If it didn't work we would go back to school in the fall and hope no one really noticed our little break. Instead, we ended up homeschooling for the next three years.

Homeschooling was hard work but it was *good* work. It was also positive work that built on successes, work that kept the pressure low but interest high, and work that John and I came to enjoy. I was daunted by the prospect of having John with me twenty-four hours a day, but it was easier than sending him to school had been. We heard no more bad news, no more feelings of constant failure. I was grateful never to have to drive to the school to pick up a tantrumming child and seeing him so distressed. Life was more affirmative. I no longer dreaded answering the phone!

I will talk more about the mechanics of homeschooling in Chapter 7 of this book but to give you a summary, after the inevitable rocky start, we had an excellent first year that brought about many changes. We found a good homeschool support group, a good bookstore, and even a small teacher supply store. I also had my eyes opened to the writings of John Holt and began to worry less about the mechanics of 'school' (worksheets, grades, busywork, ticking off each curriculum item) and began to focus more on instilling a joy in learning.

One month into our homeschooling adventure, we took John off Ritalin. We reasoned that homeschooling gave John less stress, more reasonable expectations and less sensory input, so he probably didn't need it as much. We experimented for one day without it, then a second, and then stuck the bottle of pills in the back of the cupboard, never to be used again.

Being home all day allowed me to work with John's diet too. I'd read about foods that can interfere with ability to focus and behave, and I began a food journal and a series of homespun experiments. With lots of false starts and frustrations, we discovered that some foods were in fact interfering. Eliminating them evened out John's mood somewhat and improved behavior. More about that in Chapter 9.

Since we made so many changes in a short time span, it's difficult to tease apart which actions caused which effects, but the combination of homeschooling, dropping medication, and changing diet worked together to cause a profound change in John. The progress was gradual and full of hiccups (two steps forward, one step back) but it was unmistakable. After years of no progress and even sometimes regression, seeing John make dramatic gains was the thrill of a lifetime. Having him home all the time also helped us better understand him. We didn't have the label of Asperger Syndrome, but we came to know John and how he operated, and that was by far more important.

After one year of homeschooling, we did follow my husband's career to lovely England. The countryside, with its stone churches, purple moors, village squares, and rippling brooks, was picturesque. If you've ever seen the movie *The Secret Garden* or the TV series, James Herriott's *All Creatures Great and Small*, you've seen the landscape we saw each day that we put on our wellies (English rubber boots) and took a walk.

Our new location meant that we added other experiences to our homeschooling – picking wild berries, watching the new lambs, shopping at the market stalls in the villages, dickering at Sunday boot sales (flea markets), and exploring castles, abbeys, and museums. John's little brother was old enough to enjoy it too. It should have been perfect.

However, the support I'd come to rely on in Colorado (homeschoolers' group and bookstores) was sorely missed in our rural home. The only support group I found was too religious for us, so we participated only occasionally. We learned too, that in order to get all that spectacular landscape, it has to rain – a lot.

This was also the land of the Brontë sisters. We often drove past the estate where locals said that Charlotte Brontë had once been a depressed and lonely governess. I knew how she felt. You can imagine that homeschooling took a downturn. Internet was in its infancy, and the teaching materials I'd brought were getting stale. *I* was getting stale. There is a rule of thumb in home-schooling that three years is the 'burn out' point for many homeschoolers. Maybe we ran smack up against that.

The other side of it, though, is that John's academics had blossomed so much that his questions were getting tough. He wanted to know chemistry, electronics, and other things I didn't know. My confidence started to flag. In spite of reading accounts from other homeschoolers to the contrary, I began to wonder if I was somehow doing John a disservice by keeping him out of the public school. After all, we only worked for about three hours every morning. What if what I'd assumed was good progress was mere illusion, and he had really fallen impossibly behind his peers? I had taken him out of school for his own good, but perhaps now I should put him back in?

As it happened, we had access to a very small and well-funded school affiliated with a US military base. The student–teacher ratio was 18 to 1 and it had a cozy atmosphere, with only two main hallways and a total of 180 or so pupils. I reasoned that if ever we wanted to see John cope in a regular classroom, this might be the proving ground. It felt like a fork in the road for us and an opportunity not to be missed.

John was wary of going to school, but also curious. I think school felt like the horse he had fallen off years ago, and he was scared of it, but three years of successful work had convinced him that he had come far, and I think there was a part of him that wanted to get on that horse and ride this time. I assured him that we could do it as an experiment. If it didn't work out or he didn't like it, we'd go right back to homeschooling. With that under-standing, we arranged to visit the school and also had him tested during the summer. He was at grade level, a little behind in reading but three years ahead in math!

The first day of sixth grade, he got on the school bus and never looked back. I waited with my heart in my throat for the phone to ring, to hear that John was having a meltdown and that the experiment had reached a major hitch, but the phone didn't ring. He made it that day, the next, and every day that year. My boy, who had *never once* made it through a regular school day in a regular classroom, was now surviving in school in all regular classes. The difference was, this time he was ready. We'd given him the time he needed.

There were challenges, of course. He had to learn terms he'd never heard before — attendance sheets, field trip, tardy, permission slip, hall pass, test monitors, chaperones, bleachers. He had to figure out his school locker, how to follow a class schedule (this was sixth grade but changed classes as in junior high), and find his way around the school.

Sixth grade was a watershed year in many respects. John later called it 'the year I found my brain.' He had always felt like he couldn't compete with other kids when he'd been in special education and although he'd begged me to homeschool, my taking him out of school probably also confirmed the feeling that he'd failed at it. It really bothers me to say that, since I worked so hard on combating feelings of inadequacy in whatever way I could as we homeschooled. I knew and had known all along how bright he was, and I had always told him that he hadn't failed school, school had failed him — a very true statement.

But as much as I talked about these things, it was still just mom talking. The bar he felt he had to jump was not one that was held by parents but by his peers. And when he got to sixth grade and found that he *could* compete with the other kids, a weighty burden lifted. He was jubilant to know — to see for himself — that he was capable. From that aspect, sixth grade was a tremendous success.

In other ways, I regretted my decision. The bullies soon found their victim. Anyone with Asperger Syndrome has a bull's eye plastered on his chest. My son soon found himself ostracized and ridiculed just for being himself. He was poked with umbrellas, stolen from repeatedly, and on and on. The most heartbreaking incident was when John told me that a group of kids had voted that John should kill himself. Another time, an entire busload of kids sang 'Joy to the World, when John is dead.' It was during this year that he was invited to a birthday party (only the second party invitation of his life), only to have the birthday boy tell John not to come – he had invited him only because his mother made him. What a sad night that was, as my son sat at the kitchen table with his present already bought and wrapped, trying to decide whether to go to the party or not.

While John endured abuse on the playground, I fought the school. John's English teacher saw right away what kind of unique person he was, and did her best to protect him and guide him. John said her class was the only class where kids didn't bother him. She and I agreed he needed some supports, and she recommended further testing which would lead to an individual-ized education plan (IEP: the blueprint for getting anything done). I agreed with this, but it never happened.

By now this was 1995 and Asperger Syndrome had come into existence the previous year as an official diagnosis. News of it had reached the Internet, and I had tripped over it. It was a true 'Eureka!' moment. The hair raised on the back of my neck as I read symptom after symptom, mentally ticking off each one, as nearly all the puzzle pieces of John's unique existence fell into place. The kaleidoscope bits that had floated around us for so long – the tactile problems, motor clumsiness, social difficulties, perseverative interests – *everything* slid into sharp focus. The relief was immense.

But what did it mean to the school? Nothing. No one had heard of Asperger Syndrome, and my problem was that John was not behind academically. If he'd been behind in math or reading, then he could have had some help. But he was behind in areas like social skills and communication skills; he didn't fit any mold they recognized.

I remember arriving at school for a meeting (where John's deficits would ultimately be waved away as not their problem) and through the school's office window I could see my son on the playground. Completely overstimulated, he was doing his self-stimulation thing, flapping a stick and staring at it. Sometimes he wandered up to a group of kids and would moments later be buffeted away, like a pinball hitting bumpers. Mostly he walked in circles. When the special education specialist walked in, I nearly pounced on her. '*How* can you say he doesn't need help?' I'm sure my voice quivered in anger and frustration. He needed an aide, social skills, moral support, or maybe a bodyguard – *something*! He needed a way of fitting in.

But they only knew certain pigeonholes and John didn't fit them. I knew even as they gave me the malarkey on why they couldn't give him any services, most of it was wrong and even illegal, but it didn't change the outcome a bit. They weren't budging, officially. Unofficially, they offered some one-on-one counseling and a couple other minor things. It helped. The only other thing I could do was to put John onto an incredibly long waiting list for more testing at the other end of the country, so that I could win a label for him that they couldn't ignore. We ended up moving long before our turn came up.

Meanwhile, John carried on as best he could. He enjoyed the classes, especially the stimulation of listening to his teachers, and felt absolute joy at discovering he could do the same work his peers were doing, but the friends he had planned on making in school did not materialize, and bullies seemed to outnumber even the neutral kids. He was alone outside of a couple of short-lived instances of having an occasional lunch or bus companion. School made him too busy and stressed to keep up with the swimming lessons and running that he'd done while we were homeschooling, so he even lost those positive experiences. And he began to get stressed and depressed.

As things went into a downward spiral, I would find him just sitting, wondering why he was born, and what was the point of living. It scared me. Was it all the depressing rain or had school done this? Sometimes he would get frustrated enough to injure himself. He might punch his fist on his thigh repeatedly, hit himself in the head, or bend his finger backward until I thought the poor finger would break. I suspected that part of the upset was some food reaction to Christmas candy, but the depression itself was something larger and more brooding than I had witnessed with food problems.

It did not take much of this before I decided to turn to professional help – or tried, anyway. The only psychologist available to us was not used to working with children, however. She'd also never heard of Asperger Syndrome, and did not want to listen to anything about it. I tried to tell her about his diet and also some interesting research studies I'd just found about vitamins (B6 especially) but she brushed that off very fast. I could see she thought I was a lunatic even to suggest that behavior and mood could possibly be improved by modifying diet or vitamin intake. She dismissed me to talk to John alone. When she called me back in, she announced, 'There's nothing wrong with him. He just needs some friends.'

To this day, I wish I'd had presence of mind to ask her just where I should find those mythical friends. Was there a catalog where some good ones might be ordered? Instead, I asked her if she would come to the school and observe how he interacted with his classmates firsthand so she could see what the real problem was. I told her that I'd spoken with the school counselor about starting a social skills group. She promised to call the school the following week and never did.

If you are getting the picture that services for Asperger Syndrome were hard to define and hard to find, you see what we were up against. The situation was worse back when we were going through this, but it's still no picnic. The syndrome is not readily visible, and it doesn't fit the behavioral or academic molds schools are traditionally set up for. Services are improving in pockets of society thanks to the untiring efforts of parents who are mad as hell and not willing to take it any longer, but it's still fair to say, there is a long way to go.

So I got busy and did what I could about John's depression myself. I put in an order for some mega-vitamins specifically formulated for the autistic population and heavy on the B6 and other B vitamins and magnesium. Over Christmas break I began John on the regimen.

In January, one week into the new school term, John's depression disappeared. His teacher even noticed. I will talk more about the specific vitamin regimen John uses in Chapter 9, but he still takes vitamins five years later and continues to benefit.

The only other notable event in our last year in England was that we were able to partake in a couple of university research projects having to do with autism and metabolism. We had known for years through our homespun experimentation and crude food journals that diet made a difference, but now, four years after we had begun these dietary quests, we had the chance to pit our experience against scientific study. It was all interesting information, and I will talk about these research studies too; the most interesting thing was that the studies really only verified the same diet we had figured out for ourselves. Having the verification and scientific theory behind it is nice, but if we had waited for the tests, it would have cost us four years. I do not think we did anything remarkable working these things out on our own. I have since talked with many other parents who have managed to do the same thing.

After John's sixth grade (1996), we moved back to the US. We spent six weeks in a hotel, house hunting mostly. It was miserable. Our hotel room was burglarized, our car caught fire and burned up, our credit card was frozen due to a computer glitch, and a house deal fell through. It seemed the States did not want us back.

When my husband came back to the hotel room one day and announced that we had the chance to go overseas again, it seemed like a reasonable idea. In the space of a lunch hour, the family took a vote and decided to move to Australia.

But it was another three months before we moved. Meanwhile, I enrolled the kids into school. This was a serious mistake. Within two weeks, John had been bullied and harassed. His clothes were the wrong cut and the wrong brands. He didn't fit in. He was distressed by the loud music on the school bus, the overcrowding, and when he told me someone had threatened his life, promising to cut him to ribbons the following week, I pulled both boys out of school and went back to homeschooling.

Australia is where we live now. We've been here four years. John attends private school and thrives. We've had our bullying incidents and life's challenges here and there, but it's been the best time of his life so far. I will talk more about this school and what has made it successful, in later sections of the book.

Today John is seventeen. He is in twelfth grade and is doing well. He has been a student representative on the student council, organized the school bowling team, and is a House Officer. He has taken part in music festivals, a play, and been on the social dance decoration committee. He skipped ninth grade entirely. Not bad for a kid who was supposedly mentally retarded and destined to spend his whole school career in self-contained special education.

In life beyond the schoolroom walls, he has become a terrific bowler. Besides winning several trophies over the years, he was the 2000 Northern Territory champion bowler for his age division (roughly equivalent to becoming a state champion in the US).

He also drives a car, has had babysitting and mowing jobs, has worked the odd job down at the bowling alley and hopes to get a real part-time job soon. Most importantly to John and also to me, he has found the ability to make friends. His social life is not lively compared to many of his peers, but it ticks along at a level that is comfortable for him. At the age of thirteen he met his first real friend, a classmate who became his best friend. Both avid bowlers and pizza lovers, they have kept up their friendship even though the other boy has since moved back to the US. Last summer, John was able to travel halfway around the world (alone) in order to see his friend. For someone with Asperger Syndrome, this accomplishment of maintaining true friendship is probably greater than any other.

Now I've brought you up to the present. I've shown you a boy who was handed a half dozen devastating labels, who was shuffled off to inappropriate special ed classrooms, who could not cope, who flapped and answered questions with bizarre responses, who was thought to be retarded, clumsy, and deficient in every area, who needed medication just to get through the day. And I've shown you a boy who will have a bright future. He still has Asperger Syndrome but it doesn't have *him*.

The rest of this book details how he got from one point to the other and tells of lessons learned, both from our family and occasionally from other families who have followed similar paths. I don't think our family is all that special, really. There are many other families who can tell tales similar to our experience.

The purpose of this book is not to tell you what to do in your own circumstances but simply to convince you that you can trust your own instincts and find your own path, and to offer some ideas on places to look for it. This book is not a map but I hope it may help serve as a compass as you hitchhike your own way through Asperger Syndrome.

Chapter 2
What is Asperger Syndrome?

When I searched for answers in the 1980s, Asperger Syndrome was not a diagnosis nor was it known in any English-language literature. Now, information is available, but a lot is still in flux. Researchers are still working out where the edges of Asperger Syndrome lie, and how it overlaps with other conditions.

There are at least three different official criteria used to diagnose Asperger Syndrome, depending on your doctor or the country in which you live. They are all a bit cryptic, in my opinion. Far more readable and illuminating is a scale (Garnett and Attwood 1995) for use by parents, called Australian Scale for Asperger Syndrome. (see Appendix 1 for this helpful scale and for the names of the most popular diagnostic criteria and how to find them.)

A child with Asperger Syndrome is affected in a number of areas, the prime three being problems with social situations, problems with communication, and poor imagination. Keeping in mind that no child will display every characteristic, here is a more detailed definition compiled from several sources:

> The child with Asperger Syndrome is socially awkward, has difficulty making or keeping friends and he is generally egocentric and lacking, or seeming to lack, empathy or ability to see the other person's point of view. Communication may be literal. Thinking may be black and white and lack imagination (or show unusual imagination). Speech and language skills may seem somewhat odd compared with peers. That is, speech may

seem formal or pedantic (teacher-like), or may sound somewhat unusual. Nonverbal communication is lacking, so that the child misses or misreads nonverbal signals (gestures, body language, facial expression) and is ineffectual or limited in sending them. Personal interests (collections, hobbies, preoccupations) may be unusual in subject and/or narrow in range and/or pursued intensely. In addition, the child may gravitate to or take comfort in routines, rituals, and repetition and be upset by surprises. Intelligence, however, is average or better, and initial language acquisition is within norms. There may be abnormal reactions to sensory stimuli (i.e. have acute sensitivity to light, smells, tastes, tactile sensation, or sounds). There is usually, but not always, physical clumsiness.

Now let's look at it piece by piece with a few examples.

Social

The child with Asperger Syndrome is socially awkward, has difficulty making or keeping friends.

Dr. Phil McGraw ('Dr. Phil' of Oprah Winfrey's talk show fame) says about life, 'You either get it, or you don't.' In the world of social interaction, it might be said that children with Asperger Syndrome don't get it. That is, they don't *intuitively* get it. The subtle ways people gain entry into social groups are lost on them. They find it difficult to to use friendly (but not *too* friendly) facial expressions, come up with acceptable topics of conversation, or follow the unwritten rules of making friends. Making a friend is somewhat of an art and our kids are, to put it a bit harshly, artless.

Difficulties with making friends may not be obvious in early years. Toddlers and preschoolers spend more time playing beside each other than with each other anyway, and our kids may be able to do that all right. Troubles usually start a little later, when children are expected to develop beyond parallel play and start interacting.

If someone has suggested your child might have Asperger Syndrome but you don't see social problems, keep in mind that parents can be slow to pick up on this. At home relationships are predictable and with fewer demands than in a school or playgroup setting. Also, we parents are used to our child's quirks. If junior prattles on for a half hour about light bulbs or hubcaps or Siberian tigers (in our case it was witches and animal traps), the family doesn't think much about it. That perseverative conversation at preschool, though, sets our kids apart. Family life is in most cases easier on an Asperger Syndrome child than the 'real world.' Parents are often the last to know about social problems, then, and it also explains why mom and dad are shocked when their wonderful young child steps out into the world and is soon flattened by the big yellow bus of social convention. Why isn't he getting along? He seems pretty normal at home.

With each year of primary school, the evidence of social deficit sifts in. Play dates don't go well. Your child can't cope in groups, and acts out or retreats to a corner. He may engage in self-stimulating behavior, such as flapping, rocking, or other. It looks odd. Neighborhood kids come over once or twice (a dozen times if you have a pool in your backyard) but don't reciprocate invitations. You may not know what exactly is wrong, but you realize that *something* is.

You may start to get the feeling that all the other kids are in a secret club but your child doesn't know the secret handshake or password to get in. That's really not so far off from reality. Your child really doesn't know the words or gestures that social interaction requires. It can be quite heartbreaking to see your child always on the fringes although you may mind it more than he does.

The good news is that as our children grow older, with education and practice, they do learn social rules. It's just that rather than learning them intuitively, they learn them intellectually.

The really frustrating thing is that our kids often don't display their social deficits in the doctor's office. As wrong-footed as our kids are among their peers, they frequently are able to hold wonderful conversations with doctors, who often find our kids charming. It's almost funny (or it would be if it weren't an expensive time-waster) that many inexperienced doctors reject a diagnosis of Asperger Syndrome because the child is too sociable and talkative. In my mind's eye, I picture a doctor saying, 'He seems fine to me' and then I picture the doctor's own young son spending a few minutes with the patient, tugging at his daddy's sleeve and whispering, 'What's up with that kid?' Our kids can be quite sociable, just ineptly so. It's just one reason why you should make sure that any doctor who sees your child really understands Asperger Syndrome.

As for why our kids have trouble with social skills, that's a big question. Part of it undoubtedly has to do with the way these kids process information, and with their sensory system. Social situations require strengths in areas where our children may be deficient. These areas include being able to imagine or anticipate what the other person is thinking, and also the ability to handle a rapidly dynamic situation. Many social scenes are also very stimulating (too loud, too smelly, too bright, too fast, too *much*) for our Asperger kids' acute sensory systems. This is discussed a bit later.

The other problem with social situations is that they are rarely logical and rules of social engagement are complicated and subtle. For example, one summer my son John decided to make friends by approaching strange kids in the grocery aisles. 'How old are you?' he would ask. If the startled child said the magic answer (eight), John would say, 'OK, we'll be friends then,' and would demand a phone number and ask what day the child could play. At this point I would usually enter the scene and whisk him away with an apologetic smile.

This was confusing to John. *Why* couldn't he make friends that way? I had no simple explanation. It sounded lame to say that grocery stores are not usual friend-making settings, and paranoid to say I might not like the kid's mother. I could have said that being the same age is not a reason to be friends, but schools force friendships in that exact way, don't they?

One benefit of living with a child with Asperger Syndrome is that you will be forced to examine social convention in new ways. After all, why *can't* we just walk up to someone and say, 'Let's be friends' and see where it goes? The world would be a better place if we could. Parenting a child with Asperger Syndrome assures that your own social sense gets a good stretch, and you will start gazing at social niceties with a fresh eye as you are called to consider questions such as these:

- Why can't we show the tip to the waitress and ask her if it is enough?

- If I'm not having a good time at my birthday party, why can't I go watch TV?

- Why can't I laugh at a biker with purple hair? He looks funny, doesn't he?

- Why can't I blow my brother's birthday candles out? Wax is getting on the cake.

- Why can't I flap my paper money around while I'm shopping? I like having it in my hand so I know I have it.

- Why shouldn't I wave my hands in someone's face? They can't ignore me then.

- Why can't I take all the salad? Mrs. S. said I could have all I wanted.

Examining social convention in the light of Asperger logic and honesty is not a bad thing. I sometimes wonder if the child who said 'The Emperor has no clothes!' was one of our kids.

The problem with the above examples, though, is that our children don't usually ask first. They make the inappropriate comment or action and are upset when we defy logic and say, 'Don't do that.' Unfortunately, this is the wrong response because they still won't know what they *should* do or why. Without further guidance, they may continue to use the only script they know. Interestingly, in each of the above examples, the child's action serves his purpose. Flapping one's hands in someone's face *does* get attention, after all. So if a behavior is inappropriate and needs to change, then parents need to give the child a substitute way of behaving that also works, but in a more appropriate way. The child needs a new blueprint, so to speak, and then help in following it.

> The child with Asperger Syndrome is generally egocentric and lacking, or seeming to lack, empathy or ability to see the other person's point of view.

A child with Asperger Syndrome may *seem* extremely self-centered or egocentric. I do not think that it is strictly true however. Certainly all young children have 'me' at the top of their agenda, and since Asperger Syndrome represents a developmental delay, our special kids may be stuck on the 'me thing' for longer than usual. My own son can be very generous and concerned about other people's feelings though, *when he understands them and is given time to process the situation.* I do think that he is baffled by why people do what they do, however, and may not figure it all out until it's too late to react appropriately in the situation. But this is quite different from knowing another person's view and not caring, which is an assumption the outside world often makes. Now that John is older, he has become much more skilled at assessing situations and behaving appropriately.

That was not always so. I remember one morning when John was about seven. I was annoyed about something and sent out many 'bad mood' signals – rushing through breakfast with a sour look, stomping a bit, closing cupboard doors noisily, etc. I wonder now what I was aggravated about, but at the time I just knew that anybody within ten feet of me would know exactly how I was feeling and would know to steer clear. My sweet boy witnessed my behavior for what must have been twenty minutes. Finally he had to ask, 'Are you mad, Mommy?'

I remember this small incident, partly because I regretted acting so cranky, but mostly because I was so surprised. Of course I was mad! Couldn't he see it? His little brother (aged 3) had known to make himself scarce several minutes earlier. He didn't need to be told that mommy was mad – he felt it in his bones. But John had to do it in his head, so it took longer and he had to ask to be sure. It's a small thing really, but it was just one more time when, unaware of Asperger Syndrome, I wanted to throw up my hands and ask, what is it with this kid!

If he had asked me to make pancakes at that moment (he didn't) it would have been easy to convince myself that here was a selfish kid who did not care that others were having problems and only cared about himself. In truth, he just didn't know. The difficulty in seeing the other person's viewpoint, imagining what the other person knows or feels, is sometimes called mind blindness or a Theory of Mind problem.

Communication

> Communication may be literal. Thinking may be black and white and lack imagination (or show unusual imagination).

People with Asperger Syndrome tend to take things literally and at face value. Not surprisingly, common idioms often trip our kids up. Expressions like 'hop to it' or 'shake a leg' may get you a quizzical or confused look. I have to admit that 'keep your eyes peeled' conjures up a literal and graphic picture for me so that I don't use this expression. Judging from my son's shocked face, however, that expression is no more graphic than one I used recently – 'Eat your heart out.' My son was positively repulsed by this and demanded to know just what I was saying!

The thing is, there are so very many of these expressions, and we use them quite unconsciously. Teachers should avoid them. Our kids already have difficulty with communication, and avoiding idioms is one concrete way to ease the strain. I think they are good to use at home, however. The more chances John has to hear various figures of speech, the more likely he will absorb them and begin to use them himself. At home he can ask questions or take the time he needs to process them, a luxury he doesn't have at school. I try to drop one or two into my conversation regularly. (This week it was 'seven ways to Sunday' and 'you have a lot on your plate this week.') I have listed some more expressions at the back of this. Individuals with Asperger Syndrome may enjoy a good online game that consists of guessing the meanings of expressions. Paint by Idioms is at http://www. funbrain.com/kidscenter.html.

Literalness is not restricted to idioms. When John cooks macaroni he has no need to taste it to see if it's done. 'The instructions say seven minutes and it's been seven minutes,' he explains.

Taking the world literally sets our kids up for a fall. Weather forecasters are frequently 'liars' as are parents who say, 'We'll go in just a minute'. In younger years if a mail-order package failed to arrive in five business days (or whatever the company promised), by day six John expected the post office to put a tracer on it or for me to call the company. Waiting longer made no sense to him. 'The company said we would get it in five business days'. Period.

Of course literalness has its lighter side. My son recently told me he'd lost his handing. (Well, a literal kid walking on his hands couldn't say he'd lost his footing, could he?) Literalness extends to the written word. When we recently drove past a business cleverly called 'Boomerang Rentals' my son expressed surprise that people could stay in business renting boomerangs to people. He knew it didn't sound right even as he said it (although we do live in Australia!), but he couldn't make the leap beyond the literal. He also became concerned to see bottled water at the grocery store with the catchy name of 'H$_2$GO'. He feared another chemical element might have been added to the water, and maybe the water was poisonous. The context that the water sat on the grocery shelf next to Perrier and other brands of water could not overcome the concern caused by his literal misinterpretation. A support group friend recently told of his brother-in-law with Asperger Syndrome who decided that he couldn't ride an escalator because of a sign that warned, 'Dogs Must Be Carried on Escalator'. He asked the security guard what to do because he hadn't brought a dog.

Going in another literal direction for a moment, I'm struck by author Temple Grandin's comments on language in her book, *Thinking in Pictures*, that deals with her life with autism. She comments that nouns are more understandable to her than other words. Words like 'under' and 'over' held no meaning when she was a child because there was no concrete word picture to associate (Grandin 1995, p.30). I have suspected that this trouble feeds John's occasional confusion with conversation. Anyone having difficulties explaining something to a child with Asperger Syndrome might do well to add more nouns into the conversation. 'Sit in the chair' is better than 'Sit down'.

> Speech and language skills may seem somewhat odd compared with peers. That is, speech may seem formal or pedantic (teacher-like), or may sound somewhat unusual.

What seems like ordinary everyday conversation is more than just words. The words need to fit the situation, be said in the right order, be said with a tempo and inflection that conveys meaning, and be said in a way that prompts the other person to talk too, in a give-and-take. The child with Asperger Syndrome may have a great vocabulary but it doesn't translate to good conversational skills. Listing types of dinosaurs or talking lengthily *at* someone about a narrow subject is not the same as making good conversation.

Speech pragmatics is that branch of speech therapy concerned with how speech is used to communicate. Some subtopics might be how to begin or join a conversation, take turns, choose a topic, avoid taboo topics, stay on topic, change the topic, repair a conversation, or end the discussion.

Since our kids may have difficulties figuring out what words fit the situation when they speak, it should come as no surprise that they also have trouble listening to speech and deciding how it applies to them. Double meanings, abstract concepts, and reading meaning into the manner in which something is said, all present difficulties.

Let's take the simple phrase, 'Come here.' The person with Asperger Syndrome would likely interpret it in a very factual way, and that shouldn't present much of a problem. However, depending on the inflection, volume, and so forth, it can take on many meanings:

- 'Come here,' whispered means 'Come here quietly'.

- 'Come here!' shouted in a panicky voice means 'Help, I need you'.

- 'Come here,' said with a sigh in the voice, means 'There's a problem'.

- 'Come here!' said very quickly, means 'Come here and hurry up about it'.

- 'Come HERE!' means 'You've gone to the wrong place or aren't moving fast enough'.

- 'Come here,' said to a child who has a knot in his shoelace, means 'Bring your shoe over here and I will fix it for you'.

Looking at just the last example, a child with Asperger Syndrome might easily hear 'Come here,' and obey, but leave his shoe behind because he has missed the implied meaning to bring it. Or he might think it means, 'When you get your shoe on, come here.' Instead of coming, then, he might keep working on his shoelace or become frustrated thinking, 'I can't because I can't get my shoe on!'

I discovered that John needed help in understanding group instructions. Shortly after he entered sixth grade, the teacher complained that she would tell the class to turn to page 67 in their books, and John would sit there. She would have to say, 'John, turn to page 67,' before he would comply. She said it wasn't a case of not paying attention. On a hunch I asked John, 'Do you know that when the teacher says, "Class," and tells the class to do something, that means you, too?' He said, 'Oh.' The problem was solved. Other parents have told me that they've also had this experience.

Children with Asperger Syndrome also typically have trouble on the transmitting end of speech too. Their speech may sound stiff or formal and may lack the highs and lows that make for pleasant-sounding conversation. Their speech may be a monotone or have unusual volume or speed. John speaks just a shade slower than most people. I can't hear it myself, but I heard this from a neighbor once. Of course newspaperman Bob Woodward speaks with a uniquely slow and deliberate pronunciation and he is one of Larry King's most frequent talk show guests on CNN so I'm not very concerned about it. Another boy whom I suspect may have Asperger Syndrome has a singsong way of speaking.

Volume may also be an issue. Kids with Asperger Syndrome may not adjust their voice volume as most people do. Some parents report that the volume knob is turned up all the time. John has a normal volume speaking voice (I'm happy to say); however he was a pre-teen before he caught on to whispering. It was one of those gaps in development that I had just never noticed. For years, he used a normal voice even in situations that called for a softer voice, but I thought it was a social issue – that he didn't recognize it as a soft-voice situation. When he was twelve though, we were standing in line at the Department of Motor Vehicles. The small town office was quiet when he said in a standard volume voice, 'This place smells like a toilet.' I told him softly, as I have done in the past, to keep his voice down. He responded in the same normal voice with, 'But doesn't it?' Well, the place did smell like a toilet. I murmured something non-committal like, 'I guess that's a matter of opinion' and changed the topic. Later that day when I was advising him that he should have left his toilet remark unsaid or whispered it to me it suddenly occurred to me – I had *never* heard John whisper. Could he physically do it? I asked him to whisper something for me, and sure enough, his normal-voiced response confirmed that he physically didn't know how to do it. Why had I never noticed?

It is a great example of the way even parents can assume our kids know things that they don't, because we confuse intuition and intellect. So, I immediately set out to help John master whispering. At first he overcompensated, dropping all air out of his speech. Soon though, he figured out what he needed to do to put breath into his whispers. It is still not easy for him to recognize a situation that calls for whispers, however.

> Nonverbal communication is lacking, so that the child misses or misreads nonverbal signals (gestures, body language, facial expression) and is ineffectual or limited in sending them.

The vast majority of a message's emotional meaning is expressed through facial expression, body posture or gesture, or tone of voice (Nowicki and Duke 1992, p.7). Only seven per cent is conveyed through actual words. For the person with Asperger Syndrome, it means effective communication is an uphill battle. Besides the voice issues we've already talked about, a look at assessment criteria for Asperger Syndrome shows the following types of nonverbal difficulties:

- limited facial expression

- limited ability to read facial expressions
- inappropriate expressions
- limited gestures, clumsy gestures, or inability to use gestures to convey meaning
- limited ability to interpret gestures
- limited ability to use body posture to convey meaning
- limited ability to read the body posture of others
- unusual eye contact (may be a stiff gaze, or alternatively, a reluctance or inability to maintain eye contact)
- inappropriate body space (being too close to others).

People with Asperger Syndrome and other autistic spectrum disorders are often limited in facial expression. They may appear somewhat stone-faced and unapproachable, which no doubt adds to the challenge of making friends. The other side of the coin is a limited ability to read the facial expressions of others.

Discussing characters on TV shows with your child can reveal some of the difficulties. I remember a *Mary Tyler Moore Show* where Mary twisted her ankle and Ted accidentally banged into it. I asked John how Ted felt based on his facial expression. I expected him to say 'embarrassed' or 'stupid' but he said, 'He's showing his teeth so he's laughing. He thinks it's funny.' Not quite. So we have spent a lot of time watching TV over the years and discussing these sorts of scenarios.

A recent study of thirteen individuals with Asperger Syndrome showed that they did well recognizing simple facial emotions, but with harder emotion-recognition tasks, they showed a tendency to believe words over faces (Grossman *et al.* 2000). Put another way, I would guess this means that they tend to value the seven per cent of actual words over the 93 per cent of nonverbal information. No wonder the world is confusing. I'm sure that's what makes sarcasm so difficult for our kids, and I suspect it explains why many of our Asperger children are easily duped. They readily believe what people say, and do not catch facial expressions that would otherwise give the other person's game away.

Dr. Attwood, when he assessed John a couple of years ago, mentioned a certain 'choreiform' (spasmodic or uncoordinated) way of gesturing that is typical of people with Asperger Syndrome. I have sometimes sensed that John's gestures were a bit distinctive. They gain more natural grace every year and would not raise any eyebrows today, but there is a repetitive rhythm to them, so that I suspect they do not convey as much meaning as would be helpful for him.

John often has trouble interpreting gestures or body postures. When someone pointed to something, his childhood instinct was not to look where the person was pointing but to look at the finger itself or the speaker's face. Because we know that nonverbal communication is tricky for him, his dad and I help him work through some of the issues. He might like to get a part-time job soon, so we have rehearsed job interviews with him. For instance I put my elbow on the table and rested my chin in my hand and asked him if my posture would be OK during an interview. His answer – 'It's fine as long as you look interested' – gave us a good starting point for discussions. I thought it was interesting that he knew you should look interested in the face, but did not know how that translated to the body.

Eye contact

When John was young, he often bowed his head downward and glanced up at people in an upward sidelong glance. Also, he would often look away altogether, or rather, he would already be facing away and calling his name would fail to turn his head. Many parents have their young children with Asperger Syndrome tested for deafness. We considered this, but realized he could easily hear the crinkling of candy wrappers in the next room so he couldn't be deaf.

Because these kids often do not maintain eye contact when they are listening, teachers often exclaim, 'I think he isn't listening to me because he's looking away but then later I'm surprised because he knows the material.' In truth some of our kids listen *better* when they are not having to pay attention to people's faces. Many autistic people report that looking someone in the eyes is just too much sensory input so listening shuts down. Teachers and other authority figures need to be aware of this, not only to aid in their teaching, but also to prevent misinterpretation – our society tends to equate an averted gaze with either lying or guilt, neither of which is appropriate for an individual with Asperger Syndrome. This may also explain why conversations in the car often go better than face to face in the living room.

John's special education teacher worked with him on eye contact in kindergarten and first grade. It was helpful. Some folks believe that we shouldn't interfere with some of the more autistic habits and preferences of our children, such as avoiding eye contact. If our children dislike eye contact, we should respect that and not cause them stress by trying to change it. I personally disagree, although we do need to tread carefully. Since we parents cannot easily gauge the discomfort we may be putting our children through, we do need to be sensitive about therapy. Still, I see nothing wrong with gentle encouragement. What we do with our brain every day determines which neural pathways get repaved, which connections occur, and so forth (Healy 1990, pp.74–6). If I can help my son change a little every day in a direction that helps him relate to the society he lives in, I think it is all to the good. I'm not talking about some Gestapo-like training session inflicted on our kids. My son's eye contact therapy was nothing more than gentle reminders on the teacher's part incorporated throughout the day. Mostly it amounted to praising my son when she observed him making eye contact. I concede that his eye contact issue may be milder and more amenable to this therapy than that of some kids.

Speaking of the brain changing every day, according to a recent study, the brains of several licensed taxi drivers were analyzed via Magnetic Resonance Imagery (MRI). Researchers found that one part of the brain (the posterior hippocampal region) was larger in the taxi drivers than in control subjects. Even more interesting, the volume of this region correlated with the amount of time spent as a taxi driver. By looking at the brain images, they could tell which subjects had been driving only a few years and which had been driving many years. The conclusion seems to be that the adult human brain is able to continue to change and grow in response to stimulation from the environment (Maguire *et al.* 2000). Aristotle put it in more philosophical terms – 'We are what we repeatedly do. Excellence, then, is not an act, but a habit.'

What does this have to do with eye contact? Maybe nothing. Different parts of the brain are involved, and an adult taxi driver is not an autistic child. It's the principle I'm going after. My point is that with time and practice my son became more at ease with eye contact. Maybe his brain physically underwent a subtle change? I should add that much of this work was done by age six. It's possible there is a critical window for when such therapy is most likely to result in positive changes.

Body Space

In a young child, body space issues can make it difficult to stand in the line or to sit peacefully at circle time. This child is not trying to be difficult. He just does not realize he is standing or sitting too close to his neighbor. He also may be afraid of being jostled or touched.

Body space issues invade situations out of school too. If mom has occasion to wipe the dinner table while people are still seated, likely everyone will lift their elbows except the child with Asperger Syndrome who does not interpret the dishcloth moving toward his elbows as a signal to move them. Most of us know the procedure on an elevator – get in, move to back or side, face the door. Someone with a deficit in body space issues might get on the elevator and do it 'wrong'. John needed rehearsals to be able to go through a door correctly, neither crowding others nor letting the door swing back on the next person.

Special interests

> Personal interests (collections, hobbies, preoccupations) may be unusual in subject and/or narrow in range and/or pursued intensely.

Having unusual special interests is a characteristic of Asperger Syndrome depicted in the media more than any other. It's overdone, most probably because it's easy for TV cameras to focus on interesting actions – little Bobby enthusing over a vacuum cleaner or young Andrew excitedly counting railroad cars or reciting the train schedule. It's much harder to show the other areas of Asperger Syndrome that are usually more devastating. How does one show a child *not* getting a party invitation, *not* being included in a game, or the phone *not* ringing? How does one depict the subtleties of communication difficulties – *not* understanding an idiom, for instance? So I forgive the TV news shows for dwelling on the kid who talks non-stop about dishwashers but I do wish the print media could try a little harder.

The truth is many of our kids have pretty ordinary interests. Many parents of children with Asperger Syndrome report typical kid-type interests: Pokémon®, Nintendo®, popular TV shows, movies, music, computer games, space, weather, chess, gymnastics, bowling, dinosaurs, and collecting stickers and Beanie Babies®, to name a few.

What might be unusual is simply the ardor at which they are pursued, that the interest may last an especially long time or that it is brought up in inappropriate situations. Our kids can often get rather 'stuck' on a topic. When the movie *Ace Ventura* was all the rage, John decided to 'be' Ace Ventura. He adopted the lingo, mannerisms, and walk of this movie character, and he soon earned the nickname 'Ace' at school, even handing out homemade Ace Ventura Pet Detective business cards to his classmates. We went through about a year of living with Ace. I got very sick of the dialog and had to limit it after a while, but otherwise it was relatively harmless. One UK mom reports that conversation for a while in her house revolved around her son's obsession with *The Simpsons*.

Of course, other interests may be more unusual for a child. I recently took a small survey of families affected by Asperger Syndrome. London, Japan, mules, trains, warships, gardening, bridges, manhole covers, drains, vents, vitamins, vacuum cleaners, Bill Gates, wheelchairs, and babies are just some of the interests reported.

Often collections may seem odd to the outsider but are relatively harmless or present only small problems. Sondra's nine-year-old son liked empty toilet paper tubes and also insisted on collecting boxes he would find in stores. He would become upset if he could not bring several boxes home on each shopping trip. Stephen's 13-year-old boy likes things that come in sets. This can be a minor problem when he is asked to choose just one cookie from an assortment plate. He feels compelled to take all the cookies of a particular type so they will remain in a set.

Many of our kids are packrats. One California mom whose child couldn't part with too-small clothes devised a 'camping box' to get little-used clothes at least as far as the garage. Other parents use charities as a positive way to convince kids to give up things. Recycling was the answer for Karen R. when her daughter went through a stage of cutting thousands of paper strips and wanting to keep them all.

Other special interests can cause larger problems. One New Zealand mom has a daughter who obsesses over wheelchairs. When she makes a run toward a stranger in a wheelchair, it may be perceived as rude, embarrassing, or intimidating. Sondra's daughter at age seven was the same way with baby items, such as pacifiers, bottles and especially shoes. Says Sondra, 'It was hard to go anywhere as she would run bolting to strangers to get to the baby and explore what items the baby had.'

Lindsay is an autistic adult who recalls:

> I used to be fascinated by trains. I once caught a train from Melbourne to Adelaide with no thought of what I would do when I got there or how I would get back. I was 13. The police put me on a plane to Melbourne after securing my mother's guarantee that she would meet the plane and pay the fare.

He continues, 'I'm still interested in trains. Now I know never to catch one unless I can get back.'

Sometimes what could turn into a large problem is fixed with some substitution. Sue's daughter loves animals but has difficulty behaving appropriately with them. Sue handles this by watching her closely and also by prompting her that if she needs to control an animal, she must use a stuffed animal. A Sydney mom had problems with her son taking money (both toy and real) for his money collection. Being able to see and handle his collection made him fixate too much on it so she limits the visual payoff by having him use a sealed metal bank. He can still save money, but the fascination has been eliminated and it does not tempt him to add to it in an inappropriate way.

Still, large problems seem the exception. Most parents I have talked to think the special interests are *mostly beneficial* and parents encourage or at least willingly tolerate them. I can vouch for that. John has received tremendous esteem and respect from his classmates because a special interest in bowling has garnered him several bowling trophies. When the interest is in a popular kid thing such as Pokémon® or video games, it can also lead to prestige. Theresa's son was chosen to draw a huge birthday card from his class to their teacher, because he and the teacher shared a love of whales. Lori says of her son's expertise with computer games, 'I think it's been beneficial in giving him some "coin of the realm" in terms of talking to other kids.' She notes that she does need to break up his time on these games so that he pays attention to his body's needs, like eating and sleeping.

Sarah's experience is similar. She says of her son, 'He learned a lot of social interaction by talking about video games with classmates. He has incentive to learn what they know. They admire his skills – even though they are a bit put off by his obsessive interest.' Other parents have noticed that their kids' interests have furthered motor skills (gymnastics, typing, running, karate, for example) and general knowledge and research skills (space, weather, animals, insects, geography). Often the parents learn a lot as well!

Intense interests can help a child control their fears. Karen R. says her daughter overcame a fear of bathtub and sink drains by becoming fascinated with drains of all types. Says Karen, 'This one was cyclical for many years – spring was always heralded by a renewed interest in drains.' John's obsession with witches when he was quite young may have been a way to cope with his fear of them. Years later, he also became obsessed with the O.J. Simpson trial. Of course there were many people who were darkly captivated by it, but John had difficulty talking or thinking about anything else during that long year. The courtroom drama appealed to his intellectual side but I wonder if perhaps there was also a horror to it that he needed to work out. He had a tendency of cornering houseguests on this topic, but on the bright side, he learned a whopping amount about law, court procedure, forensics, and the foibles of the US justice system.

To summarize, while special interests seem to be common in Asperger Syndrome, they are often portrayed more negatively than necessary. What Karen says about her daughter's interests can be applied to many children with Asperger Syndrome: 'Since I have yet to see an obsession or interest that hasn't helped her in some way (although that may not be immediately clear), my tendency is to encourage them and allow her to indulge them as much as possible'.

Routine

> The child may gravitate to or take comfort in routines, rituals, and repetition and be upset by surprises.

I once asked John, 'What is your definition of hell?' He said without hesitation, 'Surprises.'

There aren't too many good surprises for our kids with Asperger Syndrome. Due to mind blindness and lack of social awareness, actions and emotions of other people's are too often a surprise. Sensory issues too can make sudden sensory input (a fire drill, for instance) into a very nasty surprise, and in short, life often spins out of control. Relief can be found by artificially imposing control through insistence upon routine, ritual and repetition.

It's not an odd idea. When life gets too wild, most of us head for home to reach for the familiar – a comfort food, petting the dog, reading a favorite old book. It feels good. We are centered and soon back in control.

Our kids with Asperger Syndrome need this centering. Life outside the home can be extremely stressful, so when our kids get home they can be quite tyrannical in imposing structure. Some kids insist on taking a certain route to the store, or need a certain breakfast each day (with toast cut the same way) in front of the same TV show. When the TV station changes the cartoon line-up, the child may be inconsolable. Seen through the parents' eyes, we want to say, 'Get over it!' But the other way to look at it is that the tiny crumb of control and predictability in an otherwise chaotic world has been taken. Rather than yell at the child, we can realize that the importance of the show was not just that he liked it but that it represented safety. Even if the child can no longer have the show, we can help him establish a new routine.

I recently learned something new about a routine that my son has had for years. Since he was thirteen John has been in charge of mowing the grass. It is an immutable part of his week. He has never needed to be reminded because it's on an internal schedule for him. (I'm sure I am the envy of most homeowners in this!) In fact, if he can't mow (for rain or other reasons) it causes stress. While on a month's vacation, we'd paid a neighbor boy to mow but during the last week of vacation when John was pretty overloaded in a lot of ways, he obsessed about mowing. He mentioned it over and over. He had to mow. The grass would be high. He had to mow. When we arrived home exhausted after a Los Angles to Australia flight, the rest of the family hit the pillows but John mowed. The grass didn't need it but John did. After that, he was centered and back in control.

The surprising thing I learned recently, though, was when I complimented him on the beautiful job he does and mentioned that as much as he likes to mow he would do great as a golf course groundskeeper. He looked at me with disdain. 'I hate mowing!'

That brought me up short. I had always assumed he liked it! Now I postulate that it's not mowing he craves but the routine of it (or perhaps the physical exertion of it, which can be calming).

Adherence to routine is a good judge of stress.

> Clinical evidence suggests that the routine becomes more dominant and elaborate when the person has recently experienced changes in the key people in their life, accommodation, daily routine and expectations, or when they display signs of anxiety. (Attwood 1998, p.100).

I'm the same way with making lists. I've always liked lists, but as pressure builds, list-making does too – what to cook, household chores, errands to run, ways to save money, etc. It goes beyond not wanting to forget things. I might redo the same list many times. I used to be embarrassed by this habit but now I understand that it helps me feel centered and that's OK. It also signals that I need to reduce stressors.

Intelligence

> Intelligence, however, is average or better, and initial language acquisition is within norms.

By definition, someone with Asperger Syndrome has intelligence that is normal or better. That's how things are divided out in the diagnostics books. If someone has most of the characteristics of Asperger Syndrome but language acquisition is significantly delayed and/or intelligence is below normal, then it is usually called High Functioning Autism.

Because it's part of the definition, it is not debatable. However, I think the way intelligence is measured is. At age four, John was tested and found to have an IQ of 70. That is at the ragged edge between low normal IQ and mental retardation. My gut instinct told me that was a bunch of hogwash and it's one of the rare times I said as much out loud. I'm sure the psychologist thought I was in denial. But in fact, I knew that John's mind was very quick.

The problem is, our kids do not cope well in testing situations. Sensory, motor and linguistic issues all affect performance, and with new people and new demands, the child with Asperger Syndrome is likely to become overloaded. He may zone out, act up, or fall apart, but he will probably not do his best thinking. Whatever IQ score is handed to you for your child, I suggest that you mentally affix the words 'at least' in front of the number.

To give you some idea of how wide the gap is, the next time John tested (he was twelve), he'd gained over forty points and was now at the ragged edge of 'high normal'.

In achievement tests too, I take a skeptical view. During our homeschooling years, I ordered and administered such a test at home. One question asked on what basis one would choose a house. The possible answers were something like proximity to dad's work, proximity to the park, or proximity to church. There is a right answer to this?

This is a good time to mention Theory of Mind again. Even ridiculous questions can be answered if you can figure out what answer was intended (in the above question, I'm betting on dad's work). But mightn't a person with Asperger Syndrome have much more difficulty trying to guess the test's intended answers? A literal kid would look at his own home situation (rather than a typical family), and reason that dad works at home, and we don't go to church, so I'll choose the park. Or, if he lived with only his mom he might decide he can't answer the question at all. At any rate, scholastic achievement is hardly being measured by such fuzzy questions. Therefore I say again, test results can be useful, but they do not seal your child's fate. They are minimum scores.

Sensory

> There may be abnormal reactions to sensory stimuli (i.e. have acute sensitivity to light, smells, tastes, tactile sensation, or sounds).

I think sensory difficulties lie at the root of a lot of problems with kids acting out in preschool and school. They do not feel safe or comfortable in school, and learning is subverted by tantrums and meltdowns. Although social rules and communication difficulties add to the complexity of a school day, at least for my son I feel that sensory issues completely enveloped him and overwhelmed him on a much more primitive level.

This is not to say that all autistic people have sensory difficulties. Some studies indicate that perhaps 40 per cent of those with autism do (Attwood 1998, p.129). Another report indicates that sensory issues plague up to 70 per cent of learning disabled children (Ayres, undated). Some may have only one or two senses affected. Some may even be *less* sensitive than normal.

And what must it be like to have sensory difficulties and still be expected to perform at school? Take a moment for this exercise. Imagine having the 'volume turned up' on every sense. Imagine a day when you have premenstrual tension (for male readers, imagine early flu symptoms). Halogen lights are in your eyes.

Someone is squeaking a balloon and it's grating on your last nerve. Meanwhile, you're expected to balance your checkbook.

Now think about sitting in the middle of a parking garage. Cars rumble past inches from your feet. You have mild sunburn all over. Exhaust fumes are turning your stomach. A bird swoops and chirps too close to your ear. No place feels sturdy enough to write on but you are expected to compose a business letter.

My gut feeling is that my son's sensory system was never under *that* much assault (and certainly isn't now when he is older), but I think he spent early years in 'fight or flight' mode, at least partially caused by a too bright, too noisy, too scratchy, too stinky world.

If you are skeptical that this is 'real,' so was I until one event when John was eleven. He'd been taking swimming lessons at the town pool and we were at his first (and only) swim meet. I sat on the bleachers with a mother I'd met at an ADD meeting (her son was diagnosed with Oppositional Defiance Disorder). We chatted nervously, hoping our two boys, who didn't know each other, would each 'keep it together' in spite of the chaos. Then the whistle blew to start the first race.

Picture ten kids diving into the pool, 200 kids standing watching, and two lone boys at opposite ends of the pool hunched over, hands clapped over their ears. I had seen my son do this defensive move dozens of times before – on city streets, when the radio jumped to life as I started the car, when the speakers at an 'IMAX' cinema were too loud. He was always grouchy about something, it seemed, and although I'd know for years *intellectually* about his sensory issues, a tiny part of me thought that maybe he was just trying to wind me up, and another part of me had wanted to tell him, 'this is how noisy life is, so get over it.' But this day I got it. The other mother and I looked at each other as though we'd each gotten our acceptance letters to the same secret society on the same day. These two kids who had such difficulties getting along in the world were the only ones doubled over. It happened every race, all afternoon. I felt like 200 kids were in play mode, while our own boys were in 'fight or flight' hell, wanting to participate and trying valiantly just to hang on. What a way to live.

The most common sensory issues involve sound and touch (Attwood 1998, p.129). That was the case for John. School bathrooms can be torture chambers of sound (flushing, hand dryers, and banging metal doors) and like many with sensory difficulties John refused to enter. We had our moments at home, too. I hate ironing and avoid it so adamantly that when I finally had to bring out the iron, John looked at it with fear in his eyes and asked, 'Is that thing going to make a noise?' Of course my husband fell about on the floor laughing and tells this story on me whenever anyone mentions ironing.

John is now older. Over the years he's adjusted to city traffic and other annoying but ordinary noises. These days, he finds only a few things troublesome, such as a parade with a brass band, a noisy echoing gymnasium, or skeet shooting. At the age of seventeen, sensory issues are much, much better but not altogether gone.

Touch is the other main source of sensory discomfort. Many parents report having to clip labels out of garments or that socks must be worn inside out to avoid the toe seam. As a child John wanted long sleeved shirts and 'long sleeved pants,' always in soft materials. Hugs are to be endured, not enjoyed, for John. Many kids are extremely bothered by touch and cannot stand in line, sit in a group or have a seatmate on the bus because of anxiety over being touched. Conversely, some kids feel an extreme need to touch everything, although this seems to be less common. Firm touch is usually better tolerated (and often craved) while light touch is a big problem. John has a hair trigger startle reflex that bullies used to advantage, touching lightly on the back of the neck to see him jump. Tactile issues can make haircuts an interesting challenge.

Physical

There is usually, but not always, physical clumsiness.

Physical clumsiness can show itself in several subtle ways – clumsy or odd gait, balance and coordination issues, and poor fine motor skills are among them. Various studies indicate that the odds of having such physical issues are between 50 and 90 per cent among the Asperger population (Attwood 1998, p.103).

In John's case, handwriting has always been a problem (so much so that the schools refused to teach cursive writing to him at all), and this is quite common, even among Asperger individuals who may be artistic. In other areas, John's motor issues have been fairly subtle. His gait used to be awkward and uneven (but John Wayne's signatory walk was much more pronounced, and look how far that took him). In fifth grade year, John took up daily running, something he kept up for a few months. His gait went from fairly awkward to very normal. It was as though his body just needed extra opportunity to figure it all out.

Balance has not been a major issue for John. He did spend extra time learning to take stair steps with alternating feet, and the doctor noted he had more difficulty balancing on one leg than the other. Other balance issues that kids have might make it tricky to sit in a chair without sort of falling into it, to walk across a room without bumping into things or to learn to ride a bicycle.

One thing we discovered in John's preschool was a 'mid-line' problem. This roughly means that the two halves of the body don't work well together, and there is difficulty with the left half crossing over to the right half and vice versa. A telltale sign is if your child chooses to do two-handed things with one hand. (See Chapter 7 for tips on working with this.)

Face Blindness

The technical term for face blindness is prosopagnosia. It means impairment in recognizing faces. This is not difficulty in recalling someone's name, but rather difficulty in telling one face from another. Some (percentage unknown) individuals with Asperger Syndrome have trouble distinguishing faces. Researchers at Yale University have used brain-imaging techniques to show why. Most people process faces in a special section of the brain reserved for that purpose. However, Asperger people tested were found to process faces in a different area, the part that normally processes objects.

What does that mean? Imagine that you work with a six-person committee all one day, and then meet one of those people the next day on the street. You would get a flash of recognition. You might not recall his name, but you would recognize him. But what if you were face blind? You would have processed those six faces in the 'object' portion of your brain. Now imagine that you are in a room with six blue upholstered chairs. Even if you spent the entire morning among them, would you expect to be able to tell them apart? Would you notice if you saw one of those chairs in a different room the next day? Probably not.

If it were critically important to do so, you would probably develop little hints to tell them apart. You'd learn to notice wood grain on the arms, the wear of the upholstery and any rips. Those techniques would work for you until the chair was changed in some way. Once it got reupholstered, you would be back to square one.

This may be close to how a face-blind person feels when looking at people. Success at distinguishing faces may depend on how adept one becomes at noticing details intellectually and choosing the *right* details. Shape of the head, height and manner of walking don't change much but require close observation. Hair, beards, glasses and clothing are easier to spot but are more easily changed.

My son John is somewhat face blind. I say 'somewhat' because he has improved in this area as he has matured. I believe he has learned to use more reliable details than he used to. Here are some examples of problems he used to have:

John has seen every *Seinfeld* episode (we have taped them all), and has watched it for *years*. So, I was astounded when John asked, 'Who is that girl?' while we were watching one night. It was Elaine (one of the four main characters), sitting with Jerry and George in the coffee shop, like she does in every episode, but she had her hair up and wore glasses. Similarly, on another favorite show, the *Mary Tyler Moore Show*, when Ted grew a mustache John asked, 'Who is that?'

John was bullied by kids he didn't recognize. It wasn't just that he didn't know names. He often had no idea if they were from his class, his bus, or even his school. How bewildering for him.

I feel that facial recognition has improved greatly for John. Some of it might be general development. As he has less to deal with in terms of sensory and language issues, perhaps he can better attend to facial cues. More than that, I think we fell into a sort of therapy by accident.

When John went to a public school in sixth grade, he referred to all kids in his class by their clothing or glasses (the boy with the leather jacket, the kid in red sneakers, etc.). The following year, John went to private school that required uniforms. How would he fare in a school where everybody wore the same navy shorts, striped shirt and navy blazer?

At first, he struggled. I suspect everyone was a blur, and many times a kid would say hello and John would not know if it were someone he should know or not. But gradually things got better. He realized subconsciously that clothing clues could no longer help him and he learned new clues. Four years later, he is much improved. Of course, most school children in the US do not wear uniforms. (I wonder if face blindness is more common in the US than in the UK or Australia, where uniforms are usually worn?)

Regardless of one's situation, parents may be able to stretch a child's repertoire of clues by discussing various attributes (height, hair color, build, way of walking, shape of nose, color of eyes, etc.). The person born face blind might never process faces from the typical 'face place' in the brain, but with practice, coping skills may be much improved anyway. That's my unscientific opinion only.

Tics, stims, and stereotypies

Many people with Asperger Syndrome stand out in a crowd because of somewhat unusual movements. These movements are often called tics, stims (self-stimulating behaviors) or stereotypies (idiosyncratic movements). It's a confusing area, and even the doctors can muddle this up unless they are well trained in such matters, but here's an attempt at explaining the differences in layman's terms.

When the movement is purposeless, largely involuntary, and involves primarily the head, neck, and shoulder area, it is usually called a tic. It can sometimes be put off but only for short periods of time, similar to putting off scratching an itch, but by and large this is something over which the individual has little control. Many children (whether Asperger or not) have an occasional motor tic and it's a passing thing that doesn't require treatment.

When tics become bothersome and meet certain criteria of type and duration, the child should be assessed for a disorder known as Tourette Syndrome. Some people with Asperger Syndrome will meet the criteria for Tourette Syndrome, and a larger percentage of those with Tourette Syndrome will meet the criteria for Asperger Syndrome. The variety of tics is wide, but common ones are eye blinking, facial grimacing, throat clearing, shoulder jerking, or coughing.

John has gone through phases of eye blinking and facial grimacing but it is not worthy of a separate diagnosis. Medication can often ameliorate the ticking (although see Chapter 9 on diet and vitamins with respect to Tourette Syndrome).

The type of idiosyncratic movement that is more a feature of Asperger Syndrome itself is known as a stim (also called stereotypy, a generic term some medical folks prefer). 'Stim' is short for self-stimulating behavior. This is different from tics because the movement is more voluntary. It is usually rhythmic, often involves hands or the whole body, and may serve one or more purposes for the individual. I once interviewed Dr. Attwood about this and he indicated that there seem to be many ways in which these movements may serve the Asperger individual:

- Exploration via sensation – e.g. sifting sand through fingers; reflects natural early development but lasts longer in the autistic individual.

- A form of self-hypnosis – to exclude excessive sensory data by concentrating on one event; women use Lamaze to reduce labor pain and people with Asperger Syndrome may wiggle their fingers in front of their eyes or hum to shut out extra data.

- A means of communicating thoughts and feelings – e.g. flapping to mean 'I'm happy' takes the place of words.

- An attempt to make life predictable – light switches are delightfully predictable.

- Pure pleasure – just as rocking or swinging is pleasurable to most people. This action is not to screen things out but to enjoy; intensity can increase to agitation or euphoria.

- A compulsive act as a response to anxiety – the more anxiety, the more need for rigid rituals (this may overlap with Obsessive-Compulsive Disorder).

- A movement disorder (motor tic) – involuntary and spontaneous movement (this may overlap with Tourette). Some tics appear at the juncture between two activities or environments and, in essence, aid in 'switching gears.'

John has always 'stimmed' on anything with a flash or sparkle – water from a hose or garden fountain, fireworks, sparks and flames from barbecue grill or fireplace. As I mentioned earlier, he also wagged a stick in front of his eyes for prolonged periods of time. I used to think he liked the motor movement of wagging it, but years later John explained that he liked the strobe effect of the stick flicking in front of his eyes.

Some miscellaneous questions

Q. What is the incidence of autism and Asperger Syndrome?

Latest estimates by the National Autism Society (NAS) in the UK are that people somewhere on the autism spectrum may represent 1 in 500 people. A few years ago it was estimated at 1 in 1000 people and before that at 4–10 per 10,000. Discussions abound on whether the increase in incidence is real or a factor of better diagnosing. Asperger Syndrome is more common than classic autism but there has been such an increase in numbers of people diagnosed with it that I think the official scientific reports may be lagging behind reality.

Q. I've been told that Asperger Syndrome is a 'pervasive development disorder.' What is that and how does it fit in with other types of autism? I'm so confused!

Here's what's confusing. There's an umbrella sort of term in the official diagnostic criteria called Pervasive Developmental Disorder (PDD). Under that are four conditions – autism, Asperger Syndrome, Rett Syndrome, and Childhood Disintegrative Disorder. The latter two are severe and distinct and beyond our discussion, so let's just think about the first two – autism and Asperger Syndrome. Within autism are two subforms – classic or Kanner autism (characterized by aloofness, self-absorption, a lack of interest in being with others, mental retardation and other issues) and High Functioning Autism (HFA), which also features aloofness, but people with HFA have normal intelligence and fewer issues in general. (Note: there is also something called PDD-Not Otherwise Specified or PDD-NOS, which simply means that there are pervasive developmental issues but the criteria were not met for any specific disorder.)

And then there's Asperger Syndrome. These days it is well accepted as being on the autism spectrum yet it is listed separately. Adding to the confusion is an ongoing debate on whether Asperger Syndrome is identical to HFA. There may be subtle differences but experts don't agree on what they are, so I tend not to worry too much about which label to use. I alternatively say that my son has Asperger Syndrome, an autistic spectrum disorder, or a pervasive developmental disorder. If someone said he had HFA, I would probably not protest too much, although I personally side with the experts who characterize HFA as more aloof, less verbal and less clumsy than Asperger Syndrome. In the end, we need to work with the child and not worry too much about the exact label. Close is close enough for most purposes.

Q. How did Asperger Syndrome get its name?
Dr. Hans Asperger was an Austrian pediatrician who in 1944 wrote about several young boys he'd observed who all seemed to share a certain collection of traits. His papers were translated decades later and in 1981, the term 'Asperger Syndrome' was coined by Lorna Wing, who was doing her own studies of a group of children with similar characteristics.

Q. What is the ratio of boys to girls with Asperger Syndrome?
It's estimated that the ratio of boys to girls is four to one. Since this book is written from the perspective of the mother of a son, girls have unfortunately gotten little attention in this book (as in most books). Even more unfortunately, the same can be said about research studies. There haven't been a lot of studies specific to the female with Asperger Syndrome. Most issues appear to be similar regardless of gender, but girls seem to be quieter and less obvious about their differences, so may be delayed in getting diagnosis and help.

Q. What conditions are co-morbid with Asperger Syndrome?

A person with Asperger Syndrome has an increased chance of having some other neurological condition as compared to the general population. Some of these conditions are Tourette Syndrome, epilepsy, Obsessive-Compulsive Disorder, depression, and bi-polar disorder (formerly termed manic-depressive disorder).

Attention Deficit Disorder or Attention Deficit with Hyperactivity Disorder (ADHD) is often diagnosed in the person with Asperger Syndrome, and many children get that diagnosis first before the Asperger is spotted. I think most experts feel that attention issues are an integral part of Asperger Syndrome. That is, you can have ADD without Asperger Syndrome, but if you have Asperger Syndrome you are assumed to have attention issues, whether or not you get a separate diagnosis for them.

Q. Are there good points to Asperger Syndrome?

YES! What is too easily forgotten in the necessity to discuss problem areas is that Asperger Syndrome is also a reservoir of great gifts. Sometimes it's hard to remember that, especially on days when things are not going well, but here are just some of the good features.

Positive attributes of Asperger Syndrome
Normal or high intelligence

Many test in the high IQ ranges. Some very bright people in history are thought to have some traits of Asperger Syndrome. Many of the world's scientists, inventors, mathematicians, and computer gurus have been unusual or eccentric and some might today be diagnosed as having Asperger Syndrome. We may owe many of the world's inventions, cures, and innovations to the intellectual skills of the Asperger population.

Rote memory

Our kids often have phenomenal memories, especially for facts and dates, and concrete details are of interest to them. This stands them in good stead in pursuing hobbies, and many become walking encyclopedias on chosen subjects, especially aspects of science, history, or geography. This may give them a chance to shine in school. John's high school geography teacher has asked him more than once, 'How do you *know* all of this?' because of his good memory for geographical locations. Several state and national finalists in spelling bees and geography bees have been students who have also happened to have Asperger Syndrome.

Honesty

It's not impossible for a child with Asperger Syndrome to tell a lie but most Asperger kids are scrupulously honest. Lies don't really work for them anyway, and any attempts are apt to be clumsy and easily discovered, so there really isn't much incentive to try it often. I have learned *always* to believe my son because he has shown me that he tells the truth. Sometimes literalness gets in the way however. I told a teacher once that John was finding the school day terrible to deal with due to harassment issues. She turned to John for his opinion by asking, 'John, how do you feel when you go home from school each day?' John said, 'Terrific!' She looked triumphant and said, 'I don't see a problem.' I was momentarily confused before I realized that John was answering her literally. (On his way *home* from school he felt great, because school was over!) So I requested that she ask the question in a different way. She looked at me funny, then asked, 'John, how are things going for you at school?' He replied, 'Awful.'

Law-abiding

From what I've read over the years, the Asperger population is a law-abiding group as a whole. Life is easier, more predictable, and more manageable when there are rules in place and most have an affinity for rules. There is the occasional problem in the Asperger population, often having to do with following an interest beyond acceptable boundaries (taking something for a special collection, for instance), getting into trouble over social inappropriateness (an example might be pursuing a girlfriend too aggressively so that it crosses the line into stalking) or panicking in a violent way (such as when being restrained).

I could continue listing more positive attributes of Asperger Syndrome but if you know and love somebody who has it, you already know many of the highlights. There are tough times, surely, but there are opportunities to look at life in special ways. If I could 'cure' my son of his Asperger Syndrome, I wouldn't. I have worked to alleviate many of the problem behaviors and physical troubles my son has endured, so that he can enjoy his life more and be successful in ways that he chooses. That is different from trying to cure him of who he is. He will always have a unique way of looking at the world and dealing with the world. It's both a difficulty for him and also his strength. If I could cure anything, it would be to cure the world of its lack of understanding.

Chapter 3

Grabbing Hold

You may have a pretty good suspicion by now as to whether your child has Asperger Syndrome or not. If yes, you may ask – now what do I do?

You will probably want to follow one or more of the following avenues:

- medical assessment and therapy
- school assessment, educational placement and therapy
- survival or interim tactics – make your own informal assessment and work with your child at home.

You can do these options in any order or all at once. Americans will probably want to pursue school assessment first since it is free and medical assessment may not be (depending on your insurer). You do not have to wait until your child is school-aged in order to request consideration for assessment. If your child is found to have significant delays, he or she will qualify for early intervention preschool and various therapies will be provided. Later, the school will need to know more precisely what your child's issues are in order for him or her to continue to qualify for special services. That usually means the child will need a medical diagnosis.

Medical diagnosis will most likely come from a pediatric neurologist, child psychiatrist, developmental psychologist, or pediatrician. Referral to an autism clinic will ensure a comprehensive picture by a team of professionals that might comprise a pediatrician, psychologist, speech therapist and occupational therapist. A neurologist may suggest other tests – for example, blood work to rule out Fragile X, PKU, or other disorders; an EEG can pinpoint epilepsy; and an MRI may be requested to investigate the possibility of any brain anomalies. The doctor may also refer your child to one or more kinds of therapy (speech, physical, occupational, and/or social skills). By the way, the psychiatrist and neurologist may prescribe medication but the psychologist cannot, a point that may be important to you if you suspect medication may be needed (or if you are adamantly opposed to it).

Does the two-avenue system work? Yes, for many people, getting assessment and services has been a successful process. Marti Nelson of Minneapolis, Minnesota, for example, is well pleased with how events have unfolded for her child. After an assessment at age three and a half by the school district, her son qualified for early-intervention preschool, staffed with speech and occupational therapists, and where he receives adaptive physical education. Two autism specialists fill out the school's team, and they will be available for consultation for the next several years, until grade seven. On the medical side, recently (at age five), her son was one of the first children assessed at the University of Minnesota's new Autism Spectrum Disorder Clinic. Through medical assessment and Marti's insurance, her son is currently entitled to 60 speech therapy visits and 60 occupational therapy visits per calendar year. He also attends a social skills play therapy group (paid for privately).

I can see why Marti is happy with the support she is getting. This is an illustration of all systems working. This is what *can* be provided to our kids if the commitment of the community is there. Marti also takes her own role in her son's progress seriously. She helps him feel successful through his special interest (music – violin lessons), while his large motor skills and social skills get a workout with swimming lessons. Marti does not work outside the home and considers it her full-time job to be her son's advocate, a job she works at tenaciously. Also, her school district is regarded as being the best in the state.

Marti's case represents the most positive end of the spectrum and it's an absolute pleasure to write about it because it is encouraging for parents to see that it's possible for a great many good things to come together for a young special needs child. Her son's future is bright.

On the other hand, how many people have traveled down the assessment path with the same needs and expectations, but with less success? For them, the path has been rock-strewn, traffic-jammed, and has resulted in dead ends. Families living just a few miles from Marti might have nothing but trouble (and the waiting list at the assessment center Marti used is now at approximately ten months!).

The problem is, some of us live in settings where things don't go so smoothly. Sometimes those first two avenues take too darned long, or the pot of gold at the end turns out to be too puny for the time, effort, and money spent trying to reach it. That is why later I will also discuss the third avenue (making your own informal assessment and working with your child at home), which is a course of action for the families who cannot wait for others to come to their aid.

Why do people's experiences vary so drastically?

Parents blame themselves when things don't fall into place, but my low-tech research says it's truly a game of chance. Pam, mother to an eleven-year-old son, expresses it this way:

> The hand one draws, as far as happening to find good medical advice or good school experiences, can make a big difference, which is scary since in most cases we don't appreciate that until it's too late to affect the draw (i.e. move or change doctors).

The next several pages will outline some of the pitfalls of the medical and school pathways. The goal in presenting this is to offer you a sobering view of what can go wrong (at least my opinion of it!) and also to suggest some possible workarounds, although I can't promise miracles. Try not to panic as we go through these! At least knowing about the problems may help you avoid a few of them. Most of all, at the risk of being called a fear-monger, I hope to impress upon you the potential roughness of the road ahead. Things may go just great for you (I hope they do), but the path for some will be a morass of red tape and high weeds. I've talked with too many of people who know this first hand. At least if you know there are potential road hazards ahead, you can proceed with caution and also keep your eye out for an alternate route.

Road hazards on the medical path

Problem 1: You may be rushed through the system

This shouldn't be a problem with a full assessment at an autism clinic (these take anywhere from a half day up to a couple of days), but it may be a problem with any appointment short of that. The average American pediatrician has about 1500 patients to care for (Bykowski 1999), usually in fifteen-minute visits. The reason many parents feel rushed through doctors' appointments is because they *are* rushed.

The American Academy of Pediatrics had traditionally preferred that doctors use a 'direct observation' diagnostics test for developmental disabilities, where the doctor observes the child's functioning in key areas for himself. This sort of test usually takes thirty minutes or so, however, which is hard to fit into a fifteen minute visit. Many doctors waive these tests and opt for something quicker.

What they may be more likely to use is a checklist, asking parents if the child has met certain developmental milestones. Can your child climb stairs? Yes. With alternating feet? No. It is quick. Be aware that some milestone checklists tests are much better than others. Your doctor could even be using a test that detects fewer than 30 per cent of all children with developmental disabilities.

I'm guessing that this may be one reason why different families have such totally different experiences. If your child is one who is picked up through this sort of quick test, you will get a diagnosis or a referral for more complete assessment with blinding speed (although you may wait months for the complete assessment). If you are part of the percentage who do not get picked up, though, you can't even get that far. Your doctor, unconvinced there is a problem, may dismiss you with a 'let's wait and see' deferment that delays proper diagnosis for a few more months, until your concerns again reach critical mass. This happened to us once.

SUGGESTIONS

- A parent questionnaire such as the Parents' Evaluations of Developmental Status (PEDS) is thought to be much better (perhaps 70–80 per cent accuracy) than a milestone checklist (Kilgore 1999, p.2). In the UK, the DISCO (Diagnostic Interview for Social and Communication Disorders) is the gold standard. Ask your doctor what diagnostic tool will be used and its estimated accuracy.

- Resist being rushed. Ask for an appointment at the very end of the day when the doctor may have more time to talk, or ask for (and be prepared to pay for) a double appointment.

- Be clear about what you want to get out of the appointment, and make a list of your concerns, with examples.

Problem 2: Your family doctor may have a hard time referring you to a specialist

Many managed healthcare systems in the US make it difficult for doctors to make referrals. Figures show that around 85 per cent of the American workforce is enrolled in managed care plans

(Brown 1998). I would think that means that a lot of families are running into this hurdle in trying to see a specialist.

Doctors themselves are frustrated. A 1997 study showed that primary care physicians are having 'more trouble accessing mental health services for their patients than they are in obtaining other types of medical care.' In fact, some doctors have to bend the rules. A survey of several hundred physicians found that more than a quarter of them frequently have to exaggerate the seriousness of their patients' conditions just to procure care that they deem to be medically necessary (Zwillich 1999).

SUGGESTION

- Persistence is probably key here, as well as shopping insurance carefully. If a referral is denied, you may need to work through a caseworker at your insurance company and keep moving up the chain to the Medical Director.

Problem 3: Getting a diagnosis may take several tries

Probably because Asperger Syndrome is relatively new in the medical books, and not always obvious, it may take awhile to get the proper assessment. In the UK, according to a 1999 BBC news story, the National Autistic Society reported:

> Forty per cent of parents of children with autism or Asperger Syndrome waited more than three years for a diagnosis, and 10 per cent waited 10 or more years.

Most had to see at least three doctors.

In the US, Dr. Pauline Filipek, a professor of pediatrics and neurology who led a group of 25 researchers on a quest to make recommendations for earlier autism diagnosis, made the following statement: 'Our research found that children with autism are often not diagnosed until age 5 or 6 but have had symptoms of the disorder for years.' That statement, which originally appeared in the December 2000 issue of the *Journal of*

Autism and Developmental Disorders, was quoted in a Daily University Science News article with the depressing title, 'Thousands of Infants with Autism Go Undiagnosed.'

Lady Astor in the UK spent four years getting an autism diagnosis for her daughter. Her story may be found on the NAS website (see Appendix 2).

SUGGESTION

- Do your own reading and make sure that the doctor you visit is well versed in autistic disorders or will refer you to someone who is.

Problem 4: You may not get the diagnosis you expect

You may be expecting to hear 'Asperger Syndrome' but the specialist you see may say that your child has High Functioning Autism. As I stated in Chapter 2, HFA is a close cousin and many doctors even feel that these disorders are the same. Another label you might be handed is Pervasive Developmental Disorder – Not Otherwise Specified (PDD-NOS) if your child does not meet enough characteristics for a specific syndrome but has some pervasive development issues.

Any of these diagnoses may be reasonable to you since the conditions are all related. You should be more concerned though if the doctor feels your child has something else entirely that does not seem to be a good match to you, or seems to cover only a piece of the puzzle. Many children are first diagnosed with Attention Deficit Disorder, for instance, before getting a later and better diagnosis of Asperger Syndrome. Attention deficit is frequently a characteristic of Asperger Syndrome, but it doesn't get at the heart of what is going on.

SUGGESTION

- Do as much reading as you can so you are somewhat knowledgeable about all the parts that make up

Asperger Syndrome and the 'lesser' labels that may fit within it.

- Have in mind all the issues about your child that you feel need addressing.
- Ask for an explanation of the doctor's rationale if the label is not what you expect.

Problem 5: To go to a top diagnostic center, you may wait a long time
The length of waiting lists can be anything from a month (reasonable) to nearly two years (outrageous). Here are just a few examples, as reported by parents currently on waiting lists, as reported by the centers themselves, or according to recent news articles:

- Children's Hospital, Philadelphia – 4 months
- University of Minnesota Autism Spectrum Disorder Center – 10 months
- Child Study Center, Yale University – 13 months
- Autistic Society of South Australia, Adelaide – 1 month
- Autistic Society of Queensland, Brisbane – 12–18 months
- UK – a wait for a clinical psychologist may be up to 9 months.

SUGGESTIONS

- Get the appointment as soon as you can, obviously.
- Let the appointment desk know you could take someone's cancelled appointment on short notice.
- If you are in crisis, let them know (it can't hurt and it might help).

- If your child's school is requesting the assessment, let the doctor's office know this. It has been known to bump you up in line.

- For those in the UK: the College of Health operates a waiting list helpline at 020 8983 1133. They may be able to find quicker access for you at another location.

Problem 6: Once you do get an assessment, you may get little follow-up

The same UK report I mentioned earlier indicated that when families did finally get the diagnosis of autism or Asperger Syndrome, over 80 per cent of them got little or no information on the relative severity of the disease and nearly half of them got little information on the disability itself and no information on where to go for support and advice.

The experience is much the same in the United States. It was my experience, and also that of Susan, a mom fortunate enough to have her child evaluated at a top university research clinic in the Midwest. Although she felt the assessment was comprehensive, when she asked questions like 'Now what do I do?' she got blank looks. When she pressed them about possible services her son might need, she heard 'Let's hold off on that and see how he is doing next year.' Says Susan, 'I was completely devastated by the diagnosis and felt like I had been hung out to dry.' She doubts she is alone in this: 'It seems that every parent group meeting I attend, the major complaint is the lack of follow-up information offered by the professionals.'

Terry M. from southern California puts it even more bluntly. 'My son has had evaluations up the wazoo, but then these professionals don't know what to do.' Janet in Oregon echoes this sentiment:

> Our experience with universities has been very professional. However we were left with labels and minus deviations [test scores revealing problem areas] for Amy

beginning at 18 months of age, with no clue as to what to do to make things better. I guess everyone expects early intervention [the school program] to pick up on remediations and interventions. NOT!

SUGGESTION

- I think this problem area is slowly improving, but no matter how much they tell you at time of diagnosis, you will still crave more information. Prepare to do your own research and link up with any local support organizations, where you will find people who can tell you about whatever your local area offers, if anything (therapists, playgroups, etc.).

Problem 7: You may have to wait for therapy

This is another area of great disparity. Where I live, for example, there is no speech therapist for anyone over the age of five, so the wait for speech therapy might be a very long one. In parts of Canada, according to a 2000 news story in the *Montreal Gazette*, autistic children wait around two and a half years to get therapy. The news story featured a four-year-old who had been diagnosed two years earlier but was still waiting to be accepted into a special-needs program. He sees a speech therapist only once every two months and gets a visit from an occupational therapist once every *six* months.

The waiting list for the autism program at University Center for Developmental Disabilities in San Bernardino can stretch to a year, while the program at the autism clinic at the James Whitcomb Riley Children's Hospital in Indiana (the only comprehensive clinic in the state) currently has a six-month waiting list.

Of note, many waiting lists are for programs designed for the more classically autistic. When it comes to Asperger Syndrome, there may not be a program in existence *at all*. Put another way, the wait for a good program might be until you or someone else decides to develop it.

- Consider what you can do at home to work on various issues. This might be in the areas of sensory, motor skills, language, social skills or other. You will find ideas elsewhere in this book but also consider getting ideas from support groups and wide reading.

- Paying privately for a consultation with an occupational or physical therapist might be money well spent and can start you on your way.

- Start your own social skills group. (See Appendix 3.)

Road hazards on the school path

As disturbing as the medical route is, the school path is just as rocky. The same types of problems crop up that permeate the medical side – being inconsistent, inexperienced, slow, and so forth. I won't go into tortuous detail about it all except to say it is intensely aggravated by a few other factors.

Problem 1: Special education teachers are overwhelmed

Trends in special education are alarming. The Council for Exceptional Children, in an October 2000 report, indicated that the caseload for special education teachers is overwhelming and working with kids takes back seat to paperwork and administrative duties. Teachers report having to deal with an average of seventeen other people just to get through their paperwork. Little wonder that *special education teachers are leaving the field at nearly twice the rate of general education teachers*. The National Information Center for Children and Youth with Disabilities (NICHCY) reports a shortage in special education teachers in every state in the US, with rural and urban areas hardest hit, and suburban areas less so.

The news isn't any better elsewhere. Toronto, Canada, reports critical teacher shortages in special education. Because high numbers of teachers are retiring shortages will worsen. A similar story appeared in Australia's *Herald Sun* (April 22, 2000), when Victoria's Director of Schools said, 'Nationwide, all education systems are facing the fact that a significant proportion of the workforce is approaching the age of retirement.' An Internet search of the BBC News website will reveal several headlines on widespread teacher shortages throughout the UK. In most cases, teacher shortages are highest in fields of science, math and special education.

SUGGESTION

- There is little for the individual family to do about this problem. If you do have a good special education teacher, make sure she knows she is appreciated! Realize that she is likely as frustrated by the paperwork and layers of bureaucracy as you are.

Problem 2: Communication

If the medical profession is just becoming knowledgeable about Asperger Syndrome, you can bet that the school personnel are by and large still scratching their heads and asking what the heck you are talking about. The flip side of that is that the parents often scratch their heads when it comes to understanding the educational bureaucracy. It's a different world with a different vocabulary and where it intersects with government regulations, even the educators get lost. If you want to speak about special education to special educators, you'd better start learning the lingo. In the US this means you'd better get used to swimming in alphabet soup. Here are a few of the chunks you'll be swimming around: IDEA, IEP, IFSP, 504, FAPE, FBA, EEI, EBD, BED, SED, OHI, LD, CSE, APE, BIC, BIP, BMP, CST, IEE, ECSE, EI, EIBI, ESE, ESY, IME, SLP, OT, and PT. (Don't ask me to explain these!)

You can make a career out of understanding the bureaucratic and legal avenues of getting an education for a special needs child, and indeed, many people do make careers out of this very thing. Parents in the US often use advocates (procured free from an agency or paid for privately) or even special education lawyers to help navigate the educational maze and say the right words to make educators understand. Although I'm glad such advocates exist, to me it is sad that they should be necessary. A free and appropriate public education (FAPE) is supposedly guaranteed in the US. Can you imagine if we had to hire an advocate to use a public library? To use a public road? We should not have to enlist the services of a professional bodyguard (in the sense that we are needing somebody to protect our child's body of rights) just because it's getting so difficult to talk with and work things out with our own neighborhood school. Parents have now come to accept this as standard practice but to my mind it borders on the absurd. Yet who can blame the parents? They feel unequipped to walk into a school meeting and have a discussion with the education professionals unless so accompanied. It's not all about vocabulary of course. It's about understanding rights and process and communicating needs to the schools.

SUGGESTIONS

- If you feel intimidated or as though your rights may get stomped on, do enlist the services of an advocate or do your research.

- Do not be embarrassed if you don't understand a term that is used. Make them explain.

- Take notes and/or use a tape recorder so you can mull thing over later.

- If you can't get an advocate, bring a spouse, neighbor, or friend, to be a second pair of ears for you.

- Do not sign anything you don't fully understand. Take any paperwork home to read it at your own pace rather than being rushed into signing.

Problem 3: There's no money.

Parents are not supposed to have to worry about their school's budget, because adequate services are mandated by law and must be funded (although the federal government doesn't pay too many of the bills). School principals are not supposed to be able to say, 'We can't afford it.' Does that mean that principals need to have a counterfeiting machine in the school basement? What do they do if they are not allowed to say they can't afford it, but yet they can't? You might say, 'That's not my problem what they do,' but I think it's very much your problem, because the easiest solution is to stall. So principals put up road blocks, cancel and re-schedule meetings repeatedly, make sure their experts refute your experts, argue about whether Asperger Syndrome qualifies under autism, argue whether social deficits are his responsibility, etc. Ad nauseam. I'm no education expert but I've chatted with lots of families over the last six years and this is what I'm hearing. I'm not saying that the parents shouldn't demand. I am saying that demanding might not get the job done.

SUGGESTIONS

- Regardless of what the law entitles you to, you may get further accommodations if the school sees that you are not trying to spend all their money on one child. Be sensitive in your requests, while still getting your child what he needs.

- Prioritize. You may not get everything you want, so know what is most important to you.

- Look for accommodations that cost nothing.

- Let them know what you have tried and found to be successful. Schools are more willing to try something new if they have some indication it will be successful.

- Share information with them and stress that you are all on the same team. Instead of saying 'I want,' say, 'my child needs.'

Problem 4: Timing.

Even if you have qualified teachers and everyone agrees on what needs to be done, and the school can pay for it and is willing to, every time you think you are finally getting ahead in this bureaucratic board game, the school year ends. A couple months later it's mass amnesia and you're one more face forgotten. Linda in Texas is facing the frustration of trying to get services in place for her son who has Asperger Syndrome. She muses, 'Perhaps *next* school year. I learned with my ADHD daughter that by the time you get things in place, the year is over and wasted.' The process is long and tortuous.

SUGGESTIONS

- Look ahead. Decide if you have enough time left at a particular school to make waging the battle worthwhile.

- Use your calendar wisely. If the school is supposed to have done something by a certain day, have that date marked on your calendar so you can follow up.

- Keep good files. Don't lose things over the summer.

General advice

The above problems centered on the US, but I'm sure the same sorts of problems occur everywhere. My overall suggestion for all of these school problems is to not depend totally on the school. Certainly you will work with them to put together good goals for your child (in the US and Australia this is called the individualized education plan or IEP, in the UK it's called a statement of special educational needs or SSEN). But until someone starts *doing the actions*, nothing has been done as far as helping your child is concerned. Important-looking paperwork does not obviate the need for a good informal one-to-one relationship with the teacher. After all, you can develop a rapport with someone in a few minutes, while developing an IEP may take weeks or months. If at all possible, work together to make small informal changes on the fly (and never mind the blasted paperwork or formal meetings!). Thomas Edison once said, 'Hell, there are no rules here – we're trying to accomplish something.'

Last but not least, work as many issues as you can at home. This is leading to Avenue Three, the do-it-yourself response. But let me be clear. I am not suggesting that you relieve professionals of their responsibility within the medical or school communities. I would hate to think that someone in either setting would hand you a copy of this book and say, 'Other parents get along without a lot of outside intervention so you should too.' The fact that there are some homegrown techniques that might work does not absolve professionals of their legal and ethical duties to *do their job*. To suggest such a thing would be as inappropriate as calling for an ambulance and having a first aid manual dropped off on your doorstep.

Of course, if the ambulance is not *coming*, a first aid manual might come in handy. I suggest you use this book in the following ways:

- as a supplement to the services your child is already getting
- as a stopgap measure of things to do while waiting for formal mechanisms to kick in
- as a set of suggested things to do when formal systems are failing or not living out their promises
- as a set of things to do when you consciously choose to avoid formal mechanisms.

Finally, although there are serious potholes in the medical and educational paths, I hope you don't see them as hopeless. They are not. Probably *most* parents who seek diagnosis and services will achieve most of what they're looking for. The system *does* work for a significant portion of the autistic spectrum population. I just can't tell you what the portion is, or what *your* odds of having an excellent experience might be. No one knows what hand you will be dealt. Now let's look at the third avenue.

Survival and interim tactics

With or without formal diagnosis, decide for yourself if you think your child has Asperger Syndrome, and see for yourself what kind of things you can do.

If it looks, sounds, and acts like a duck, call it a duck. And if you feel Asperger Syndrome is a good fit for your child's issues, start operating from that viewpoint. Don't be afraid. Resist the temptation to put all decisions on hold while awaiting experts. That can kill time and your child needs help, the sooner the better.

If the idea of somehow 'diagnosing' your own child, even in your own mind, seems irresponsible, please consider the following.

In many ways you already do diagnose your own child

Whether it was you or someone else who first spotted your child's differences, once alerted you were the one to do research, including picking up this book and probably others. Chances are you are already more knowledgeable about Asperger Syndrome than your family doctor is. In fact, you may as well start getting used to thinking of yourself as an expert because in most situations, you will be.

You may not only be more expert than your family doctor, you may even know more than some specialists

The numbers of experts in the field of Asperger Syndrome is growing, and autism clinics will have top-notch experts. However, in the entire United States, there is only one graduate program for Asperger Syndrome (University of Kansas), and only a handful for autism. One autism specialist I talked to a couple of years ago assured me that most neurologists have never had a course in either Asperger Syndrome or Tourette Syndrome. With rare exceptions, any knowledge would have been dependent upon individual initiative in outside reading. I doubt if circumstances are better in other countries.

You know your child

You see your child every day in all sorts of situations – one-on-one, small groups, large groups, etc. The doctor doesn't. The doctor will have a calm, one-on-one conversation with your child and then may dismiss Asperger Syndrome as a diagnosis because your child communicates well or maintains some eye contact under those circumstances. And you will reject these findings and get another doctor, and another, until you get the diagnosis you believe is right (so who diagnosed your child?). Or, that first doctor may realize his or her view is limited and will ask for your input. *Your* observations then will provide much of the basis on which the doctor does the diagnosing. Again, in many ways the diagnosis comes from you.

Please don't misunderstand. Don't fake forms, lie, or be any less diligent in procuring actual diagnosis from a professional. I am suggesting, however, that you take a proactive attitude. Instead of waiting for experts to give you license to seek help for your child, give yourself that permission and move forward. Specifically, the steps might look like this:

- Step 1: say out loud, 'Yes, my child has Asperger Syndrome.'

- Step 2: begin examining your options (therapy, school, daycare) in light of this quasi-diagnosis.

- Step 3: read everything you can and start working issues both at school and at home using this book and any other resources you can get your hands on.

When I first learned of Asperger Syndrome in 1994, I knew it described my son. From that moment on, if asked, I simply said, 'He has Asperger Syndrome.' I might or might not add, 'And we're awaiting formal diagnosis.' Because I was sure, people accepted it.

I also sent an information sheet on it to all of John's teachers. All but one teacher (there's always one) readily accepted that John had Asperger Syndrome. I say this because even though John had no formal label (the waiting list was too long) and hence could not receive services formally, we still got some minor services. For instance, the counselor suggested that he could see John weekly for social skills work; his social studies teacher promised to make sure John had enough time to answer essay tests and said he would not mark answers wrong because of messy handwriting, which had formerly been an issue; his English teacher renewed her conviction that John would not be teased. In truth, at this stage, those would have been the main accommodations I'd have gone after anyway.

Appendix 2 will give you several good contacts for further information on Asperger Syndrome, the IEP process, and more. If you have access to Internet, you already have access to all the information you need, but for those who don't, addresses and phone numbers have been included. And of course, most of the rest of this book is devoted to presenting ways you can take the reins and work various issues yourself.

Chapter 4

Coming to Terms, Moving Forward

I can't tell you what most parents go through when they discover their child has a disability. I can only tell you my perspective. If you feel scared, or mad, or worried, so did I. You might feel alone too, but having this book in hand should tell you that you're not.

Parents are not automatons. You may perform superhuman feats in doing what's best for your child, but it doesn't make you superhuman. Maybe you manage to put up a brave face through the day as you deal with teachers, family members, doctors, and so forth. After the drapes are drawn for the night, though, you just might have to spend that last ounce of energy wrestling some mental gremlins.

There are a few nasty head gremlins lying in wait for you – denial, grief, guilt and a few more. They sap your strength and leave you indecisive and numb if you let them. Ask me how I know. Worse than that, they waste your time, so they are expensive boarders to feed. You can't afford to keep them longer than necessary. So turn on the lights and confront them. Send them packing or at least tie them up in the attic so their impact is minimal. Here are some tactics that may help.

Denial

Ever catch yourself saying one of these or hearing one from someone else about your child?

- 'I don't think there's anything wrong with this child. Teachers (or kids or daycare workers) just don't like him.'

- 'He's just having a bad day.'
- 'I was just like him as a child and look at me. I'm fine. He'll be fine.'
- 'He may have some problems, but he just needs [discipline, limits, a swat on the behind] and he'll straighten out.'
- 'Those doctors don't know anything. They're just looking for problems to treat.'

When these statements come from neighbors, friends, or casual acquaintances, it's no big deal. When they come from school staff, it means you have a fight on your hands. And if it comes from you, your spouse, or your family, these statements are signposts to the land of denial. It's a pretty common side trip for parents, actually, and usually one parent spends a lot more time in this wasteland than the other.

My husband and I were both in denial at first, because we didn't see what others saw. John was our first child, he seemed bright and content at home, we were used to his quirks, and with our busy schedules – poor excuse – we had never really stopped to watch John's demeanor outside the home. If we had, we might have seen that John was marching to a different drummer. Instead, we were initially shocked to hear of problems.

Being the nurturer and family worrywart, though, I was the one who followed up on the red flags when they appeared. I talked to daycare people, saw the family doctor and took John to assessments. Watching my son interact (or rather, not interact) with playmates, then seeing him act so puzzlingly during assessments, soon opened my eyes. It was hard to stay in denial too long.

My husband, on the other hand, wasn't buying it at first. Maybe he could better afford denial since he was not the one dealing with those 'other people'. I'm sure he didn't see problems as directly as I did. He mostly heard things second-hand through me. Perhaps if I'd forced him to go with me, or had been a better interpreter, he would have been less skeptical. Once he did get beyond the denial, I'm happy to report he was an active participant and champion for John, but I think even he will admit it was hard for him to get to that point.

Fathers seem to be in denial longer than mothers as a rule, but it probably depends on who is more involved in daily care giving. Typically dads are not up to their knees in daily kid interactions the way moms are.

Dads may need time for other reasons – the 'chip off the old block' sort of male pride may require an adjustment period. (Or am I just furthering outmoded stereotypes? I don't really know. I'm just throwing out ideas here for your evaluation.) Too, I have the impression that males embrace problems best if the problems seem fixable. We all know the old joke about males being unwilling to ask for directions or help. Maybe it's harder to acknowledge a problem in which there is no easy fix and they are going to have to ask for help.

As long as I'm already out on a skinny limb making generalizations, let me make one more. Studies show that for every child with Asperger Syndrome, there are usually more relatives in the family tree who show tendencies. Since those are most likely to be males, a lot of dads of children with Asperger Syndrome probably have a dash of it themselves. If so, they may have a different mental yardstick of what is 'normal' and 'not normal'. They may be slow to pick up on social oddities, for example. Dad may also feel that if he himself survived childhood while having these traits, his child will too, so why put a label on it at all? You could only make an argument for that if both parent and child each just have 'a dash' of Asperger Syndrome, however.

Whatever the cause, denial can cause a rift between parents. If the two of you can't agree on what is going on with your child, you also can't agree on what to do next. Lack of consistency doesn't do the child any good either and it increases the chance that you won't do anything at all.

To get around all this denial, seeing is believing. If your spouse doubts anything is wrong but is amenable to at least doing his (or her) own investigating, get him out of the buffer zone of home and closer to the lines of battle. That is, arrange for your spouse to observe your child in the classroom or daycare. It can be a real eye opener to see your child in a social setting and side by side with same-age peers. Have your spouse attend school meetings and speak with the teachers. He may come home with a new impression.

If your spouse is unwilling to do that, your job is tougher but not impossible. Perhaps he does not like facing outside people. If so, continue being the main communicator with doctor and school, but try one of these:

- Have your child video- or audio-recorded. Bill still recalls the shock from an audiotape of our overstimulated son at daycare. It was John's voice, but *not* the John he knew.

- Discuss with your spouse any chats you have with teachers.

- Ask your spouse to attend meetings with you but don't expect him to take a leading role.

- Make available any handouts, reports, or articles that might shed light for him.

I have to confess that Bill was not fond of being handed reading materials but he did read them. I also used to read aloud those Internet emails from parents of other kids whose characteristics were similar to our own son's. I would often say, 'Hey, listen to this!' then read aloud about some other boy and wait for my husband to exclaim, 'That sounds like John!' After a few instances of knowing there were other families out there in similar circumstances, we were both more comfortable with admitting the problems we were having and putting a label to them.

One reason for denial is when we get conflicting views from people who are supposed to be the experts. One doctor says *X* diagnosis and another doctor says *Y* diagnosis, so how can you believe either one? No one ever spoke to us about the concept of *pervasive* developmental disability, which would have connected the dots for us. Each separate label (sensory issues, motor issues) was like being shown an individual star in a big dark sky, but no one ever showed us that they were all part of one constellation. If they had, we would have gotten our bearings sooner.

An added problem was that we knew the label of mental retardation was wrong (it was), so that gave us a toehold to discount everything. Bill would throw up his hands and exclaim, 'These bozos don't know anything!' and I would agree. I even wrote an article for the *Denver Post* in which I voiced my frustration and misgivings. We had allowed our son to be part of the early intervention preschool by that time, but in my article I wondered if we had placed our child in the hands of 'modern-day witch doctors and Dr. Frankensteins, anxious to put hard-earned degrees to use.' Some years later when I met with the superintendent of schools and he opened my son's file folder, that clipping fluttered out. I'm not sure who was more embarrassed.

So I'm hardly one to tell other people not to be in denial, but I guess I will say this. Try not to throw the baby out with the bathwater. If one part of the diagnosis seems wrong, fine, throw that out, but do not necessarily throw out the rest. The doctors aren't perfect, and also, I've learned that when it comes to this area of neurology, little is 'all or nothing'. A child never fits a diagnosis perfectly, so expect fuzzy areas, dual diagnoses, areas of overlap, and things that don't quite fit. It is a much messier business than the crisp black-and-white DSM-IV (the doctor's diagnostics guide: APA 1994) would lead you to believe. Just work with what does fit. In the end, you do not live with a label; you live with a child. If the label helps you access services, it has done its work. Worry about the picture, not the frame.

Speaking of labels, I guess here is as good as any place to talk about the stigma of labels. Some folks hate the thought of any label being put on their child. A label feels superficial, inadequate, self-limiting, and like a pigeonhole. True, true, true, and true. However, labels do have these three things going for them:

- Finding the right label prevents the wrong label being assumed. Once your child hits the classroom, he will get a label, but it could end up being a label like 'problem kid' or 'pain in the you-know-what,' and you will have the label 'rotten parent' in the bargain. If you are going to have to live with labels then, it's far better to have a label that has a hope of pointing to the correct issues.

- Labels point you in the right directions to find support groups, research papers, helpful articles and books, and parenting techniques.

- Labels get your child services.

In the end, a label is a tool. Use it if you can, don't be used by it.

The last thing I've learned about denial is that it comes and goes. Even *years* after you believe the diagnosis, you will be tempted to doubt it from time to time. It's usually when things are on a roll. Life is good at home, the school hasn't called you in awhile, and maybe your child tells you he has a friend. You start to wonder if you were all wrong about the diagnosis. Did you dream it up? Could your child have somehow gotten over it?

Asperger Syndrome is a lifelong condition, a way of looking at and processing the world. That won't change. What probably really happened was that the school had nothing new to relate and they're busy so they didn't bother to communicate. Or, perhaps your child's school experience really is improving because he has a gem of a teacher who understands what it takes to spell success for an Asperger child. Maybe your child does have a friend at long last. Good things do happen! Even so, it's a mistake to fall into the trap of thinking 'finally, we're over the hump.' It is not a hump. It is a lifelong journey, as any adult with Asperger Syndrome will tell you. It's just that the incline of the road may be gentle right now or your child has developed more coping skills (better muscles to make the journey, so to speak).

Enjoy the break and catch your breath, but do not believe that the trek is over.

If I were to hazard a guess, the antidote for this type of denial is probably to gather all the information on Asperger Syndrome you can, particularly the writings of adults with Asperger Syndrome. Their often poignant, direct, and even very eloquent observations will illustrate to you the many facets of Asperger Syndrome that remain challenging no matter how much time passes.

Grief

This is a toughie. People have different ways of grieving and there doesn't seem to be any right or wrong to it. And I suspect most parents of disabled children go through it. So just go through it as best you can, and try to let your partner go through it too, not necessarily in the same way. My husband seemed to clam up, and when pressed, he would tend to get angry and soon after would go to bed with a headache. That's just his style. Me, I had to talk about it, write about it, read about it, and talk some more. It can be a very rocky time. I have no solution here, just a warning. Be gentle with one another if you can. For the one who needs to talk more than the spouse is willing to, Internet support groups and face-to-face support groups are the ticket. Find them and you will soon feel less alone and have a place to bare your soul if need be. For the partner who needs to retreat and process things alone, usually time and some peace and quiet are the main requirements.

One thing that may help a bit is advice a friend of mine gave about the diagnosis process. She said, 'Just remember, no matter what the diagnosis is, that kid sitting in front of you is the same one as before. *He* hasn't changed. You just know better how to help him.' Good thinking.

What else about grief? Like denial, it will ebb away, but comes rippling back from time to time. For the most part, after the first big shock, we all learn to get on with the business of raising our children, and we deal with the daily frustrations and learn to take pleasure in the progress. We learn to push back that huge wave of grief that we had at the beginning. Still, once in awhile little sorrows catch us quite by surprise.

Some of these sorrows are predictable. At each major milestone, whether the first day of kindergarten or a birthday or the last day of high school, we tend to take stock. And we tend not to look just at our child but also to the left and right of him, making comparisons with other kids and being reminded that our children (and by extension, we) don't fit in. I feel like Roger Ebert reviewing one of those predictable teen horror movies. I want to yell, 'You know the monster is in the basement so *don't go in the basement!*' And it is the same with these sorts of comparisons. Don't put yourself through it. Your child is unique with his own timetable, so doing a comparison with other classmates is unfair to you and your child. A much better idea is to find a happier comparison. Instead of looking at the other kids, look at your own kid and think back to how very far he has come. Has he overcome a big issue that you were worried about last year – potty training? Getting on the bus? You will see tremendous progress with this sort of comparison, and it will give you a great deal more pleasure and optimism for future successes.

I have known some parents who say they grieve for their child's condition because it signals the 'death of their dreams' or the 'death of the child they thought they were going to have.' No parent knows what her child is going to be or do, so don't sell him short. His future may be brighter than you're giving him credit for. It is not his job to fulfill your dreams in any case. He'll be too busy trying to fulfill his own dreams. So-called 'normal' kids are just as uncooperative when it comes to fulfilling parents' dreams!

So I understand this sort of grief to some extent, but it is selfish indulgence. Rather than focus on self we need to remember that this is about our children. But wait, I said earlier that we should be kind to one another about our grief. OK, if you want to feel crushed about the death of your dreams, well, go right ahead.

Have a good cry, but then get on with helping your child realize his own dreams.

Guilt

I would like to dismiss guilt with one sentence. Don't waste your time. But that might not be enough discussion for you, so here are a couple of comments. When one finally absorbs the diagnosis of one's child, we do all seem to ask ourselves, how did this happen? What did I do, or not do, to cause my child to have Asperger Syndrome?

Chances are you didn't do anything wrong, or if you did no one can tell you what that was. There are lots of theories, and a ton of research, but the $64,000 question remains – what causes Asperger Syndrome and other autism spectrum disorders?

You will have no trouble finding enough research to wallpaper your house if you do a bit of scratching around Internet. It's beyond the scope of this book (and beyond the scope of my non-scientific background) to get into a technical discussion. However, there are a few big schools of thought having to do with genetics and some physical differences in the brain. Some other theories have to do with gastrointestinal (food absorption and digestion) issues, vaccinations, environmental assaults, and brain chemistry. I think there may be several subtypes of autism spectrum disorders that are caused by one or more of the above variables which would explain why things like diet can help one autistic person but not another. Some attempts have been made to figure out ways in which there may be interplay among the afore-mentioned variables so that they may all be contributors or feed off one another. Most researchers seem to have tunnel vision in this regard however so there isn't as much effort made to integrate the various theories as one would think. Dr. Paul Shattock gives the best discussion I have seen in this regard. (See Appendix 7 for his website address.)

Given that there may be several contributing causes then, here is my simplistic analogy. I liken the origin of Asperger Syndrome

to the popular dice game called Yahtzee. Yes, I'm serious. It's all in
the roll of the dice. Maybe one die represents a child's genetic
make-up. Another couple of dice might represent environmental
factors and prenatal issues. The next one might represent diet or
allergies. The last die might represent birth trauma or vaccination
reaction. Roll all the dice and if they land just right you get
Yahtzee – or rather, autism or Asperger Syndrome. Extending this
analogy further, perhaps if you get all sixes you get one type of
autism, and all fives would give you another subtype. Who
knows? This analogy is ridiculously simplistic, but perhaps it's
enough to help you keep these hard questions at arm's length and
not worry about them. If the researchers get it all figured out, I'm
sure they'll let us know.

To be honest, I never felt guilty about possibly causing my
son's issues, because I knew that I tried to have the healthiest
pregnancy I could. I don't smoke, and as soon as I found out I was
expecting, I made sure not to take alcohol or any medications. I
took prenatal vitamins, saw my doctor, and switched to decaf
coffee and tea. Even so, no pregnancy is perfect! I worked shift
work so was short on sleep; I worked around electrical
equipment; we lived near a toxic waste site; I drank gallons of
milk (which my child is sensitive to). The doctor gave me drugs to
induce labor, and also some pain medication during labor that has
since been taken off the market. I drank alcohol the week before I
discovered I was pregnant. And, of course, I gave John my genes,
although there's not much I could have done about that.

Even though we try to do things right, something interferes. I
can't beat myself up about it. Whatever I did wrong, if anything,
was done inadvertently and in good faith. I am truly at peace with
this and I sincerely wish that for other parents. Guilt is pointless.

Inertia

Inertia (in my opinion) might be caused by panic, depression,
complacency, being overwhelmed, or having a fatalistic view that
'what will be, will be'. Whatever the cause, your child will suffer

from your inertia so once again, try to get over it as soon as possible.

I think the antidote is to take a small step, and then another and then another. If you are overwhelmed, close your books and websites and forget trying to solve the great mysteries of Asperger Syndrome. Just tackle a little issue. Teach your child one idiom today, practice catching the ball, read him a story, talk about his day, or cook a pancake together. All of these are noble actions that go far in teaching him language, motor skills, social skills, and life skills.

Panic and complacency are different sides of the same coin, and we need to figure out a way to balance it. If you are panicked, please rest assured that things are probably not so bleak as you fear. Your child will grow and develop and things will get steadily better. So don't panic.

But, don't be complacent either! You can't assume things will improve without your direct daily involvement. You can't dismiss the importance of your role, or say that educating your child and overcoming various issues is the school's responsibility. It may be their job but it's your responsibility. If they don't do their job, or do it well enough, it's not good enough to spend your time writing letters of complaint and waiting for replies, or filing a lawsuit against the school system that ties up two years of your time and causes you to take a second job to pay the lawyers. None of these things means *anything* to your child today. And today is what counts. This day. Do not be complacent. A board game with your son will probably be more productive than a meeting of the school board.

Some helpful emotions
Relief

You might have felt an intense sense of relief to have a label. I know that after searching through a zillion unsatisfactory answers, I was overjoyed finally to put a name to the issues. I finally had validation of all those unsettling suspicions I had been juggling in my mind for months. Finally figuring things out puts boundaries around the unknown, and lays to rest a lot of other labels that you no longer have to think about. It contains the amorphous worries into something definite you can work with; and it absolves you of the mantle of rotten parenthood and self-doubt once and for all. Enjoy the relief, and use it to empower you to tackle the jobs that need doing.

Optimism

Yes, there is optimism to be had. You may feel devastated at first to feel the limitations implied by all the various issues that are involved in a pervasive developmental disorder. It can be overwhelming to think about the length of the row you have to hoe. But it's not that bad.

After I wrote my article in the *Denver Post* (John was four then) in which I bemoaned my son's many special needs and worried about what his future would hold, I got a beautiful, handwritten letter from a mother named Heather, sent to me in care of the newspaper. The letter spanned seven pages in which she described her own son and the success he was now having after having once been in the same special education classes my son was in. The letter was meant to be encouraging but all I could feel was bitterness and fear. Her son 'only' had ADD but was otherwise able to cope with classes and sports and so forth. My son seemed ten times more disabled and I was so angry at her blind assumption that my son would ever – ever – be as successful as hers. I knew that I should write to thank her, but I was too bitter to find the words. I threw her letter into a box.

Thirteen years later the letter is still in a box, unanswered, but when I find it again I am finally going to respond to her and tell her our own story. For all of my son's seemingly profound deficits at the age of three and four, these days life is good.

So, although you may be reading this paragraph with an urge to cry, resist it. You may want to holler at me, 'Well my son is obviously worse off than yours! How dare you promise me a bright future when all I see is despair!' Well, I can't promise anything, and our kids are all going to turn out differently. All I can say is, if you approach your parenting job with tremendous optimism and perseverance, good things will happen.

Of course, as hard as I wanted to shake Heather for her Pollyanna viewpoint that did not seem to fit my world, I cannot say enough about optimism and its importance. Although I believed that my son had much greater issues than Heather's son did, I was still adamantly determined that John was going to go as far as he possibly could and I would never hold him back through diminished expectations. I am a firm believer in the power of self-fulfilling prophesy, and I would never ever suggest to John that he couldn't do anything he set his mind to.

Persistence

Next to optimism, persistence is your greatest asset. You will need to be persistent in getting a diagnosis, in resolving medication or diet issues, in dealing with obstinate schools, and in working with your child each and every day. You will need to try different approaches to behavior and learning, since our kids often do not respond to conventional parenting books and do not learn the way most kids learn. You will need persistence in breaking down social situations into small pieces so that lessons can be learned from them.

All of these action items take hard work and tenacity. But even just making small inroads every day, the progress can be astounding. Luckily, you probably have a great role model for persistence in your own household – your child with Asperger Syndrome. John has shown me the power of persevering in a hundred different ways. He started as the most inept bowler in the league and ended up as state champion. He didn't learn to skip until he was twelve but he learned to do skips and cartwheels and front flips through sheer determination, by logging hundreds of hours out on the front lawn, willing to fall and get up again as many times as it took. How could I do any less than be willing to fall down and get back up again myself?

Seeing Asperger Syndrome in yourself

Many of us who have discovered Asperger Syndrome in our children can pinpoint some traits in ourselves. Whether we parents go on own path of self-discovery and eventually seek formal diagnosis, or simply see a few signs here and there, the introspective journey can be worth taking.

I do not feel that my husband and I have Asperger Syndrome, but the shadows are there. As a young child I had quite a wild flappy dance when I was excited, I was miserable at team sports, and had few friends. I have waxing and waning compulsive tendencies (counting, checking, list-making), have mild face blindness, and have always had difficulty dealing with anything new. My husband is extremely logical, black and white in his thinking, and he has a great need for order. We are not joiners by nature, although when we are among others we can have a good time. When we got married, we chose a secret civil ceremony at the courthouse. We brought no one with us and had to borrow a courthouse secretary to be our witness (I remember she wore lime green stretch pants). Bill and I are probably more alike than different, ignore fashion trends, and our idea of a nice Friday night is generally watching reruns of favorite movies or sharing a thermos of coffee between our two side-by-side computers.

Probably we are just a bit eccentric – which may be the extreme mildest end of Asperger Syndrome? If nothing else, our personal connections to Asperger Syndrome, however tenuous or debatable, help us connect with John. For one thing, I can understand my son's wish for more friends and the difficulty in finding them. I hope it helps him to know that I faced similar challenges trying to fit in, and I learned the joy of not having to fit into any particular group and to respect my individuality and need for space away from the crowd. It's really OK to be different.

I used to worry about John's future because I saw it as this great unknown. However, Dr. Attwood told John he thought life would likely become easier as he goes along. Part of this happy prognosis is because John will continue to hone coping skills and gain social graces as he matures, but also, as an adult he will be able to make choices that suit him. Adults, after all, can live their own life. A narrow pursuit is called a specialty when you're an adult, which sounds much nicer than a perseverative interest or obsession. No one cares if all you read is nonfiction and no one makes you play a team sport. I'd say adulthood has a lot going for the individual with Asperger Syndrome.

Telling your child about Asperger Syndrome

Our big discussion took place when my John was twelve, but we had led up to the topic in a number of ways before that. I think a good start for a young child is to talk about the fact that everybody is different and that's OK. Quite young kids can understand how boring it would be if everyone were the same.

This can lead to discussion on *how* everyone is different, and that some people are good at some things and not so good at other things. If your child is not good at catching a ball, for example, you can remind him how much he knows about dinosaurs.

We stayed at this juncture for years. Eventually, though, John became particularly down on himself and frustrated. He knew that he wasn't coping in school the way other kids did. At this point, we discussed that he also learned in a different way from most people. When that made him upset, we reminded him that everyone has something to deal with and we talked about various people we knew and the things they had to deal with – a lisp, a bad ear, lazy eye, allergies, asthma, and so forth. No one has everything just the way they want it and it's OK to have problems because everyone has them.

We had these talks many times over the years, and that's how we dealt with the various problem areas John had to deal with –

his school problems, his friend problems, etc. Then, when he was twelve, he asked me point blank if there were something 'really wrong' with him that made him different from all the other kids.

At this point, we discussed Asperger Syndrome. I told him that there was a name for what made him different, but that it was really just the collection of things we'd talked about over the years – the messy handwriting, the different way of learning, the social problems. I thought he would be upset to hear this big official name, but the relief was visible on his face. He said, 'You mean there's a reason I have messy handwriting? A reason I can't make friends? I thought it was just me!'

Rather than be upset by hearing that he had a syndrome, he felt better to have a reason for things and a relief that he no longer needed to blame himself. In some ways, I probably should have told him earlier, but I didn't know these things were worrying him. Anyway, I'd only known about it for about a year myself.

He also felt better when I told him all the good things about Asperger Syndrome. I told him he was very special, with a good brain and a good memory, and a logical way of looking at things. We talked about other people who were smart but different – Thomas Edison and Albert Einstein, for example, and Bill Gates. He ended up feeling quite OK about the discussion.

You will need to follow your own instinct. Although I might have told John a bit earlier, I would still advise not rushing. You don't want to dump everything at once onto your child, and I definitely advise waiting until you are comfortable with the diagnosis and have come to terms with it. You need to be able to talk about it without looking upset or scared, to be able to talk about it realistically but also optimistically, and to be able to see the good side of Asperger Syndrome yourself.

When Dr. Attwood later confirmed to John that he had Asperger Syndrome, he also was upbeat. In fact, he said, 'Congratulations,' and shook John's hand. He also told John that he is a hero, because every day at school he does two jobs (thinking about both academics and social issues), while most kids only have to do one job. I couldn't agree more.

Siblings

I have only recently told John's little brother Jay a bit about Asperger Syndrome. I've tried on a few occasions but he doesn't seem to be curious or want to know about it. He's twelve now, but maybe still isn't ready to absorb much.

I think he thinks that Asperger Syndrome just means that his brother gets to be rigid while he must be the flexible one. It is true to a certain extent. Since Jay is easy going, he gets asked to be the one to bend, probably more often than should happen.

There are a few areas of contention. Jay has lots of friends. It is annoying to John to have phones and doorbells ringing all the time, and sometimes he is jealous.

Beyond that, they are just two very different kids and they butt heads a lot. They do have tender moments though. When Jay was eight he seemed to get birthday party invitations about every other week, much to John's frustration. When yet another one arrived, Jay said, 'Let's not tell John. He'll get upset.' Then he looked at it more closely and grinned broadly. 'It's for John! YES!' I started to cry, both from happiness at John being invited to a party and also from seeing the love Jay had for his brother.

Dealing with others – family

A family's reaction to the news of your child's diagnosis can be pretty surprising and often hurtful, so be prepared. I count myself lucky to have a family that is supportive no matter what. My folks do not tell me what to do and seem to trust that I will do what's best for my kids.

A lot of people have less happy tales. Frequently the child's grandparent or other relative does the denial thing, or offers various solutions that usually amount to various forms of discipline or anti-mollycoddling. The fact that you have already tried those techniques to no avail, rolls off of them like a tennis ball down a driveway.

You can spend time and energy trying to educate them, and continue to keep them informed of developments in the hope they will eventually get it. Some family members will actually get it, and may turn out to be your staunchest supporters.

The other choice is to realize that some people aren't ever going to get it. With those, you just have to deal with it as best you can. You can try to ignore remarks from insensitive family members. Or you can be generous and choose to interpret remarks in their most positive light (Aunt Sarah is only trying to be helpful, Uncle George's denial is really an attempt to make us feel better). Sometimes you have to overlook misguided remarks for the sake of family harmony.

If every family gathering ends in disaster and bickering, though, you might want to put perimeters on your child's exposure to them. This might mean cutting visits short, leaving children home with one parent or a competent babysitter, or forgoing some family events entirely. Limiting exposure serves a few purposes – it is less stressful on the child, who can easily be wound up or overwhelmed by a family gathering; it is less stressful on the parent, who otherwise spends all day trying to avert crises; and it gives less ammunition to those critical family members who just love to see a child spun out of control so they can offer unsolicited advice on how they would fix that kid! Also, a few short but successful experiences are going to help your child's social skills much more than one long fiasco.

Sadly, some families find such lack of support among the extended family members that at some point all ties are severed. This is very sad, but when every family gathering results in damaged feelings, relationships put on hold may be the best you can do. Ties can perhaps be re-established at a later point.

Dealing with others – friends

Friends can seem in short supply when you have a child diagnosed with a disability of any type. Folks don't know what to say and feel awkward. Just as your child may rarely get birthday party invitations from classmates, you may start feeling shunned by folks you thought were your friends too. At least, this is what I've heard.

Frankly, my husband and I have never been social butterflies and have a very small circle of friends who accept our kids along with us, warts and all, so our true friends are still our true friends.

Sometimes our friends have had to be persistent with us though. In true Asperger style, when my husband and I face a dilemma, we tend to roll down the tent flaps and become rather inaccessible. When we were going through the early days of knowing something was wrong but not knowing what, we needed time to sort things out. It was not a time to throw parties or go to them. We were too exhausted (mentally, physically, emotionally) to want to be social. I don't think we formed these thoughts consciously in our minds, of course. It was just that when an invitation to do something came up, we often weren't up to it.

Another sort of self-imposed isolation occurred too. When John was much younger, I used to see him be shunned by other people's kids. It put a frosty edge on the relationships that I had, or might have had, with those kids' parents. I couldn't help feeling hurt and resentful. Of course I knew I couldn't force other kids to like my kid, so there was nothing really to be done about it. But it stopped me from being very chatty and friendly. I know of no adult who ever snubbed me, but I think in some ways I found myself pre-emptively snubbing others. Perhaps on some other level I was envious that other parents had such an easy time of it, and fearful and embarrassed (in our pre-diagnosis days) that I just didn't have the parenting skills they did and that it would be only a matter of time before they figured out I was a clueless idiot of a parent. Then surely they would ostracize me just as their kids ostracized John, so why should I bother getting to know them at all? It was easy to isolate oneself.

So regardless of who started it, one's world does seem to get smaller and less friendly than it used to be. If there is an antidote, I suppose realizing that a lot of the isolation is self-imposed can help. Also, reaching out to support groups is good. You will find people who are in the same boat and who won't judge you in the same way that others will. They won't raise an eyebrow over a child who is flapping or walking in circles, and a meltdown tantrum won't throw them.

Dealing with the community

Sometimes you wonder how much of your child's disability to disclose. Do you tell the babysitter? The baseball coach? The summer camp staff? The parks department swimming instructor? Your neighbors? You certainly don't go around telling everyone that you come in contact with about it. How do you decide whom to tell?

It depends on the amount of time and responsibility the other person will have with your child. When it came to swimming lessons, my son enjoyed the lessons, they were short and I was always nearby, so it seemed unnecessary to discuss special issues unless I saw a problem developing (I didn't). On the other hand, John was involved in two different scout troops and disclosure or non-disclosure was possibly the deal-breaker for John's success. With the first troop, I discussed things with the leader. The leader was superb in easing John into the troop, finding buddies for him, and patiently explaining items that were confusing or of concern to John, such as *exactly* what was to happen on an overnight (the complete menus, all activities, etc.). It was a successful experience. The following year we moved and changed troops. This time I opted not to tell the leader. John lasted two meetings before refusing to attend again. Now this troop was also more chaotic, but I wonder if things would have gone better with some more disclosure. One can only guess.

Although I will talk about school in Chapters 5 and 6, here's one more comment. At the beginning of each school year (for the years that John has attended conventional school), I have endeavored to reach all of John's teachers to explain his unique style and Asperger Syndrome in general. Inevitably I miss one or two teachers, and usually it is with one of these teachers that I end up locking horns later. Sometimes we can iron things out, but often the die is cast for a miserable relationship, and I sorely wish I'd gotten to them *before* things went awry.

Now my bottom line is, when in doubt, I have a talk.

Chapter 5
School in General

When Chris was young and having his greatest difficulties (first and second grades), there was no label called Asperger Syndrome, and consequently no books, therapies, websites, or anything else to guide us. What were we supposed to do with this child? I read everything I could, and eventually found guidance in the writings of two smart men – John Holt, a teacher, and Abraham Maslow, a psychologist, neither of whom ever focused on special needs children or ever heard of Asperger Syndrome. Yet they taught me what was wrong with John's school (and most if not all schools) and also how to proceed.

Holt spent many years as a grade school teacher, observing average kids in his classes. Mostly he observed how they *failed* to learn in spite of his best efforts. That he could want so very much to teach these kids and still fail troubled him deeply. He determined to study the issue and write his observations. All of his books are worth reading but his book *How Children Fail* (1982) rearranged my thinking about schools and learning, and solidified my resolve to follow our own education path.

One fundamental finding of Holt's is that fear predominates the school experience.

> There are very few children who do not feel…an amount of fear, anxiety, and tension that most adults would find intolerable. It is no coincidence at all that in many of their worst nightmares, adults find themselves back in school. (Holt 1982, p.115)

The idea that fear interferes with learning, attention, memory, and intelligence is certainly not news. Who among us hasn't shown up for a test only to discover that our brain has shut down? Or has gotten so flustered that we forget our own phone number? Holt's observations on fear made a connection for me with John. If kids are anxious in the classroom, how do they learn anything? And if average kids are anxious in the classroom, what must it be like for the child with Asperger Syndrome?

At that early time I had little understanding of the issues John had – the language pragmatics difficulties, literal thinking, mind blindness and so forth. But after reading Holt, I started to realize that John was telling me through his actions in the classroom – his barking, growling, spitting, swearing, biting – that he was feeling terrified and besieged.

All of this connected with recollections of a college lecture years earlier on psychologist Abraham Maslow's Hierarchy of Needs. Briefly, the main tenet of his theory is that individuals are motivated to satisfy various needs in stages, and one stage needs to be largely fulfilled before the next stage can be effectively reached for. This is often depicted as a pyramid or ladder, but the order is as follows:

1   physiological: food, water, and air

2   safety: security, stability, protection, need for structure, and freedom from fear, anxiety, and chaos

3   belongingness and love: giving/receiving love, friendship, finding a place in a group or family

4   esteem: competency, achievement, adequacy, self-esteem, recognition

5   self-actualization: having the 'peak' experience of doing what one is meant to do, reaching one's individual's potential.

We don't need to worry much about Step 1 since families reading this book will most likely know where their next meal is coming from. What about Step 2? Do our kids feel safe? Holt says that at school most do not! And what about Step 3 – belonging to the group? The hallmark of Asperger children is not belonging to the group. Our schools want kids to learn and achieve but that doesn't come until Step 4.

What I drew from this with respect to my son's experience in primary school was that he was being asked to skip from Step 1 to Step 4. It was no surprise that John couldn't focus on anything, that he tantrummed to be removed from the classroom, and was in grade two but only doing kindergarten work. Hadn't Holt and Maslow both said the same thing? John was stalled, terrified, at Step 2. The schools were trying to teach a boy to swim while he was busy drowning.

Now, on *top* of the basic fear/safety issue you could layer all the other issues that we have come to know about Asperger Syndrome – the misread social cues, motor clumsiness, sensory integration stuff. All of these issues just help to explain why John was chronically anxious. But at the time, I didn't really understand those things. I could only deal with the fact that he was anxious and try to do something about it.

Safety

How big an issue is safety? I think it is huge. Holt's observations led him to conclude that *all* students are fearful in the classroom and that the emotion is powerful enough to bring effective learning to its knees. Maslow believed that the issue of safety and security was second only to food, water and air in importance. If either had known about children with Asperger Syndrome, I think they would have been appalled to think of the added issues our kids have to deal with that directly connect to feelings of fear and chaos. These include:

- sounds, sights, smells, and tactile input, which are overwhelming to our usually hypersensitive kids
- Theory of Mind problems, rendering people's actions and reactions unpredictable and mysterious to our kids
- literalness, which increases the chances our kids will misinterpret verbal communication and be easily lost
- social skills deficits, which cause our children to be ostracized from peer groups and eventually teased and bullied.

Now that John is older, I look back through our experiences and judge them through this filter of fear. That is, I try to imagine John's filter, because after all, it has nothing to do with the parent's view of 'safe versus unsafe' and everything to do with the child's perception. We adults have the insight to understand that a flushing toilet or buzzing overhead light is not a threat, but if the child feels unsafe, the fear flag is most decidedly up. I think back to the day I visited John's second grade class when they were learning to make apple sauce using a blender. All John learned that day is that even if you cry and whimper at the back of the room because of that horrible scary noise, they won't turn it off and they won't let you leave. He did not learn to make apple sauce.

I don't have any pat answers here. My intent is merely to raise awareness, whether parents choose to homeschool their child or they choose to enroll them in some sort of class situation. If Holt and Maslow, both great and respected thinkers, are correct in their assessment of the great influence of fear and corresponding need for safety *before* higher level learning can effectively take place, then this is something that we as parents ought to regard not just as a concern, but as a *primary* concern.

What does this mean in practical terms? It means that in selecting schools, writing education plans, and sorting out behavior issues, the safety and security questions should *lead* the discussion. Never mind for the moment *what* is going to be taught. There is time enough later to talk about whether Johnny will learn reading through phonics or whole language, or whether this is the year he conquers his multiplication tables. My view is, stick all of that on the shelf until you have made dead sure he won't spend his entire school year in fight or flight mode. Work the scary issues.

As I think about it, it's clear most schools work from the outside in, where everything is planned ahead of time and students are added in at the last minute irrespective of their needs. Rarely is the child considered first and even more rarely are things looked at from the child's point of view. Ideally, it should be the other way around.

Homeschooling, to its credit, does do it the other way around. Children are at the center of the process, not as in 'spoiled and catered to' but also not wedged in as an afterthought. They just naturally work from a base of comfort and security with people they most trust and understand. That frees the children then to reach out to other things – geography, astronomy, learning math and whatever else. It is only one of the reasons why many families of children with Asperger Syndrome choose homeschooling, but it's probably a big reason why so many are astounded at the progress their child makes.

Even if you do not choose to homeschool, though, you can work toward a more child-centered approach. Before you meet with any school team or write down any learning goals, you can spend some time looking through your child's eyes. What are your child's special issues? What are the scary parts of the day? What hurts or is uncomfortable? Where is there uncertainty over what to do? When is it that other kids are most likely to cause problems? How does each part of the day feel?

In the next chapter I talk about specific hints to make a school experience more user-friendly to the Asperger child, but that is only one person's view of common problems. More important is that you think about your own child and decide what are the main issues that need addressing, whether it is sensory issues, a need for structure, visual helps, the comfort of an aide, a shortened day, or other. Make school not a scary place and your child will have a chance to move past Step 2 of Maslow's hierarchy. It only makes sense to pull a drowning child out of the deep end and deposit him in the shallow end before you can hope to teach him to swim.

Belongingness and love

After handling the safety/fear issue, the next gap to be filled is Step 3, the need to belong and feel loved, which includes giving and receiving love, friendship, and finding a place in a group or family.

Once again, homeschooling has a built-in advantage. Unless the family is extremely dysfunctional, the child already feels belongingness and love, and knows without question that he or she is part of the family. So now homeschooled children are two steps ahead of the game because they have both safety and belongingness needs met. No wonder these children can more effectively reach out and enjoy learning and achievements of all types.

In terms of regular school settings for the child with Asperger Syndrome, we can still strive to give the child a feeling of belonging. To me that means that the teacher's attitude toward the child is critical. She must like and want to work with the child or the game is lost from the start. Our kids (regardless of their social deficits) sense whether they are welcome in class or not. Plus, the teacher's attitude determines how the rest of the class responds to the child. If the teacher does not like the child, the rest of the class will pick up on it and act accordingly. Not that all peer interactions are within a teacher's control, of course, but attitude and demeanor define the tone of the classroom as caring and inclusive (family-like) – or not.

Some factors to consider:

- Tolerance for, or ignoring of bullying: this doesn't just mean physical encounters, but also subtle bullying – i.e. name-calling, ridicule, excluding someone from the group, or other subtle put-downs.

- Competitiveness: sometimes competitions (spelling bees, and so forth) are fun, but too much pits one student against another.

- Celebration of diversity: there should be frequent discussions to the effect that being different is OK and we all need to help each other. The child with Asperger need not be identified in these discussions, but he should be made to feel accepted for who he is and included in the fold.

- Accommodating different learning styles: a teacher's ability to accommodate various styles (visual, auditory, hands-on, etc.) will make all students feel more integrated into the group.

The other part of belongingness has to do with social skills work. Parents and school need a teamwork approach to help the child learn the skills needed to fit in, to make and keep friends and function in the group. In every case I have ever heard of in the school system (after kindergarten, that is), social skills work either is not offered at all or takes a far back seat to academics. Parents usually have to beg and grovel for it, often even having to design and run the programs themselves. Schools sometimes try to assert that social skills training is beyond their responsibility (even though almost all school mission statements talk about their commitment to help all students reach their full potential). Why should this ignoring of social skills occur? If one believes Maslow (or my interpretation of Maslow), and understands the problems of Asperger Syndrome, the schools will do themselves a huge favor by tackling – *embracing* – the issues rather than attempting to ignore or skip them.

I make a modest proposal. Rather than treating social deficits as an afterthought, social skills education (along with safety/fear considerations) should be given a *front seat* in all discussions of individual education plans. And lest this suggestion be twisted into a program to 'fix' behavior for the school's convenience, I want to be clear that the proper intent for this social skills training is not to serve the school. I am not talking about Behavior 101 or a behavioral delays (BD) class. Social skills class should be a welcomed resource in which our kids can get information *they* need and a safe place to practice it – how to read body gestures, facial expressions, how to make a friend or start a conversation, win and lose a game, and so forth. Sometimes it may mean that a given social situation needs to be broken down into pieces and discussed, and that a child's actions will indeed change and improve as a result, but the overriding theme of such a class should *not* be to imply to the kid, 'Your behavior stands out. We're here to fix you.' It should be a positive experience, a means for getting our kids interacting with others, and a chance for them to belong. The class should send out the message, 'You look like you could use a hand. Will this help?'

When John was in grade seven, he was paired with an older student to act as a tutor for English, John's weakest subject. He was already so stressed with school I wasn't crazy to heap more on him during study hall, but if the school said he needed help, well OK. I kept a close eye on it. The first two weeks he and his tutor played Hangman. This seemed barely English-related, but I reasoned it was probably an icebreaker. The next week the tutor brought in a chessboard and they played chess the whole period. Whoa, I thought. This is not on the agenda. I nearly blew the whistle on it before I realized with a slap to the forehead what a gift we'd been handed. Hooray! For my son to have a buddy to play a game with and just talk to was gold – maybe platinum. Instead of complaining, I crossed fingers that some teacher wouldn't come in and close them down. It had become an impromptu social skills class, and I was glad for it. The thing is, this sort of thing should not have to depend on a happy accident and a schoolboy's shenanigans for it to occur.

The perfect school

Is there such a thing as a perfect school? People talk about 'good schools' and 'bad schools' and parents are always on the lookout for the best neighborhood based on school reports. Some folks are willing to move to find such a place. But what is best?

Unfortunately 'best' may have a lot of definitions and only a few may translate to what is good for your child. A school with a strong academic standing may be right for the Asperger child who sparks to heavy academics, but the competition may be fierce, and it says nothing about the school's ability to accommodate special learning situations. It's important to ask about any helps you think your child may need. Several parents have gotten rather chilly receptions when they have approached highly competitive private schools and asked those sorts of questions, but it's better to know upfront if you're going to have problems.

People usually think a school in a high-priced neighborhood means a better program. If the money goes to hiring aides, providing learning spaces for special needs kids, or keeping the student to teacher ratio low, that's useful. If the money goes for a new football field, big deal.

Sometimes a well-funded school with lots of things to make learning interesting can be great, but you need to make sure there is a commitment to use them. Otherwise they are just toys on display to impress visitors. When we first visited the school where John spent his sixth grade, John was excited that the school had a weather station and a greenhouse. The principal also proudly showed off a satellite dish for long-distance education and banks of personal computers along several walls. This all helped to sell us on the school. As the year progressed, though, we saw that this stuff was only so much window-dressing. John did use the computers a bit for word processing but mostly they sat idle. Many were not even hooked up. He saw the satellite dish used once for a French lesson, the weather station was never used and the only things grown in the greenhouse were two tomato plants that a teacher was raising for his own use. We had been duped.

Contrast that with John's next school. Every time I go to this school (grades seven through twelve), I sense earnest activity – lathes and kilns and potter's wheels in use; pungent smells coming out of the chemistry labs; computer labs full of students. I feel like the school is made up of verbs and not adjectives, and that they know how to put their money to use for the students' benefits. Perhaps that is the difference between a government school and a privately funded school? I don't know. I personally think it's a difference in leadership. That is the biggest point I want to make. The best school has the best people and you have to meet them.

School size and class size

As for the perfect size of the school, Tony Attwood has written, 'It does not matter how old the teacher is, how big the school, or whether it is a government or private school. What is important is the size of the classroom.'

I agree that the size of the class is important. For an Asperger child, the smaller the class size, usually, the greater chance for a calm and anxiety-free atmosphere and more one-on-one direction from the teacher. My son in the early primary grades could at least function in a class of six or so students, while a mainstream class was impossible until later years.

I think the size of the entire school is important too, however, and once again, smaller is better. School size is important because often our kids are the most vulnerable when they are not in class at all but elsewhere on school property. Time and time again, the most vicious bullying and most overwhelming chaos occurs during lunch, recess, before and after school, or en route (either at the bus stop, on the bus, or walking to and from school). Incidents that occur during these times have nothing to do with class size but may have a lot to do with the size of the school.

A small school has the further advantage that teachers are more likely to know everyone, so bullies cannot hide behind anonymity and are more likely to be seen, named, and held accountable for their reprehensible behavior. Teachers are more likely to know our kids too, understand how they tick, and watch out for them. In a small school, hallways and playgrounds are less crowded, cafeterias less deafening, and bus stops less confusing (the fear/safety thing).

All schools, small or large, are going to have some bullying, but our own experience has been that the first year in a small school was the worst and each year got better. My theory on this is that kids eventually adjust to each other, reaching a state of either truce or indifference, and after awhile there's a boredom factor (especially if your child doesn't react to the bullying), so that it's more tempting for hoodlums to go after fresh meat. In a large school, conversely, every year presents a greater chance to be with a different mix of kids. Each year the Asperger child is 'fresh meat' to someone.

A large school does have some positives, however. There is a greater chance the school will have other kids with Asperger Syndrome. This may increase chances for friendship, especially if a teacher helps these kids find each other. More students with similar needs can help drive programs. Bigger schools mean more teachers so if your child gets a 'lemon', there will be alternatives.

Some parents feel that in a large school, relative anonymity provides a fresh start for their child each year. This rationale doesn't impress me, partly because of the fresh meat bully factor I mentioned above, and also because I suspect that in some cases this parental thinking actually reflects an impatient wish that 'this school year will be the year Johnny passes for normal'. It could happen, of course, since our kids are learning coping skills all the time and do learn to fit in better as time goes on, but the price is high for this sort of thinking. It fosters a pressure that our kids don't need and over something that can't be rushed along. If anything, continually giving our kids new kids and teachers to cope with probably only adds to the fear and belonging factor and holds them back. They don't need this.

Of course, each situation has unique circumstances, and differing personalities make my generalizations perhaps of little value. In the end, you need to decide what factors are the most important and see for yourself. Visit any prospective school while it's in session so you can see how it operates. Meet your child's proposed teacher(s), meet the principal, and ask every question you can think of. You'll make the right decision.

Working with the school

Everyone has their own style, and mine is non-confrontational unless pushed to the wall. I truly believe that you get more flies with honey than with vinegar and this approach has worked very well for me. I concede that it is not everyone's style and that it may not work in every school. Take this for what it's worth, then, but here is what has been helpful for me:

1. *I have never gone into a new school expecting problems.* I always go in with the expectation that all the adults involved want the same thing – for my child to succeed.

2. *I tell teachers up front that I do not want anything held back, nor do I want things sugar-coated.* If my son is doing something inappropriate, I want to be able to work on it and I try to convey the sentiment that, far from jumping down their throats or getting defensive, I will truly appreciate knowing. I cannot work with him on something if I don't know what it is. I acknowledge that teachers sometimes see behaviors that I'm not in a position to see.

3. *I speak to teachers about Asperger Syndrome and John at the beginning of every year.* I aim for about the second or third week of school. I try to see a few at once if someone (usually the special education or resource person) will coordinate it, but I will also speak with teachers

individually. By the second week, they have sometimes gotten an inkling that my son takes a special brand of teaching, but it's early enough that they probably haven't had time to misconstrue the situation and come up with misconceptions. I have sometimes gotten lazy about trying to catch every teacher and it is usually a mistake. If I miss a teacher, I can just about predict which class John will have trouble in later.

4. *I am very nice.* I bring cookies and thank the teachers for their time. They are usually missing lunch for my meeting. Regardless of the issues that may come between us, teachers are an overworked and underpaid group who can do with a kind word.

5. *When I give my talk on Asperger Syndrome, I give handouts for each teacher to keep.* I highlight any things of particular importance. I also type up a page of examples of how Asperger Syndrome affects John.

6. *If there is a problem, I do not offer my ideas* on what teachers should do, at least not at first. I usually present the issue and then ask that we all brainstorm together. I have found (by chance) that teachers appreciate being consulted, and they often see the same solution that I do. If I suggest that action, however, it can feel like I'm trying to shove something down their throats. No one likes that. When it is their idea, they are enthusiastic and willing to do their part. If I don't like their suggestion, I have the chance to stop it before it starts, and learn about potential problem attitudes.

8. *Teachers listen to themselves better than they listen to me.* At the end of one year I interviewed teachers about my son to prepare for a doctor's appointment. Later I realized how useful the information would be for new teachers. If *I* say, 'Punishing for something minor only agitates John further. It's better to just let him leave the room and calm

down,' teachers look at me like I'm trying to let my son get away with something. But if a *teacher* says this, they understand it as an effective management technique and take it on board.

8. *I do not bring an advocate or a tape recorder to meetings.* OK, now some readers are probably standing on their chairs wanting to argue with me. That's fine. *You* know your situation, the current climate at your school, the issues involved, and so forth. So if *you* feel you should bring an advocate, lawyer, fingerprinting kit or anything else that makes you feel more secure and on a legally sound footing, by all means, do so! I know many parents who would not consider showing up at a meeting without a posse of advocates and so forth. Fine. You have your reasons.

    My perspective is different. My family has lived in foreign lands, we have moved around, and we have not taken advantage (if it is an advantage) of any formal process such as an IEP since John was very small. Everything we have gotten for John for the last several years has been through informal means. If a problem crops up, I make a phone call or write a letter to the principal and we work it out.

    I know this will drive a lot of people batty, but to me, showing up at a school meeting with a lawyer before there are any problems is like bringing a policeman with you to meet the neighbors, or inviting your divorce attorney to the wedding. I think it sets an ugly tone and an expectation of trouble that is soon fulfilled. You are free to disagree, of course.

    I also feel that being too heavy-handed in making demands can work to your disadvantage. People who get pushed around dig in their heels. It's human nature. A friend of ours used to have a neighbor who kept asking him when he was going to repaint his house. Our friend would politely say, 'Oh, one of these days.' He actually did want to paint the house, and told us, 'If he'd just quit telling me to paint the house, I'd paint it!' He finally painted it after the neighbor moved.

My point is, of course, that you might have some goals on paper, and they might even get technically met, but it still comes down to people and personalities. If the teachers who deal with your child feel bullied, they are going to start to resent your child's presence, and to make the classroom experience miserable for him. Almost any small incident in class can be interpreted in a number of ways, after all, so it isn't hard to do. You know that if you send your steak back to the cook too many times, he's going to drop it 'accidentally' on the floor, right? I suggest that if you enter a school relationship with an aggressive attitude, fight over petty issues, find fault constantly, and try to dictate on every movement your child's teachers make your kid's education is also going to get dropped on the floor.

9. *I save my silver bullets.* I try not to waste the school's time over things that don't make a difference to my kids' education. By that I mean I would not make a big deal over something like a dress code rule or a school lunch price increase. Sometimes I have to bite my tongue over what I think are dumb school rules, but I think you burn bridges when you are on the end of the phone complaining every week. Your power is diluted. I want the school to know that when I call it's important.

When things go sour

If your child's schooling is not working out, there are a few different avenues you can take.

Avenue 1

Work with the school to improve things. You can do this via formal mechanisms (reconvene the IEP team) or informally (chat with the teacher). As well as asking for things, do your part to work on issues at home. If necessary, tell yourself that 'this too shall pass' and that sometimes we (and that includes our children) get 'opportunities for growth' that we hadn't bargained for. Most situations are temporary. Minimize the impact if you can. See Chapter 6 for ideas on handling some of the more common problems.

Avenue 2

Escalate your grievances and head for Legal-land. I have no experience in this area but understand that you may want to try one or more of these things:

- Casually mention the name of a special education lawyer in your next conversation with the principal and see if that improves his or her cooperation.

- Hire an advocate and buy that tape recorder after all.

- Document everything. Follow up phone calls with a letter outlining what you understood to have been discussed. Or, insist on no phone calls, only written communication.

- Write formal complaint letters, and send copies to everyone you can think of.

- File a formal complaint at which point the school district will likely suggest mediation, which is an arbitration process that is free to you.

- If mediation fails, the next step is 'due process,' which means you go to court. At this point you will need to have a lawyer and possibly expert witnesses. In other words, you will need to have money. (You may or may not recoup costs depending on whether you win.)

I've given you only the very quick and dirty synopsis of procedures. For more authoritative information, see Appendix 2.

Avenue 3

Go the do-it-yourself route. Decide that the current situation may be unacceptable, but a court fight is not worth the aggravation. Decide that you can better handle things in your own way because you know what you want. This may mean turning to private schools or therapies on your own (and paying for them yourself, assuming you are done fighting with the schools), or homeschooling.

Frankly, it would take something truly extraordinary to get me into a big legal scuffle, because in my view taking the school district to court has high stakes I would not willingly pay. My views are in line with Susan from Seattle, who chose to homeschool her nine-year-old daughter rather than go to court. She writes:

> I worked really hard when Becky was in kindergarten, first, and second grades, trying to get the school district to treat her as the individual she is, and they just don't have the time to do it. Even when there are people at the school who really believed in doing the right things for Becky, they just were stretched too thin. When I had Becky in regular public school, there were several times I could have sued the district for not really individualizing her education at all, but I knew that it wasn't worth it, for me, for Becky, or anybody. It wouldn't change the fact that, basically, she's just a kid who needs to have somebody work with her one-on-one most of the time if she's going to succeed in learning. Mostly parents need to just trust their own judgment and their gut and forget about all the fights and hassles. It was better for me to take her education into my own hands and tailor it to her personality.

Lest you think Susan is unaware or intimidated by the legal process, she was a lawyer for five years and is currently a law librarian. She just knows that for her, her energy is better spent on her child than in lengthy litigation.

Why isn't court an option for everybody?

I'm glad to see parents pick up the gauntlet and take schools to court on the issue of special education rights where it is warranted, where rights are abused and where children are suffering, but I think always looking to the court system to fix everything is a victim-oriented viewpoint. 'Sue!' seems to be the battle cry of many parents whenever the least little thing goes wrong and that is counterproductive. While there's no question that in many cases you perhaps *can* sue, it doesn't always mean you should. I don't think the schools will ever solve all parents' problems nor should they. Regardless if they are entitled by law, I resent parents who want everything even if the school goes broke. I know the thinking is that squeezing the schools dry will ultimately 'trickle up' to the federal government, which is not kicking in all the money it should, but I have little faith that this will occur.

You should not feel guilty if you decide not to take your case to court. This is a personal decision and there are a number of reasons why launching a legal attack may not be feasible or desirable, even if there are legal grounds.

- Financial reasons: it's not unusual to spend several thousand dollars. Schools have the best lawyers and it is not unusual for the parents to lose.

- Timing: kids graduate or age out of schools. The average American family moves every five years. By the time some families realize rights are being violated, it is too late to take up the battle.

- Family crises. Illness. Unemployment. Divorce. Coping with aging parents. Another court case. As important as our children's education problems are, sometimes they must be weighed against other heavy burdens.

- Special situations: what if you work for the school district you want to sue? It's not impossible but definitely awkward.

- Personal reasons: you may not feel equal to the task, whether due to depression, anxiety, shyness, lack of education, or other.

- Your spouse is against it: if your spouse is in denial and does not believe your child has a problem or needs special education services, the legal road will be a very difficult path. Similarly, if your child is going to refuse the service, it may not be worth fighting for.

- Protective reasons: you may fear your child will (wrongly) blame himself for being the 'cause' of so much strife between you and the school system. Parents may fear retaliation and animosity toward their child. You also may not want your child hanging in limbo, waiting out a decision for months and not knowing where he is going to end up. I think these are very real concerns.

In the end, you may decide there are better options. As an example, let's say you want your child to have a simplistic word-processing tool called an Alphasmart keyboard, to overcome handwriting difficulties. You can attend a school meeting to request it, agree to have your child tested for 'adaptive technology' needs, wait for results, reconvene to discuss results and write it into the plan, wait for the school to buy the keyboard, remind them a couple of times, possibly pay your lawyer to write a nasty letter, and several months later finally receive it for your child to use for what is left of the school year and then give it back to the school. *Or*, you can order a keyboard for about $200, get it in a week and give it to your child for his use forever.

I choose option B. If that is not the politically correct choice, if I neglected to make my school do its job for the benefit of all kids everywhere, I am sorry. I don't make my child suffer if I can help it, not even for the greater good. The better future I am working toward is producing a happy, productive and successful young adult into the world. Time enough for bigger issues after that. If that is completely selfish, so be it. I have seen many parents take the legal path (some would say the higher moral path) to the detriment of their kids' progress, waiting for the government to come and do the right thing (to pay for services, to provide promised transportation, to do testing, to find placements, to start programs, blah, blah). Well my view is that the government isn't coming to the rescue, and what is supposed to work doesn't work. Now what? Suppose your child is drowning in the city pool. You surely wouldn't stand idly just because the pool is supposed to have a lifeguard on duty but doesn't. You'd jump in the water and save your kid.

Chapter 6

School Specifics

Here are things you can possibly do on a personal level to improve things for your child. It's about small things – wise choices, minor adjustments, homemade solutions, and work-arounds, using what you've got. Not all the things I suggest will work for every person, but I hope it helps spark some ideas.

Starting with the earliest group situation your child may have to contend with (daycare), and working up through the school years, here are a few issues one might encounter.

Daycare and after-school care

If you cannot be home with your child, or leave your child with a family member or trusted neighbor, you'll need to use daycare. Daycares seem to be either big or little. I prefer the little ones but there are pros and cons to both types.

The big daycare is the franchise or institutional daycare. It typically has its own building, a large staff and lots of kids. We were asked to leave both of the large daycares we tried. By definition, large daycares have a prescribed way of doing things and John clearly didn't fit the mold. No one took a personal interest. They had a waiting list of kids, so there was no incentive for them to try to make it work for John.

Large daycares do have good points. They operate on schedules and are organized. That predictability is nice for our kids, although frequent staff changes may negate this advantage. Franchise daycares are open most of the time, unlike mom-run daycares that may close unpredictably.

If you are considering a big daycare, pay attention to the noise level. After measuring noise levels at 25 daycare facilities that each cared for 4–16 children, University of Montreal researchers found evidence that 'children may be at risk of noise-induced hearing loss dependent on the length of stay in the day-care centers.' They also noted that the kids often had to shout to be heard (Picard and Boudreau 1999).

The researchers' primary concern was hearing loss, but it raises a huge red flag for any Asperger kids with acute hearing. No wonder John usually lay in a far corner of the playroom when I would come to pick him up, faced away from the group with a blanket or jacket over his head. Far from being able to learn how to play with the other children, he couldn't tolerate being near them.

The 'little' daycares are generally less chaotic. These smaller operations generally consist of one mom and a handful of kids, often including the mother's own. Quality varies greatly, but with a careful check of references and a liberal drop-in policy (always insist on being able to drop in whenever you want to and then do it), a good mom-type daycare is my preference. It's not only calmer but feels more comfortable. Also, you will not have to deal with rotating staff so you can build a relationship. I would look for a mom that seems in friendly control, who takes an involved role with the kids (rather than just letting them loose in a playroom), and who has a bit of structure built into the day.

Even with the better atmosphere and personal care, I confess these did not always work for us. The first daycare mom we used told me she was quitting the business soon after we started with her. A couple weeks after she supposedly quit, I stopped in to retrieve something and discovered her daycare business was thriving and John had been replaced.

The second mom lasted a year or better as John's after-school caregiver, but it was a bad time for John. School issues were coming to a head. He would arrive at the mom's house stressed and on the down side of his Ritalin. Food issues hadn't been resolved, and his behavior was poor and erratic. He used threatening talk and wouldn't listen. He smashed her glass coffee table. I couldn't blame her when she told me she couldn't handle him.

With the writing on the wall for the fourth time, my husband and I came to the joint decision that I needed to quit work. My neighbor watched John the last few weeks until I could stay home. She had known him since birth and loved him for who he was. Thank heavens for her. He gave her a rough time too, but the one-on-one atmosphere did him good. The ultimate answer for us, though, was for me to stay home with him.

I wish I had better news about daycare, but we lived in a major metropolitan area and could not find daycare that would work. My experience is dated, but not much has changed. Just the other day I learned of a woman so stressed by her inability to get daycare for her disabled child that she's made it the subject of her master's thesis. Meanwhile, I get the feeling that in any area where there are waiting lists for daycare (and it's a seller's market), patience quickly wears thin for any child who takes extra work. You may have better luck than I did or your child may be better able to deal with daycare than my son ever was. Otherwise, try the following suggestions:

1. Look for a calm, quiet, atmosphere, with as few children as possible.

2. Find places within the daycare for your child to sit quietly. Identify them to your child.

3. Give the daycare provider insight into your child's issues.

4. Choose a place close to work, rather than close to home. Your child will have more time with you and less time at daycare.

5. Try for the least number of transitions. John went to daycare, school, then daycare each day. It would have been better to avoid so much shuffling.

6. If all else fails, consider quitting work to stay home with your child, at least until he is school age. (See Chapter 7 on going from two incomes to one.)

The lower grades (primary school or grade school)

Depending on when your child is assessed, he may start school in a normal classroom or he may be in a self-contained special education classroom, or perhaps a mix of the two. If he has been assessed as requiring a special class and one is not available at your local school, he might need to be bused to a school other than your neighborhood one.

In some parts of the world such as the UK, special needs children have traditionally gone off to a separate school, but that trend is changing. In the US all schools must follow a policy of providing education in the 'least restrictive environment'. Unfortunately, some districts interpret that to mean 'everybody back to the classroom'. This knee-jerk response makes it easier on school budgets than paying for separate classes or private schooling, but it misses the point. A child is supposed to be educated in the most normal (least restrictive) setting *that works*. For kids with Asperger Syndrome it's a very iffy proposition. John's experience in the regular classroom was a disaster in the early years, even with an aide, but yet it worked fine in later years. Each case needs individual care.

Karen R. tells of having two years with a good program in Maryland (her daughter was in regular class for just one subject and in a smaller special class the remainder of the day), but the following year, the principal lumped every student into regular classes, some having 40 students. Karen homeschooled her daughter the rest of the year, waiting on better placement. Her daughter ultimately went to a private school at public expense. But why did things have to get worse before they got better? The child hadn't changed, only school policy.

The normal classroom

If your child is headed for a normal classroom, for better or worse, here are ways to make the best of the situation:

- Avoid 'open plan' classrooms. They're noisy and distracting.

- A single class combining two grade levels can be a good choice since our kids' varied skills may span two or more grades.

- A teacher who is organized, friendly but firm, and relatively soft-spoken is good. Shouters are not.

An aide

Sometimes the normal classroom works with the help of an aide. This can be a one-on-one aide for your child or one assigned to help the whole class. John shared an aide in his special class; however, when they tried to introduce him into a normal classroom experience, that aide was his personal assistant.

School districts may be reluctant to offer an aide, due to the expense or difficulty in hiring them. Linda in Texas said about her school meeting to request services, 'I said "aide" and the room fell silent.'

Be warned that many aides have little training. Do not assume an aide understands Asperger Syndrome. If you get an aide, ask that the aide be included in training and discussions. Sometimes they are left out because of their part-time or non-professional status, but since they have daily dealings with your child, they may have valuable information to contribute. If they cannot attend meetings, chat with them informally ahead of time. If you send information in to the school, make sure the aide gets her own copy. Also, do not get too attached to any one particular aide. It seems that there is an incredible amount of job turnover.

Special classes

If your child is offered a place in a special class, be aware that the schools may offer you an existing class that may not be a good fit. What commonly happens (and happened in our case) is that schools typically have two types of special classes already set up. One is for children who are academically slow. The other is for those with behavioral or emotional difficulties. These latter classes may have names like BED (behaviorally or emotionally delayed) or SED (severe emotional delays). Neither of these classes is arranged with the Asperger child in mind!

Our kids, by definition, have average or better intelligence so a slow class is usually not appropriate. And, the reward-and-punishment sort of model that is used in the behavior classes assumes that the kids already understand the rules but need motivating. Our kids are already motivated to follow the rules. They need incremental instruction and opportunity to practice. It's a different paradigm. Moreover, they need good peer role models, not likely to be found in behavior class.

What is needed is a third choice, with emphasis on education and not coercion (reward/punish). School districts are just beginning to provide classes for kids with Asperger Syndrome or other autistic spectrum disorders. It's a bit ironic that just when some communities are figuring out how to create an appropriate class, other school districts are gung-ho to put kids back into regular classrooms.

If you are in a situation where the right class is non-existent or still months from reality, you need to choose the lesser of two evils or leave your child in a full-sized conventional classroom. It's impossible to say which one is the better choice without visiting each classroom.

Other options

When discussing school options, be creative. Whatever you and your school district can work out is what you can do. This may include a lot of different options: shortened days, use of resource rooms, another neighborhood school, home tutoring, online classes, skipping a grade or taking courses across a few grades, and more. Vouchers and charter schools are possibilities in some states. Private school is often a great solution, if finances can be worked out (either out of pocket or paid for by the school district). And of course, there's always homeschooling. Of all the schooling years John has had, the three years in which we homeschooled made the greatest difference for him.

Therapies

Regardless of what sort of a classroom setting your child is in, he or she may qualify for various therapies. Most kids with Asperger Syndrome seem to benefit from a combination of speech therapy (for language pragmatics and social skills), occupational therapy and/or physical therapy. Sensory work should be included.

If you are sure your child needs therapy but can't get it in the near future, see Chapter 7 for things that you might try at home. Also, try to access therapy time through the medical pathway. If your pediatrician or neurologist writes a prescription for therapy services, you may be able to access them through your health plan. Get the OK from your insurance provider in writing *before* using the services.

As great as therapies sound, too often they come in tiny dabs. Parents consider it a victory to get even thirty minutes every other week in some schools. If your child qualifies, here are ways to maximize therapy time:

- Talk with each therapist individually rather than only in group meetings. One mother tapes her discussions with her son's physical therapist so she can review the conversation at home. This is an excellent idea! Therapists use technical language, so we may miss a lot otherwise.

- Ask the therapist for ideas on things to work on at home.

- Ask to visit school on therapy days and watch what goes on firsthand.

- Be sure not to schedule a dental or other appointment during one of these sessions.

- Keep *close* tabs on the amount of time your child sees a therapist. More than one parent has sent in a note to the therapist only to find out she left on maternity leave or moved away months previously, and no one told the parent. Get a schedule of days and speak frequently to the therapist.

Dealing with a classroom that is too stimulating

- Turn loudspeakers in the classroom down or off.
- Pull blinds nearest child.
- If chairs squeaking on floors is a problem, glue carpet on chair legs, lay carpet tiles, or put chair legs into old slit tennis balls.
- Ask to have rattling fans, pipes or radiators fixed.
- If the room is overly decorated, perhaps some of the clutter can be removed.
- Play soothing music during parts of the day.
- Keep bothersome kids away, especially those who engage in unwanted touch.
- Turn lights off when they aren't needed.
- Have a quiet corner where your child can de-stress. This can be a beanbag chair, soft couch or pillow area with a few books.

Increasing your child's ability to pay attention

- Seat your child away from windows and doors and toward the front of the class.

- If your child cannot sit still, provide a trinket to fiddle with. A bendable figure, knobby ball, Koosh ball, uninflated balloon filled with flour, and other small toys are some possibilities. Just make sure it is quiet. John never used one of these, but it might have been nice.

- To provide therapy for tactile issues, on heavy-weight cardboard glue materials with tactile value – velvet, satin, plastic, sandpaper, plastic mesh, fur, etc. Place this card either inside the desk or attach underneath the desk.

Dealing with recess:

Recess can be the roughest part of the day for a child with Asperger Syndrome. There is little structure, a potential for unwanted touching and unexpected noises, and it's the first place a child is likely to be bullied.

There are several ways recess can be improved:

- Make sure every adult on playground duty knows your child and about Asperger Syndrome.

- Ask for an aide who will watch out for your child for this timeframe, if possible.

- Investigate a buddy system with someone your child likes in his class.

- Ask that an older student or two be assigned as buddies. They could perhaps earn extra credit.

- Provide structure. Often our kids get into trouble because they have no idea what they should be doing. Discuss with your child (or have the teacher discuss) ahead of time what he will do at recess. (Warning: make sure that his choice is actually something he will be allowed to do or discuss a backup option.)

- Volunteer to be a parent playground monitor.

- Ask the person on duty to organize activities and make sure your child is included. This can be outdoor games, races, scavenger hunt, obstacle course, outdoor art (chalk, squirt gun water pictures), etc.

- Start a small club to meet during recess – running, gymnastics, science, chess club, etc.

- To avoid certain recurring problems, work with the teacher to restrict your child to a certain area. This will give your child a boundary, help the playground monitor to keep better track, and allow distance from kids or activities that are a current problem.

- Reduce sensory input. If the outdoors is too chaotic, think of things inside the school – going to the library or resource room, having a snack, reading quietly.

- Allow your child to choose a buddy to come inside to play a special board game or do a puzzle as a special privilege.

- Give your child a job. Outdoors, he could be on litter patrol, hand out equipment, inflate basketballs, and set up games (nets, boundary markers). Indoors, he can take down bulletin boards, straighten desks, move books or wheel the TV cart. Good physical use of muscles!

Optimizing the lunchroom

The cafeteria or lunch area is just about as rich in sensory experiences as recess, and taste and smell can be added bothers.

- In packed lunches, provide small amounts of a few things, to increase your child's list of foods. Provide a variety of tastes and textures.

- If your child is highly bothered by lunchroom smells (some children can get to the point of gagging), prepare a cotton ball with a nice scent on it (cinnamon, peppermint, lemon, or vanilla might be good choices).

Put it into a sealed plastic bag. If he ends up sitting next to someone whose lunch bothers him, he can take a whiff of his cotton ball and feel in control.

- Standing in line is often really hard for our kids, who may get overanxious at the thought of someone bumping into them. One end of the line or the other is better than the middle. Better yet is to let them go to lunch several minutes early.

- Sitting at a separate table with handpicked kids often works better than releasing our kids to the mayhem of the general cafeteria.

- Eating in a classroom, resource room, or teachers' cafeteria are other ideas to explore.

Improving the bus experience

I personally hate the bus. It has a *Lord of the Flies* atmosphere and is a hotbed of sensory input – kids being noisy, roaring engine, squeaking brakes, stinky fumes of gas and exhaust, often a radio blaring, being jostled, sitting next to people you don't choose to sit next to, temperatures that are often very hot or quite cold, and often a very bouncy ride. What more could there be?

John hated the bus so much that when we got a heavy snowfall, he disappeared outside with a shovel and told me that evening that he'd made a barricade so the bus couldn't stop in front of the house. Since John was only seven at the time, I didn't take it very seriously and never even peeked outside – until the next morning, when I heard the bus spinning its wheels and trying to get off the very large snow bank in the middle of the road!

As much as the bus situation gives parents cause for worry, statistically school bus accidents are rare. (It's just that when there is an accident anywhere in the world, we hear about it!) Anyway, maybe one of the following suggestions will ease this issue:

- Drive your child to school. This not only ensures your child doesn't have any safety issues, but also ensures your child reaches school in a pleasant and receptive mood, instead of agitated. The school district may owe your child transportation by law, but if it causes major trauma, what is the point?

- Carpool, for the same reasons as above.

- Ask for a special bus or van. It should have fewer children and more staff.

- Ask for an aide or other adult to ride the bus with him.

- Try to have the bus driver educated in Asperger Syndrome.

- Choose the shortest route available. You don't often have a choice in this, but sometimes one bus makes more stops than another, or adds a leg to the route. Sometimes the route will be shorter if you pick up the bus in a slightly different location.

- Provide earplugs to muffle sounds of a too-loud bus.

- Let your child listen to music through headphones.

- Have your child sit in the front of the bus, away from bullies (important!).

- Assign a buddy to sit with your child.

- Explain to your child exactly what he should do on the bus. Use 'do' words and not 'don't' words.

- Have someone make sure he comes off the bus without incident, and with all of his things.

Handling field trips or excursions

Unusual days of any kind are a special challenge for our kids. All predictability is out the window and new experiences can be expected. To make things a little easier, consider the following ideas:

- Don't go. All field trips are not created equal and not all will be worth the upset in routine. The school should always assume that the child is going though, and make sure plans are in place.

- Attend with your child. Some teachers will ask you to attend, or you may just feel easier if you do. You can ride the bus or you and your child can meet everyone there. I found that this was a good way of seeing how John dealt with things. Being there but staying apart from him for the most part gave me some insight into how he coped in group situations.

- Have an aide assigned to your child for the day. He does not have to know that the aide is for him.

- Have a buddy system in place.

- Have a plan in place in the event the child becomes upset. Can he be picked up early? Will there be someplace (a nurse's station or office) to regroup? Might he bring a book and read?

- Discuss the field trip ahead of time. Discuss any problem areas. Will he be allowed to touch things? Pet the animals? Must he stay behind ropes? Only on the sidewalk? Discuss with the teacher what the expectations will be and discuss them with your child.

- Minimize 'stuff' to keep track of. A hooded jacket is better than an umbrella; lunch should be disposable to avoid carrying it around all afternoon; and unnecessary jewelry, glasses, money, or keys should be left at home to avoid losing them.

- Minimize field-trip related assignments. John was getting high grades so it shocked one teacher when he got an F on the worksheet that he was to fill out during a field trip to a museum. He was just too overwhelmed to deal with everything else *and* fill out a worksheet. He might have done better with a buddy, or reading the worksheet the day before the trip and filling it out afterwards at home.

Coping with homework

If there is one issue that drives me wild, it is homework. Much of it is inferior. The instructions often don't make sense; the worksheets are sometimes barely legible; the work often has little or no bearing on what is being discussed in school; and it is too often busywork. Worst of all it takes time away from my family and inserts havoc and upset into our few hours together.

From an Asperger perspective, our kids are washed out by the time they finish a school day. They've had to do double-duty working on both academics and social situations and they need downtime in the evenings.

My son also has strong views about homework. One particular bugbear for him is the unpredictability of it. He knows roughly how his day will go from 8 a.m. to 3:30 p.m. and he knows what he has planned for the evening. Everything is under control until – wham – he is blindsided by some assignment. Besides the surprise aspect, it offends his sense of fair play because he feels evenings should be for us. And, right or wrong, he feels that many of the homework assignments are dreamed up on the spur of the moment or are busywork.

With my distaste for homework clearly in mind, then, here are suggestions for making it as tolerable as possible:

- If your child is taking a great deal of time over homework, ask the teacher how long she intends the homework to take. If it's meant to be a 15-minute assignment, let your child work for 15 minutes and stop. Write a note to explain what you are doing.

- If instructions are not clear or do not make sense, do not have your child try to do the assignment. Write a note.

- If you have a special family night planned, do not let homework interfere. Write a note. Most teachers do not intend to ruin family quality time (it just turns out that way). They will usually give your child an extra day to get it done.

- Ask for substitutions. Sometimes our kids choose a book that is far too advanced or otherwise unsuitable.

- Often the teacher offers choices for report topics, reading books, or type of presentation (oral vs. written, etc.). Help your child make a good decision.

- If faced with too many math problems, have your child do every other row, or every other problem, and write a note to the teacher.

- Use graph paper to keep math problems lined up.

- Allow your child to type homework on the computer. Or, you can type from your child's dictation or rough draft, being careful not to editorialize.

- Have a spare set of schoolbooks at home. This ensures a critical book won't be left at school and it also lets you preview lessons.

- Request that the teacher *ask* for homework the day it is due. Many teachers simply keep a box on their desk and assume kids will remember. Our kids have too many things to remember as it is. This is a little accommodation that can help a great deal.

- Ask that the teacher write the homework assignment down in the upper right corner of the chalkboard or whiteboard every day. This visual reminder in a predictable place is much better than just hearing the assignment.

- School diaries are helpful both for writing down homework and for passing notes to the teacher. They are only good if used, however. This is a habit worth enforcing in your child. If you use a homework diary, require that 'something' be written each day. The written remark 'no homework' tells more than a blank page.

Calming your agitated child at school

Part of the immense upset our kids feel is having feelings but being unable to identify or express them. They need practice naming emotions and talking about them. We did a lot of work with John when he was little. It helped. When we saw his frustration mounting, we furnished words to say. 'I can see you are mad, John. Tell Mommy "I'm mad! It's raining and I'm mad about it!"' This helped to head off a tantrum or stop him from hitting out. Later on, we would just remind him to 'Use your words.' If this works for your child, explain this technique to your child's teacher.

- Allow the child to excuse himself from class and go to a resourse room, nurse's office or other place where he can quietly sort through his emotions and feel better. He and a teacher can develop sign language to indicate this.

- The teachers may tell your child to work off his anger by running a lap around the track, or walking the halls or perimeter of the school. John told me that sometimes he just feels like he has to use his muscles so this is a relief for him.

- Teachers may ask your child to run an errand, such as delivering a book or taking attendence records to the office. Again, it's a chance to use some muscles. Also leaving the classroom can remove tension and give everyone some space. John's teachers have used this technique to good effect.

- Teach your child peaceful ways to deal with anger. This includes taking slow, deep breaths, meditating, saying

positive statements to oneself, doing a few stretches or
neck rolls, or writing down what is bothering him.

Dealing with 'stims'

When young, John would tense up all of his muscles into an odd
posture when presented with something visually stimulating.
This little quirk really didn't bother us; however, it set him apart
from others, and all activities (such as walking along a sidewalk)
were stalled during this process. We broke this habit by teaching
John to clap his hands and holler 'Great!' when he got excited. We
also reminded him 'No muscles,' when we saw him tensing up.
The school joined us with these reminders and the behavior
dropped away.

The stick-wagging stim also was not really bothering anyone,
but it looked a bit menacing if he did it on the playground. Also, it
kept him from doing two-handed things. To reduce that stim, we
reduced access to it. I removed all the sticks from the house and
put them in the backyard. Any time John wanted to stim with a
stick, he had to do it in the backyard. He gradually reduced his
stimming.

I'm no expert when it comes to stims, but since they often serve
a purpose for the child, a teacher should be somewhat understanding. If she were really against a particular stim, rather than
trying to eliminate it, have her try reducing it by specifying where
it needs to be done (only outside, only during bathroom breaks,
etc.) Some parents have found that when one stim is removed,
another pops up. We just have to use our best judgment.

The upper grades (secondary school or junior/senior high school)

One of the biggest challenges is dealing with a wide assortment
of teachers. It's hard enough to work with one or two teachers,
but in the upper grades there is a different teacher for every class.
My son's school here in Australia does not mind getting all or
most of John's teachers together at the beginning of the year and

letting me talk about his learning style and Asperger Syndrome in general.

Group projects

In the upper grades students often work in groups on large projects. Groups can be pretty overstimulating and the mix of the group can make or break it for our kids. If kids self-select their own groups, our kids can be left sitting by themselves or feel like 'leftovers' in the choosing process. Our kids also sometimes have a hard time figuring out what role they are to play in the group. They may only know how to lead and expect others to follow. They may get angry if their idea is rejected. Some groups like to fiddle around and if your child is focused solely on getting the job done, sparks may soon fly. To work around these potential problems, consider one or more of these approaches:

- Have the teacher choose the groups, keeping troublemakers away from our kids.
- Allow a choice of either group work or working individually.
- Have the teacher choose your child to be the teacher's assistant rather than work in any one group.
- Ask if the teacher could sit close to your child's group, to head off problems.

Long writing assignments

Our kids typically find that doing a lot of handwriting is time-consuming and tiring, and the results don't please the English teachers anyway. This year we discovered a great alternative. John has been using an Alphasmart keyboard. It is the size of a laptop computer but is specifically for word processing. It is lightweight, runs on AA batteries, and is a perfect tool for note-taking and rough drafts. John types into it during the day, and then downloads his work onto our personal computer for polishing and printing. It is a great buy at only around $200. (For more information see Appendix 6.)

- Another option to avoid copious note-taking is to use a tape recorder or have an arrangement to always use a buddy's notes.

Bullying in school

My son is probably one of the few kids with Asperger Syndrome who has been bullied on three continents, so I can tell you it's a worldwide problem. Still, don't let teachers and principals throw up their hands and tell you that nothing can be done. There are a few things that can be done and ways that bullying situations can be improved.

A bully-resistant environment

My younger son Jay (not Asperger) spent Years Five and Six at a government primary school in Australia where bullying was at a very low level. I'm sure no school is perfect, but I wish more schools took anti-bullying as seriously as this school did.

It began with a top-down emphasis from the school's principal, and she had one policy that applied to the entire school and that was set out clearly for all. Any sort of 'put down' constituted an offense against school policy. This standard applied for every student everywhere in the school (not just classrooms, but playgrounds too) and – here is the key – *it was enforced.*

The principal was committed to the idea that even something as minor as an insult must not be ignored. Offenders were initially warned, then were sat down for a talk about choices. After that they might lose privileges and have to spend some of their recess picking up litter, or ultimately sit in lunchtime detention. Kids learned what the rules were, and it was seldom an issue at all.

One might wonder what would happen if a child with Asperger Syndrome is the one to make a rude remark because he doesn't understand these social rules? Yes, that might be a concern. The benefit, though, is that he's going to be in an environment of good peer role models, will be less likely to pick up bullying habits, and he will be in a safe atmosphere where he will not be provoked into poor behavior. What constitutes a breach of rules will have to be clearly defined and if he makes a mistake, he will learn. As long as the teachers understand the difficulties, it shouldn't be a problem. I would personally have no qualms about instituting a bully-free policy such as outlined above.

The school also has a few other characteristics that may be in its favor in fostering a bully-resistant environment. It is a small school where most kids are known to school staff. The playground is well monitored and is shared with a school for children with severe disabilities, so children learn to accept differences from an early age. Maybe these are key features. I don't know. I just know that it seems to be possible to start kids off on the right foot.

Some anti-bullying ideas for you and your child
IF YOUR CHILD IS BEING BULLIED, REPORT IT

Ask that a teacher be assigned to actively watch the situation for a couple of days. If they keep their eyes on your child, they will soon ferret out the troublemakers by catching them in the act. Mark is a US high school guidance counselor who has had good results with this technique. It is called 'shadowing' at his school, and it is a confidential technique where neither the bullied child nor the aggressor know it is being done. This avoids one child being branded a snitch.

TEACH YOUR CHILD TO AVOID BULLY-PRONE AREAS

My son used to try to hide from bullies at lunchtime by finding a quiet corner of the schoolyard to eat his lunch. It seemed reasonable to him, but it was the equivalent of walking down a dark alley. You just don't do it. Things improved greatly when he sat on a bench in plain view.

SAFETY LOVES COMPANY

Finding just one person to sit with can keep the punks off your child's neck. Bullies are cowards who know that loners are the easiest marks. Encourage your child to look for another kid at school who usually sits alone and go sit by him. Teachers might prompt this sort of relationship, too, or perhaps assign an older 'big brother' to be nearby. Another tactic John used successfully was to eat his lunch quickly and sit in the library. There were adults there and a reasonable assurance of safety.

Improving the bully situation at your child's school
TAKE A TOP-DOWN VIEW

Instead of focusing on the kids who are doing it, focus on the adults who are allowing it to happen.

FIND OUT SCHOOL POLICY

Ask for a written statement of commitment. What are they doing to stop bullying and who at the school is in charge of it? Make sure that your school knows your child has a disability and absolutely must be protected from harmful bullying, including teasing.

FIND OUT IF YOUR CHILD'S TEACHER IS A BULLY

Without even realizing it, the teacher could be engaging in subtle or silent put-downs. These might include ignoring the student, communicating impatience (rolling eyes, smirking) to his classmates, or conveniently forgetting the student when it comes to special events. Some parents have told me their children have been excluded from class parties, valentine exchanges, field trips, or musical performances. Not only is the child being discriminated against, but if the other students see that your child is somehow 'lesser' in the eyes of the teacher, I believe they will interpret that as silent permission to treat your child with less respect.

MAKE SURE YOUR CHILD'S TEACHER IS SERIOUS ABOUT STOPPING
BULLYING

Another way of giving silent permission to bullying is when a
teacher turns a blind eye to incidents. John had one wonderful
teacher who clearly saw he was a frequent victim. She told me
once, 'If I had to put up with what John puts up with, I would
refuse to come to school.' She was outraged enough that she
gathered the worst offenders and laid down the law. She insti-
tuted an absolute 'hands off' policy when it came to John. It must
have worked pretty well because John commented to me, 'It's the
only class where I have any peace.' Teachers *can* make a difference, if they want to.

BEWARE OF THE 'GOTCHA'

We've heard the horror stories where a child is bullied by a group
at school until one day he snaps, and the next thing you know, we
are reading about it in the newspapers. These are extreme cases,
but to a lesser extent this happens to kids with Asperger
Syndrome every day. The punks of the school see our kids as an
easy mark and start pulling tricks. They know how to stay below
the teacher's radar, however, so the teacher is seldom aware of
what's going on. The child with Asperger Syndrome doesn't have
the same degree of guile. When he acts out in retaliation it is
without any subterfuge. He gets caught, of course! The bullies
know this and play it to advantage. They tease and tease until our
kids lash out, and then sit back and watch our kids be the ones
punished. Mission accomplished. Gotcha! It helps to see it for
exactly what it is, and to bring it to the teacher's attention in
exactly those terms.

KEEP A RECORD

I tried to handle some incidents as they happened with a phone
call or letter, but let's face it, a lot goes on that is just enough to
keep our kids on edge, but not enough to involve the parent every
day. John did not want me to be involved anyway. My alternative
method was to keep a record on my computer of bullying

incidents as I found out about them. When John was involved in a 'gotcha' incident in the eighth grade, I was ready. The school called me in to put me on the spot about the single action my son took (he bloodied a kid's nose on the bus) and I was ready with my own list of grievances. If memory serves, there were thirty-four items. The school got a new perspective.

BEWARE OF THE COMMON DENOMINATOR PROBLEM

If your child should be bullied by one classmate on Monday, by another on Tuesday, and so forth, by Friday some teachers will think your child is the common denominator to the problems. He is, of course, but that doesn't mean he is at fault. Unfortunately, the teacher tends to think that the problem must be him.

TEACHERS DON'T WANT TO GET TO THE BOTTOM OF THINGS: THEY JUST WANT IT TO STOP

On more than one occasion, John reported a problem only to be told to sit down, or found himself punished equally with the offender. In one ridiculous episode, a boy pushed his books off his desk. John did the same thing to the other boy. The annoyed teacher hollered at both of them. When John tried to explain, she said that he should have just reported it to her rather than trying to retaliate. Fair enough. The next day, the other boy pushed John's books again. This time John raised his hand and reported it. She got angry and declared, 'I'm so sick of this! You boys are both in detention!'

I guess you could call that 'Son of Gotcha'. I appreciate that teachers do not have time to play cop and detective, so the issue is complex from their viewpoint. It's easy from my viewpoint, however. I know my child and know whom to believe. A teacher who comes to appreciate and believe John's innocent candor makes her job infinitely easier too. A teacher who truly understands Asperger Syndrome is one who will understand the dynamics behind these episodes and that should help avoid these situations.

BULLYING IS MORE THAN HITTING

It's not enough to ensure your child doesn't come home with bruises. Here are some of the many ways our kids can be made miserable that I've compiled from a few articles on the topic. These are all types of bullying: hitting, kicking, spreading rumors, threats, rude gestures, pushing, tripping, stalking, excluding, silent treatment, insults, unwanted touching, making fun of, hurtful comments, staring, damage to personal belongings, name calling, encouraging or daring to do something wrong. Only two of these categories would produce a bruise!

One would think that that's a pretty hefty list, but they forgot a few. To give you a more vivid picture, here are some of the things my own son has endured. I hope teachers all over the world are reading this, because every incident happened on school property:

- books, calculator, money, lunch stolen (many episodes)
- repeatedly touched on the back of the neck, causing a startle reflex
- sand poured in his ear
- moths put down his back
- kept from his locker by four kids
- given a 'wedgie'
- soda poured all over him
- mustard packet squished on him
- banana peels and other things thrown at him
- rude caricatures drawn of him
- books pushed to floor
- lunch box hidden in tree
- dead poisonous snake put in his locker
- ink and paint put on his shirt.

THE BULLY COPS ARE IN THE WRONG PLACE

Teachers are usually given prime responsibility for overseeing the bully situation. They do a terrific job of making sure that bullying doesn't happen in the classroom, but it's kind of like the old joke of the drunk looking for his keys in the dark. He lost them in the backyard but he looks for them under the streetlight out on the corner. Why? Because the light's better. I feel that that is the way bullying is handled in many schools. They talk about it in the classroom and in the assemblies, and teachers watch out for it in class. The light's better there. But bullying happens in the in-between times and places. A recent study in Melbourne, Australia showed prime locations and times to be after school, lunchtime, before school, and on public transportation, rather than in the classrooms. I could probably also add a few other locations, including locker rooms, bathrooms, playgrounds, bus stops, hallways, and stairwells. If schools are serious about stopping it, they ought to look for it in the right places. As my younger son would say, 'Duh.'

There are legal avenues. We never took legal action for any bullying incident. It is an option for serious cases or for those who are fond of the courts. These avenues are out of my league, but see Appendix 2 for further information on support organizations for legal matters.

Specific subject areas and issues

Here are some special issues that might crop up. For each subject area, you will find some comments, a list of social issues, sensory issues, or motor skills that may present problems, and suggestions to make the class go a little better. This is based on John's experience and also that of other Asperger kids.

Math

Many of our kids do well at math, but some have difficulties, particularly with story problems. Estimating is a hard concept since our kids expect, and like to give, exact answers. Too many math problems assigned after the concept is learned can be frustrating. They may also not see the point in doing a problem by hand that could be more easily done via calculator, or the point of showing their work.

- Social issues: occasional group projects, such as devising a budget or playing mock stock market.

- Sensory issues: none.

- Motor skills: using compass, protractors, calculator; drawing precise angles and shapes; writing out math problems neatly.

SUGGESTIONS

Graph paper can keep numbers lined up. Rationale for estimating, showing one's work, or doing work without a calculator may need to be explained a few times. The teacher might be willing to compromise or help to explain them. Covering up all but one row of math problems at a time can help keep a student from becoming overwhelmed.

Science

Science is of great interest to most kids with Asperger Syndrome. They may shine on particular topics of interest and earn the respect of classmates. On the downside, they may correct the teacher, ask too many questions, or perseverate on particular topics. Equipment or lab animals may be distracting. Lab days may be overstimulating.

- Social issues: working with lab partners.

- Sensory issues: chemical smells (olfactory), possible gooey substances, protective gloves, aprons, or safety goggles (tactile); dissecting frogs, worms or other (gross-out factor!); looking into microscopes or telescopes, or at Bunsen burners or flames (visually stimulating).

- Motor skills: handling tongs, pipettes, test tubes, and scalpels; dissecting, measuring precisely, preparing slides, weighing, pouring, writing up results.

SUGGESTIONS

Choose lab partners wisely. Step-by-step written instructions may help add structure to lab days. Some skills may be practiced at home.

English

English can be one of the more challenging classes. Longer papers are required in the upper grades, so organization and pacing become key issues. Our kids seem to be either obsessively organized or chronically disorganized. Some plow ahead, barreling to finish and occasionally misinterpreting the teacher's instructions or getting off-track. Most have the opposite problem and don't know how to begin at all.

Rules of grammar are not usually a problem, but abstract concepts and literary analysis are. Our kids usually prefer non-fiction in their choice of books. In working with fiction, the Theory of Mind difficulties of Asperger Syndrome make it tough to see character motivation or the author's subtext, and so analysis tends to center more on concrete plot details.

- Social issues: group work.

- Sensory issues: none.

- Motor skills: handwriting large amounts, keyboarding.

SUGGESTIONS

See general comments on group work, handwriting, and longer assignments, on page 197.

Social studies or humanities

These subjects have highs and lows. Good memory skills help our kids to excel at recalling geography facts, names, and dates. The 'what' of this class is not the difficulty, it's the 'why' that causes trouble. Our kids may know the salient facts of an event (who, what, when, where), but not be able to state why it happened or why people behaved as they did. There may be a great deal of writing in this class as well.

- Social issues: lots of group work; field trips to historical spots or museums; surveys or field research in current world topics.
- Sensory issues: not usually a problem except during field trips.
- Motor skills: note-taking, writing.

SUGGESTIONS

Discuss field trips in advance and devise coping strategies (having a buddy, being trailed by teacher, sitting in front of bus, identifying a way to take a break, parent chaperone).

Computers and information technology

This is usually a pretty good class for our kids. Interacting with a keyboard and monitor can be easier than interacting with kids. The exactness and predictability of the computer can be comforting; however, computer crashes or lost data can provide intense frustration.

- Social issues: sharing computer terminals.
- Sensory issues: depending on the computer program, there may be various colors or actions on the screen (visual). Possibly working with speakers or headphones (auditory).
- Motor skills: typing skills.

SUGGESTIONS

Keyboarding can be practiced at home with software or a typing manual.

Physical education and extracurricular sports

Physical education (PE) is an assault on virtually every front. The sensory ambush can be overwhelming, social requirements of team dynamics are a frustrating mystery, and motor skills of all sorts come into play. Nevertheless, many of the kids, especially younger ones, like PE or are at least attracted to it. This is probably because they enjoy the physical exercise, which can be very calming and integrating. Also, kids may like the *idea* of playing a sport, even if the reality of the experience is unsuccessful. The best activities in this class are usually those without team interaction or complicated rules. The various types of sports can probably be divided something like this:

- *Best activities* (individual sport, repetitive movement): track and field, swimming, archery, weight lifting, bowling, golf, gymnastics, bicycling, karate. Karate is excellent when practiced solo and when the emphasis in on self-defense only. John loves practicing moves on his own, but got upset in a class when it came to actual body contact with others.

- *Next best activities* (team sport but with simpler rules and little or no body contact): volleyball, badminton, and tennis.

- *Most challenging activities* (complicated team sports involving quick decisions and many different skills): basketball, football, soccer, rugby, cricket, netball, hockey, and broom hockey.

- Social issues: competition, learning how to win and lose, turn-taking, following the team leader, complicated game rules, changing clothes around others, potential for bullying in the locker room.

- Sensory issues: body contact, uniforms, sometimes hats and sunscreen, taking showers (tactile); echoing showers and gymnasiums, banging lockers, coach's whistles, cheering, bouncing balls, squeaking sneakers (auditory); locker room smells (olfactory).

- Motor skills: running, jumping, hopping, balance, dribbling balls, batting, eye–hand coordination, upper body strength.

SUGGESTIONS:

Child may change clothes separate from the others. Teacher can limit whistle-blowing and prohibit the teams from hollering different directions at the child (when John got the basketball, no one was allowed to holler at him). Choosing teams can be done by the teacher. Child's group should go last, not first, doing any new skill so he can watch a bit. Teacher can join child's team to stick close by. Child can be teacher's assistant.

Art

Some kids develop an aversion to art from when they were forced to do crayon work or deal with gooey things like paste in younger years. Others of the Asperger population can be quite artistic.

- Social issues: loose nature of the class may lead to idle chatter and casual interaction.

- Sensory issues: glue, paste, finger paint, clay, charcoal, pastels, papier mâché, craft dough, and other sticky or gooey substances (tactile, olfactory).

- Motor skills: drawing, painting, cutting, molding, kneading, folding.

SUGGESTIONS

Work with some of these materials at home.

Applied technology (woodworking, metal shop)

This class can be full of distracting influences. There are lots of sensory issues and potential problems with motor skills. The class is done in a lab setting.

- Social issues: working with a shop partner, sharing equipment.

- Sensory issues: wood, metal, glue, varnish, paint (olfactory, tactile); machinery of various sorts, usually loud and often spinning or flashing (auditory, visual).

- Motor skills: measuring, sawing, bending, soldering, sanding, drilling, hammering, planing, polishing, painting.

SUGGESTIONS

Earplugs should be worn. Practice some skills at home if necessary. Have teacher watch for signs of distress.

Cooking

The class climate may be hectic on cooking days. The right partner can keep a slightly overstimulated child on task. The wrong one can agitate things.

- Social issues: working with one or more cooking partners, sharing duties, sharing food, taking turns and dividing labor.

- Sensory issues: cracking egg yolks, kneading dough, forming meat loaf or cookie balls, working with sticky pastry or frosting (tactile); food smells (olfactory); blenders, mixers (auditory).

- Motor skills: chopping, grating, peeling, slicing, stirring, lifting, turning cakes, rolling dough, flipping fried foods, weighing, measuring.

SUGGESTIONS

Find out what they will be cooking to head off any allergy or gagging problems. Practice some skills at home. Have teacher keep an eye on the partner situation.

Sewing

There are few specific issues to deal with, but the class may be quite loosely structured, which could be stressful.

- Social issues: there is rarely group work; partners usually share a sewing machine, however.
- Sensory issues: different fabrics (tactile); sewing machine (auditory).
- Motor skills: scissor work and dealing with seam rippers, needles, pins, buttons, snaps and paper patterns. Working the sewing machine requires using two hands plus either a foot or knee to operate the power. Folding material, measuring, cutting, pinning, turning casings, ironing, hand sewing.

SUGGESTIONS

If there is anxiety about the sewing machine, arrange to let your child use one at home first, where there are fewer distractions. Practice motor skills if necessary.

Foreign languages

Many parents assume their Asperger child will have trouble with foreign language class, possibly because of communication difficulties in English. Most parents I've spoken with have been pleasantly surprised. Our kids often have a fascination with words, a wide vocabulary that may help them sort out foreign words, and an excellent facility for memorization. Our kids do especially well in the first and second years when language lessons consist mostly of simple memorization and simple sentences. Starting in about third year, though, the emphasis is on conversational skills, idioms, and spontaneous conversation. Don't be surprised if grades dip then or your child loses enthusiasm.

You may need to protect your child's access to foreign language instruction. Special classes (speech therapy, physical therapy, social skills, resource room or remedial classes) are very often pullout classes and what the child is pulled out of is foreign language. Watch out for this. The school's rationale is probably that *most* kids who need remedial help don't want or need the added intellectual strain of a foreign language class (and perhaps assumes that these kids are not college-bound), but as usual, what works for *most* special needs kids has no relevance to our kids and that should be pointed out to the school. If our kids need to be pulled out of a class, there are other more logical choices – just ask our kids! They'd do better to skip PE, art, music, applied tech, or some other class that they have either difficulties with or no interest in. Keep in mind that many of our kids will be able to go to college, and entrance into college is made easier with some foreign language under one's belt.

- Social skills: possible interaction in skits, rehearsed or spontaneous conversations, songs or games.
- Sensory issues: language labs may use tape recorders, microphones and headphones (tactile and auditory).
- Motor skills: handwriting issues of special alphabets or ideographs.

Are all languages equal? Whatever language appeals to your child is probably the one to try. Romance languages are typical, but consider these if offered.

CHINESE AND JAPANESE

Being able to hear and replicate the specific tones of Asian languages might be challenging (but also perhaps good exercise?). Writing the special language characters may be difficult, from a motor skill standpoint. Difference in culture offers opportunities to compare social customs, and discuss social situations intellectually, which can be beneficial for our kids.

RUSSIAN

There is a new alphabet to learn, which may present a small motor skills challenge. Grammar is straightforward, however.

LATIN

Latin is making a comeback. It is a language to be written and read, so there is not the emphasis on pronunciation and conversation that you find in other languages. It is also quite regular and rule-based. Learning word roots is great for increasing vocabulary in English. Latin is probably a particularly excellent choice for our kids.

SUGGESTIONS:

Find out from the teacher what sort of language course will be taught. Is it mostly oral or written? A predominantly oral class may be more difficult for our kids. If headphones are required, consider getting your child used to the feel of them beforehand.

Drama

Our kids often do well in drama. Their memorization skills come in handy for learning lines, and the physical nature of the class can be a stress release. From our own experience and reports from other parents, it seems that nervousness of going onstage is not usually a problem. Perhaps nervousness is a social cue so our kids don't pick it up as easily as most folks? Some suggest that in some ways our kids spend the whole day acting anyway, so this is not so different. The culture of drama clubs and theatre groups can be very tolerating of people with differences and our kids may find acceptance and friendship here. One possible downside of drama class is the lack of structure, which may be too stimulating for some kids.

- Social skills: group work, interpreting emotions of play characters.

- Sensory issues: make-up; paint; close contact with other people.

- Motor skills: dance, movement, balance.

SUGGESTIONS:

Discuss with the teacher the problems that lack of structure may cause for your child. Suggest that she be fairly specific in describing what is to be done, and that she keep a watchful eye on group work. Physical movement may be a helpful diversion for the agitated child. This is a good place to teach relaxation techniques as well.

Music

Some of our kids seem to do well playing instruments or singing and are a successful part of a band, orchestra or choir. Others, because of hyperacute hearing, find music classes to be quite overwhelming.

- Social skills: playing in a group; possible excursions to play in other cities.

- Sensory issues: lots of noise, sour notes, vibration of instruments on lips, teeth, etc.

- Motor skills: whatever motions are involved with a specific instrument (covering holes, plucking strings, gliding bows, etc.)

SUGGESTIONS:

Work with the child on developing a sense of rhythm. If your child has hyperacute hearing, consider excusing from this class, depending on what the exact topic is. Listening to different types of recorded music may be fine, for example, whereas standing in a loud choir may be too much. The teacher should be made aware of any signs of sensory overload, and allow the child to take a break.

Chapter 7

Homeschooling and Home Helps

Here is the nitty-gritty on our homeschooling experience – what I feel were the turnaround years for my son and how we went about it. During those three years (part of year two, and all of grades three, four, and five), we virtually dropped out of the system – we discontinued Ritalin, dropped insurance fights, dropped special education and, over the protests of the school system, pulled our son out of school. With little support from anywhere, we made *incredible* gains.

Homeschooling is not for everyone, but it is an option that parents should not gloss over. In my opinion, it is worthy of serious consideration and I do not feel my son would be where he is today without it. In Chapter 1, I talked about all the things that led us to explore homeschooling. This chapter will talk about the mechanics of homeschooling and also I will mention some things that anyone can do at home, whether homeschooling or not. These are not whiz-bang tricks. They are just reminders of ways to work with kids that will increase sensory, motor, communication, social, and academic skills. Some take only a few minutes but can reap great benefits. Most are common sense and free or very low cost. Unfortunately, I'm afraid a lot of people think that if the advice doesn't cost thousands or involve fancy equipment and technical jargon, it mustn't be all that good. I heartily disagree.

Is it legal?

Homeschooling is legal in all fifty US states, in the UK, Australia, New Zealand, Canada, and many more places. Some places have more restrictions than others. In some places, you need permission from the school authority to do it, in which case you may also need to submit information on what subjects you will cover and how (will you teach the material yourself or will you use a correspondence course, tutor, or other?). Other places you just need to inform the authorities of your intent to homeschool. Requirements vary greatly.

You will usually need to keep and show attendance records, but this can be as simple as marking a calendar or keeping a daily journal of your activities. You may also need to show that your child is making progress. Depending on local rules, this may mean working with an advisor who works for the school district, assembling a portfolio of your child's work, or submitting your child to periodic standardized testing. Where we lived in Colorado, the rule was standardized testing every two years. If test results were below a certain score John could have been forced back into the public school system. It was a low cutoff score, but I worried that John would not be able to pass it. It also did not seem fair. The way I looked at it, the school system had shown little progress over the years, yet they were never penalized. Why on earth should we be? To avoid this, I enrolled John into an umbrella school. Umbrella schools are private schools whose primary role is working with homeschoolers. They keep attendance records for you, advise on curriculum choices and assist in dealings with school officials. Most people do not need an umbrella school; however, it is nice support, and you may get other benefits such as a newsletter and connections with other homeschoolers. And, being in a private school rendered John officially beyond the jurisdiction of the state school's testing requirements. In a humorous sidelight, just about the time I signed up for this school, a writer from the *Denver Post* wrote a scathing article on umbrella schools. In it he implied (or maybe said) that these schools were a disgrace because they acted as fronts to allow homeschoolers to take advantage of legal loopholes. All I can say is, three cheers for whoever found the loophole. I did *not* cancel my check.

As a final note on legalities, laws are changing all the time. If the last time you looked into homeschooling there were restrictions or requirements you felt you couldn't meet, I urge you to look again. And if you have been put off homeschooling because of the religious overtones it has historically had, I'd say that times have changed and there are plenty of homeschoolers out there who are not doing it only on religious grounds. Families with special needs kids are a rapidly growing segment of the home education population.

If you decide to try it you should find plenty of support. There are more resources and support for homeschoolers (including special needs homeschoolers) than ever before. Websites and addresses are listed in Appendix 6 of this book to help you begin your research into this, and an Internet search will likely reveal more sites. Also, do not forget local support groups. These are usually the very best places to learn about the ins and outs of requirements in your immediate area.

Finances

Many families would like to homeschool but have gotten used to a two-paycheck income and in fact can't imagine life without both income sources. Can you live on only one income? The answer might be no, that you absolutely need two paychecks in order to survive, but I have seen time after time how families have cut their income in order to have one parent home, and they have lived to tell the tale. We are one of those families. When I quit work, our income dropped by more than half. I also know some single parents who homeschool. More about that later.

Living on a single income

Living on a single income looked impossible to us at first. We owned both our cars, but we had a hefty house mortgage and of course two kids to feed. We had also recently remodeled my husband's mother's 100-year-old house and owed several thousand dollars on it. Our savings account was paltry – it could handle car repairs and Christmas bills, but it certainly couldn't sustain us. And it wasn't as though losing my paycheck represented only a fraction of our household income. I was making $46,000 and my husband was making $27,000, so we were talking about dropping our income by 63 per cent. Kind of scary.

But we did it anyhow. Very carefully, of course. If you are contemplating such a step, I urge nothing less than careful consideration. It may not be doable for every family. I daresay, though, that it is far more feasible than most two-income families think.

Below, our family finances are bared to you, not because I'm a financial exhibitionist but because I really want to show you step-by-step how we figured out that I could be a stay-at-home mom and we wouldn't starve. Keep in mind that the numbers are rough, based on 1990 figures and in US dollars. It won't translate well to today's costs, but it is the *process* that is important. Here's what we did.

Step 1: start by calculating how much money that paycheck is really bringing in
AFTER TAXES

Although my yearly income was roughly $46,000, federal taxes immediately whittled that down to $38,800, and after state taxes the paycheck was closer to $36,800. My retirement fund took up $2800. That left us with $34,000. Medicare tax was around $700. Now the paycheck I was thinking about cutting was down to $33,300.

AFTER EXPENSES

Going to work always entails some overhead expenses, but you may be chagrined to see just how very much expense is involved. Consider work clothes, extra schooling, briefcases or tools, and transportation. Daycare took two large bites but there were many items that added up to considerable expense:

- Before and after-school care (John): $60/wk x 50 = $3000
- Daycare (John's brother Jay): $90/wk x 50 = $4500
- Gasoline to work and back: $10/wk = $500
- Daily lunches: $25/wk x 50 = $1250
- Business clothes, shoes, nylons, purses, jewelry, dry cleaning = $650
- Office extras (coffee fund, gifts, office parties, business lunches) = $500
- Vending machines: $10/wk x 50 = $500
- Fast food dinners (because I was too tired to cook): $30/wk x 50 = $1500
- Total work-related expenses = $12,400

My paycheck was now looking more like $20,900 in real income, quite a comedown from the original $46,000. It was depressing to think that my fat paycheck and hard work yielded so little, but on the upside, it seemed easier to cope with losing my paycheck when it was now less than half its original size. It redoubled our conviction to become a single-income family. Now the question became, could we make up a $20,900 loss?

Step 2: look for gains you can make

One nice part about reducing family income is that it often reduces one's tax bracket. In our case, my husband got to keep about 5% more of his paycheck, resulting in something like $1350 that he didn't have to pay to Uncle Sam. We then looked at some money-saving strategies. A top priority was paying off credit cards because interest payments alone were eating $100 per month out of our income (sad, but true). Luckily, one bonus of leaving my job was that I got back my retirement fund contributions. That lump sum was enough to pay off our credit card bills, which would save another $1200 in interest we no longer had to pay. We refinanced our house loan for savings of about $3000 per year. The dollar cost for me to stay home was now looking more like $15,350 instead of the original $46,000. When my husband got the opportunity to do shift work ($4000 gain) and we knew a promotion was not too far off ($2000), we felt we could make it. I resigned my job and came home.

Step 3: economize

This aspect may amaze you the most. It's shocking how much economizing can be done if you put your mind to it. Could you cancel cable or satellite TV options? Contrary to popular belief, these are *not* necessities. Can you drop magazine subscriptions? Shop for cheaper insurance or better long distance rates? Cut the kids' hair yourself? (Given the tactile sensitivities and stress triggers of many kids with Asperger Syndrome, haircutting at home is often a less frightening option than a salon cut anyway.) These are just a few cost-cutting hints. See Appendix 5 for a further list of 55 money-saving ideas, nearly all of which we have done and in many cases still do.

Step 4: be flexible

Our ways may not work for you, but maybe some other options would. You might decide to sell a car or motorcycle, move to a more modest neighborhood, or ask your parents for your inheritance early. You might look into debt consolidation loans, running a home-based business, or putting some things on hold, such as family vacation or college night classes.

Step 5: have faith

I'm pleased to tell you the happy ending to this story. After I quit work and we trembled through a brief adjustment period, everything went smoothly. We survived. In fact, we not only survived but also soon reached a firmer economic standing than we'd ever had before. Our bills were fewer, our needs were simpler, our debts were non-existent, we had less clutter around the house (because we bought less), and our priorities were straight. Man cannot live on bread alone, but how many of us really need this year's model car?

Can a single parent homeschool?

One of the most inspiring letters I have read comes from Kendra who has graciously allowed me to print it here.

> I was actually forced to homeschool. Leo was having so many problems in school – everything from detention and suspensions in the first grade to getting expelled on his eighth birthday from second grade. To give you an idea on how long he made it in the second grade, school started in the beginning of September and his birthday is October 5th. After being expelled, he was placed in a 'special' ed. school. That was such a mistake. The reason he was having so much difficulty was that he wouldn't sit still, he hummed during class, couldn't deal with 'circle time', and basically annoyed the teachers to no end. He was never violent. This 'special' school was for behavioral disorders and had a lot of children that were too violent for regular school. Every day Leo either came home beat up or with some new 'trick' he learned from another student. The staff did their best, but they still weren't teaching him. They insisted that he was working at second grade level, but I had him tested and he was barely at mid first grade level. I figured at that rate, he might be up to third grade level by the time he graduated high school. This was completely unacceptable. He is way too

bright to be left behind because he couldn't sit still. At this time, I lost my good paying full time job because I was either taking time off to deal with Leo's school or having to take him to work with me because he had been suspended again.

Since I didn't have a job, I took him out of school to home school. Best decision I ever made. In October of 2000, we had his behavior stabilized enough and his lesson schedule ingrained enough to enable me to go back to work. I work 20 hours per week at $12/hr. I don't have a lot of money, but I have enough to barely scrape by and a very understanding landlord. I also am doing things that get me extra money on Internet. I believe that home schooling Leo is more important than having lots of things. I don't have a car, and our house isn't the best in the neighborhood, and I can't remember the last time I got new clothes, but Leo is now reading at the fourth grade level and doing fifth grade math and we've only been home schooling since the beginning of last June. Yes, I have had to get creative in finding ways to keep the food on the table, and I am always on the look out for ways to make more money without giving up time outside of the house, and they are out there. I guess it comes down to priorities.

Don't you have to give up your life to homeschooling? I don't think I could do that

A friend put it nicely in perspective for me. She said, 'I may live another fifty years. Is it such a sacrifice to spend the next few years concentrating on my kids?'

My feelings about it had darker overtones. I remember standing in my shower, debating over whether to pull my son out of school, which clearly wasn't working for him. The thought of homeschooling was absolutely daunting and I had no idea if it would go well, but I remember thinking to myself that if my son turned out 'bad' (however that was defined, I really didn't know), I could at least live with myself if I knew I'd tried to do everything possible to alter the outcome. If not, the thought that I hadn't done everything possible would be painful to live with.

As far as being with one's kids twenty-four hours a day goes, some parents do not think they can handle homeschooling because they have already seen the problems that the school has been having (and they are the experts, aren't they?). Others see the opposite. Their child holds it together during the day but the moment he gets off the school bus he becomes a veritable fire-cracker just waiting to get into the house and explode. So parents think that the school knows better how to handle their child and the parents should just let them do it. When they see their child coming into the house like a tornado they can't imagine trying to cope with having their child home all the time, much less trying to teach him.

Keep in mind that in most cases, it's a case of Contents Under Pressure. Sometimes John would fall apart in school, other times he would save it until he got home, but in either case, once we pulled him out to homeschool, the pressure was released and he became a kid we could enjoy being with. We still had our moments, of course, but the fact that we were able to take him off Ritalin almost immediately should let you know that the overload of school had been a large part of what was driving him over the edge, regardless of where the actual upset took place every day, school or home. The child you see under the stressful conditions of school is not necessarily the same child you would see when he is learning at home in manageable and successful bites. When a child is allowed to be himself, learn at his own pace, and follow his interests, he may well be easier to live with.

Choosing a style of homeschooling

There are several approaches to homeschooling and I'll describe some of them briefly here.

Traditional school-at-home

This is taking the same format of regular classroom teaching, and doing it at home. It's easy for most parents to visualize, because it's a routine we grew up with. Most folks who follow this format purchase a packaged curriculum a year at a time from an education publisher. There are many correspondence schools or publishers that provide materials for each grade, the equivalent of 'fourth grade in a box.' The material is organized, sequential, and may have the benefit of reputation. That is, the mention of a certain curriculum will cause other homeschoolers to say 'ah' and recognize what you are talking about. Public school officials recognize well-established programs, too, and may ask you fewer questions about what you are intending to teach.

Teaching materials and schedules with these programs are set fairly firmly, however, and there may be rigid homework and testing standards. This can be good or bad, depending on your child's temperament and ability. An older child with more maturity and development or a child who genuinely enjoys worksheets and seat work may thrive in such a system. A child with handwriting issues, attention problems or an aversion to traditional schooling methods (which may include many of our kids) could well have problems. Modifications may need to be made in order to avoid bringing home the same problems your child may have had in the classroom.

Another problem is that some correspondence courses, textbooks, and workbooks can be dull or expensive or both. If your kids are reluctant learners, need a different pace or learn best using hands-on methods or real life experiences, consider other methods.

It should be noted that more and more curricula are being offered as computer programs or offered online through Internet. Both of these may make learning more colorful, fun, and interactive. Then again, I've seen some computer courses that are nothing more than textbooks on a screen. Caveat emptor. Ask around for recommendations and review it before you buy it.

Unit study

The unit study method is the intensive studying of one particular subject at a time and from many angles. Unit studies seem custom-made for the student who likes to focus intently on a particular topic. In other words, it may be well suited for the student with Asperger Syndrome. A child's current special interest, whether it's tornadoes or Egypt, acid rain or the Great Barrier Reef, can be used to promote learning. The unit study can last a few days or much longer. Through unit study, you will find ways to incorporate reading, math, science, social studies and many other subjects.

To give you an example, one of the unit studies John and I devised was on Japan. John loved karate at the time, and by extension, Japan. Using that as a cue, we read a children's book together on life in Japan (thus accomplishing both reading and social studies); we learned how to use an abacus (math); John decorated a folder with the flag of Japan, a picture of Mount Fuji and a traced map (art and geography); we learned about Kite-Flying Day in Japan and made our own kite and flew it (art, social studies, science, physical education); we cooked a Japanese meal to eat with chopsticks (home economics, math, fine motor skills); John tried some Japanese writing with black poster paint (language arts and art); he folded an origami frog (art, math, fine motor skills); he learned some karate from a *Karate for Kids* video tape (physical education), and we watched *The Karate Kid* movies (fun!).

What if your child's special interest seems trivial or mundane – collecting paperclips, for instance? Well, then you build a unit study on paperclips! You can study the history of it. Who made the first one, and what did the first paperclip look like? Your child can make one out of wire, and come up with different designs. He can collect them from different companies. Perhaps he can write off for information or free samples. He can learn math by counting sets of different kinds, estimating how many are in a jar, measuring individual ones or by making long chains of them to different lengths. He can look at weight. How many paperclips to the ounce or gram? He can sort his collection and graph it. He can conduct science experiments. How strong is each type? How flexible? Which rusts faster, a paperclip or a nail? Do magnets work with them? Are there advantages of metal paperclips over plastic ones? Would a wooden paperclip work? He can devise an exhibit or scrapbook of the different types. He can do art with them. And so forth. The lowly paperclip has launched you both into new worlds and probably off to other tangents. Maybe your studies will touch on patents, inventors, the World's Fair, or World War II. Were paperclips available during wartime metal shortages? I have no idea but maybe you'll find out. Unit studies can be marvelous.

If there are disadvantages to the unit study, one is that the parent needs to be a little creative to pull ideas, resources and supplies together. There are pre-made unit studies available for purchase these days, but you may end up spending a lot of money and find them rather tame (usually a set of worksheets). Somewhat better are the unit studies that are found these days on Internet. There are hundreds of them, but the quality varies greatly and you may spend hours looking before finding the one you need. And you may never find one on paperclips! But you can always devise your own.

Devising one's own unit studies has other advantages. You can accommodate learning styles and ability levels. You can play to strengths and make it hands-on. You can make it fun, incorporate field trips, and you can follow those tangents that invariably come up.

As you can probably tell by my enthusiasm, I like unit studies. The only real problem I had was that once in a while I spent time pulling one together only to find out that John was not that interested. My son was fascinated by his dad's tales of working in a shoe factory as a teen, but he was not interested in learning how shoes were made, which I'd wrongly assumed. I discovered that if I put too much of myself into planning and didn't get rewarded with enthusiasm, I tended to become irritable. So gradually I learned that less is more. I relaxed and stopped over-planning. When I let things flow organically and tried to stay only two steps ahead instead of twenty, we were both happier.

Unschooling

Other terms for this type of education are 'life education,' 'natural learning,' or 'child-led learning.' The purest of unschoolers do not engage in 'school' at all, only life and the learning that entails. Parents trust that their children's interests will naturally lead to the best and most relevant learning, and they adhere to the premise that only the child can determine what he needs to know at any particular moment. As John Holt, the father of unschooling noted, 'He may not do it very well, but he can do it a hundred times better than we can' (Holt 1982, p.294).

Holt wrote eloquently on the subject of natural learning. While his writings were geared toward 'every child' rather than those with particular needs, the observations he made about learning seem no less apt. I could quote volumes from this gifted educator, but one small thing he said in passing has stuck with me for a decade and led me well: 'To rescue a man lost in the woods, you must get to where he is' (Holt 1982, p.133).

If I could, I would carve this on the desktop of every teacher in the world. Whether unschooling or engaging in traditional schooling methods, what better way is there to work with a child who has Asperger Syndrome (or any child) than to make the effort to see life from where he is standing? Not that we can do a perfect job, but the effort is always worthwhile.

Eclectic method

For those who are not committed to any one method or who see advantages to each of the above techniques, the eclectic method is for you. This just means choosing a little of everything and moving different methods in and out of one's homeschooling life as you see fit. It is having the best of each world, in my opinion. And that's how we actually proceeded.

The day-to-day experience of homeschooling

Many years ago, I wrote a small article entitled 'A Day in the Life' for a homeschooler newsletter. I asked nineteen homeschooling families to 'FREEZE!' and describe their day. The aim was to illustrate that there is no one right way to do things. Some families' school day had a distinct beginning time and end time and ran like well-oiled machinery. Other families had a day that was somewhat structured but loose. They used a hodgepodge of resources including workbooks, experiments, computer programs, games, personal reading, and other bits, some selected by the parent and some by the child.

Other families just lived their lives, seamlessly weaving learning into normal daily activities and trusting that that was enough. They ran errands, shopped, cleaned, pursued hobbies, gardened, cooked, discussed news, played in the park, attended club functions, ran home-based businesses, got involved in civic projects, and so forth. One family ended up spending the day in the emergency room, and another family was down with the flu. Not every day is a prize. But that was valuable information too.

In many ways the diversity in that article reflects the long-term profile of our homeschooling experiences. We went through periods that ran like well-oiled machinery, periods of hodgepodge experiences within a loose framework, days when we abandoned *trying* to learn and just let it happen. And of course, days with the flu. The first day we homeschooled, I thought I would follow John's lead, and started by asking about all the things he would like to learn. He got a worried look on his face and told me that that's not what they did at school and I was doing it wrong. I realized that John expected a more traditional approach and sure enough, he was quite relieved when I brought out some workbooks. I was a bit disappointed, but I had wanted to follow John's lead and that was where he led. He wanted the comfort of the format he knew about. Gradually though, we relaxed and expanded. After a trial and error period that took many months, John and I settled into a routine that looked something like this:

Each morning we started with a warm-up activity. This might be quizzing from a favorite deck of trivia cards, working on a maze or word game, or doing a small jigsaw puzzle, such as of US or world maps.

We then chose activities for the day. As with many kids with Asperger Syndrome, John never liked surprises, so discussing the day in advance was important. He also coped better if he had a bit of control over it. Therefore we got into a habit of taking turns choosing the order of the day's activities. We would usually plan only three or four activities. Since he generally chose math and science-type activities, I would gap-fill by choosing a language arts activity plus something else (geography, art etc.).

Our official work ended by noon each day. Following that was unschooling, unbeknown to John. Bill, John's dad, often got into the act in a lot of unplanned and fantastic ways. Many evenings, John and Bill would discuss politics, religion, statistics, astronomy, or whatever topic happened to come up. Bill is good at explaining and John is good at asking so they often stayed up until midnight just talking. I would secretly record these seminars in our school log book under the proper category of social studies, math, science or whatever. I did this with everything. When they played games (poker, chess, checkers), it was counted as math, logic, or social skills. Work around the house (fixing appliances, building a shelf, soldering something) became applied tech. When Bill would play guitar in the evenings and challenge John to keep the beat or sing along, I wrote it down for the valuable learning experience it was. And it seemed like I was always writing down 'physical education' because they often swam, wrestled, or hiked together, had nightly games of catch, and so forth. No one said, 'We'd better talk about social studies tonight' or anything remotely planned, but it was astonishing how full and well rounded these times were.

Afternoons were for errands, excursions, and whatever John wanted to do. I only insisted that he not watch TV or play video games. I discovered that these unschooled afternoons were often more educational than his mornings, so after awhile we took Fridays off too, under the same rules. When John did his own thing I quietly wrote it down. Here are some of the terrific self-initiated projects that John did during unschooled afternoons:

- worked through three *Karate for Kids* video instruction tapes (*physical education*)

- built and rebuilt wooden forts (*carpentry*)

- did all 30 experiments in an electronics kit (*science, fine motor*)

- turned our spare bedroom into a museum, making several exhibits out of feathers, bones, a squirrel skeleton, bird's nest, old coins, and other treasures; he typed up display cards and sold tickets to the neighbors (*language arts, typing, science, math*)

- made a video: he made the title cards, developed the plot, chose the music, rehearsed with his brother, and then had me shoot the film (*writing, drama, art*)

- built a pea-fence with me out of slats and twine (*carpentry*)

- worked on Lego structures, home-made kites and paper airplanes (*fine motor, math, science*)

- ran a lemonade stand (*art, cooking, math*)

- conducted dozens of science experiments (*science*)

- learned to use a sewing machine (*home economics, fine motor*)

- played lots of computer games (*various*)

- played board games – Yahtzee®, Monopoly®, Racko®, Multiplication Bingo®, etc. (*math*)

- became interested in magic and learned some tricks (*fine motor, reading*)

- played in the park, rode his bike, took up running, and developed a personal fitness routine (*physical education*)

- got interested in nutrition, looked up facts and made himself a notebook (*health, typing, research*)

- made cookies, cakes, drinks, biscuits, easy dishes (*cooking, math, fine motor*)

- learned about fingerprinting and made a family file of them (*science, fine motor*)

- used art kits such as candle-making, rubber stamps, and painting kits (*science, art, fine motor, sensory*)

- read catalogs and counted his money (*reading, math*)

And what about socialization?

'If there were no other reason for wanting to keep kids out of school, the social life would be reason enough' (Holt 1982, p.44).

Any parent of a child older than six knows the kind of mean-spirited teasing and harassment that goes on, and how it colors a child's mood and destroys self-esteem. Yet whenever a family actually decides to sidestep those landmines by choosing homeschooling, it seems that there is one question that is asked of them by every casual observer – but what about socialization?

I suppose the word 'homeschool' sounds like the parent and child sit at home all the time, which is what starts people worrying about isolation. But homeschoolers *do* generally lead social lives. They still live in neighborhoods, still have friends and go to the clubs and religious meeting places that they did when they were in school. But now they have other outlets too.

When we homeschooled, we belonged to a great home-schooler group made up of all average kids, plus John and one other kid who I now think also had Asperger Syndrome. We met this group weekly and enjoyed games, swimming, roller skating parties, kite-making, art projects, picnics, trips to places like the zoo, etc.

The difference between this type of socialization and the type you get at school was that this social stuff was *gradually* introduced to John. Sometimes we only stayed a little while because he soon had 'enough.' I was there to monitor the situation and we could leave while it was still a successful experience. It never ended in disaster or failure, as school experiences too often had.

In fact, I credit homeschooling with John finally being able to cope with groups. Remember that he had never managed to cope with a mainstream classroom at all prior to our pulling him out of school. But during homeschooling, John was able to attend a gymnastics class in a class of only three kids. He also bowled and took swimming lessons. That's not to say that we didn't have aborted attempts at classes that didn't work out for us (judo, karate, magic class, Lego® class). But those we just quit and never looked back. I've mentioned scouting earlier, and we also belonged to a babysitting co-op during some of that time, which meant that he helped me babysit younger kids and had the chance to have play dates at other people's houses (that I chose). I hope you are getting the idea that homeschooling can be very social indeed. It's actually one of its greatest strengths.

Isn't homeschooling expensive?

It does not have to be expensive. There are many books and programs marketed toward homeschoolers these days, and it's certainly possible to spend a lot of money on these things, but I do not recommend it. If you spend a great deal of money on a program, you will feel like you have to use it even if it doesn't work. Far better that you go for a few cheaper alternatives, especially until you learn what kinds of things will work or not work for your child. The unit study, unschooling and eclectic methods are all very inexpensive. There are many very good resources on

Internet, and local homeschooling support groups often share, swap, or sell resources. I procured many of our working materials from discount stores, yard sales, the library, and from the school district's 'morgue' of textbooks that they periodically gave away to anyone who wanted them.

The biggest expense for us was in computer software. John responded well to computer instructions because he could set his own pace, get immediate feedback, not have to worry about handwriting, and he could also have fun. Although I spent a fair bit of money on software, just think of the money that I was not spending on school lunches, school resource fees, backpacks, school supplies, school clothes, and Ritalin.

How do I know what my child's learning style is?

There is nothing like trying out several things and seeing what clicks. One thing that struck me about John is that he needed both structure and flexibility. Having a loose schedule each day kept him feeling in control, but variety within that schedule kept him interested. In many ways, it was a push-me-pull-me routine. He liked to be stimulated intellectually but if things were too challenging he would shut down. I learned early that less is more. If I presented ten math problems, he might balk and not want to do any of them. If I just asked for one, he would do it and feel good about it, and then he would do another one and then a few more. Either way, we probably got the same number done but ended on a high note, so that he was proud of himself and ready to tackle more another day.

What if my child has a fit over wrong answers? How can I teach him anything new if he can't ever be wrong?

It seems pretty common for our Asperger kids to have a wide streak of perfectionism built into them. John would get upset over the tiniest error, erasing holes in his paper, crumpling it up or pitching a fit.

My answer was to teach John about how good mistakes were. It may sound corny, but I dug up a few sayings about making mistakes, and taped them up on our kitchen walls. Some of my favorites were:

- 'If you can't make a mistake, you can't make anything.'
- 'You can't make an omelet without breaking some eggs.'
- 'If you don't make at least one mistake a day, you're not trying.'

We also studied Thomas Edison. John learned that young Tom lasted only a few weeks in school before his teacher called him 'addle-brained' and his mother pulled him out of school to teach him herself. And we learned about the many dead ends Edison reached while trying to make a filament for his invention, the light bulb. Edison had said he didn't feel like he failed so many hundreds of times with his unsuccessful experiments. He felt that he'd made that many discoveries – all about what wouldn't work. It's all in the attitude.

I also explained to John that if he got a lot of answers wrong on a worksheet, that meant I'd given him something too hard, but if I gave him a worksheet and he got *everything* right, then it was too easy! Getting one or two wrong was really just perfect because it meant we were at the right level. Once John absorbed that, things were much easier. He was no longer upset by a couple of mistakes. It saved us a lot of meltdowns.

How do I know if I'm teaching everything I should?

There are many places to answer this question:

- Your own school district. Ask them for their 'Scope and Sequence,' 'curriculum objectives,' or 'course of study' list.

- Search the web. Here are a couple helpful sites to get you started:

- http://homeschooling.about.com/education/homeschool
  ing/library/weekly/aa081500a.htm
- http://www.tea.state.tx.us/teks/#Grade

- Look in the bookstore. Books with this sort of
  information include the Core Knowledge Series of
  books by E.D. Hirsch (*What your First Grader Should
  Know* (1997) and so forth) and several books by Ruth
  Beechik (see References).

*Are there any special problems homeschooling a special needs child?
Do you lose special services?*

This varies from state to state. At the time of this writing, I know
parents who homeschool their kids but go to the local school for
speech therapy or other special services. Minnesota is one such
state. Unfortunately, other states are currently attempting to pass
legislation to relieve them of the responsibility to provide any
services at all to homeschooled children. *Shame on them.* So, this is
something to consider. Depending on where you live, once you
begin homeschooling you could lose whatever therapy services
the school was providing. On the other hand, in many cases it
really doesn't amount to much. You will have to evaluate your
own circumstances.

*Can a homeschooled child get a high school diploma/certificate
and/or go on to college or university?*

Certainly. There are many ways to do this. In the US you can pass
an equivalency test and obtain a diploma. Or, sign up for some
junior college courses. Once you pass those, no one much cares if
you have a high school diploma or not. You can work with an ac-
credited high school and have them evaluate your work and
assign credits. Or, you can simply type up homemade transcripts
based on work you have done and apply directly to a college with
them. Many colleges are open to homeschoolers. I highly
recommend a book by friend and mentor Cafi Cohen, entitled

And What About College? (2000) in which she answers these questions in detail. Her (not Asperger) son was the first home-schooler appointed to the United States Air Force Academy.

Where are some good resources for unit studies, worksheets, and curricula?

See Appendix 6 for these resources.

What are some good ways to teach various subjects?

Ideas for improving reading

Go to the library regularly. Read to your child every night. Take turns reading alternating sentences aloud, or read aloud along with books on tape. To reduce page glare, add colored acetate to the top of the reading material (let your child choose the color). Read in comfortable places (on pillows, porch swing, bean bag, for example). Take advantage of the terrific software available (John loved the Reader Rabbit series).

Note: there has traditionally been a debate on whole language versus phonics for years but among the experts anyway, the debate may be over. The National Reading Panel (an independent panel appointed by US Congress) published their findings last year after considering the best (most scientific) studies from over 100,000 reading studies conducted since 1966. The clear conclusion was that systematic phonics instruction provides the means for greatest improvement in reading. Period. You can read this report yourself at http://www.nationalreadingpanel.org. /Documents/pr_final report.htm

The report came too late for us, but I chose phonics for John ten years ago after reading *Why Johnny Can't Read* by Rudolph Flesch (1955; see also Flesch 1981). This terrific book details many studies, and as an added bonus it includes graduated word lists to do your own phonics instruction. It is simple and it worked for us.

Ideas to make writing more appealing

Use colored pens, markers, squiggly pens, skinny pens and fat pens. The toy Magna Doodle® is tons of fun and has a thin stylus that is nice for small hands. Try dry erase boards and chalkboards, colored paper, pretty stationery, and graph paper. Using a ruler can help line things up. Adding a triangular grip to a pencil or using a flat or multi-sided pencil can aid in gripping, as can wrapping some fine sandpaper or other tactile material around the pencil. Pens are less fatiguing than pencils.

What about working on special issues having to do with Asperger Syndrome? Am I qualified?

Let me preface my remarks by reminding you that I am a mom, not a trained therapist or a trained anything, and these are my opinions, which you are free to disagree with or disregard.

Whether you homeschool or your child attends regular school, home is still a great place to work on some of the extra challenges that come with Asperger Syndrome. It's nice if you can get testing done by professionals to let you know exactly which issues need work, but a little of that goes a long way. Too much testing can be stressful for your child and with diminishing returns.

Honestly, I think most parents know a lot of it by gut instinct and a lot more can be learned by carefully observing one's child. It's not rocket science to realize your child has trouble throwing a ball or that he freaks out when he gets his hands gooey, and those are issues you can work on (gently, in a fun way). I'm not saying don't get testing or professional therapists, I'm saying don't wait for these things. Some pointers from a qualified therapist would undoubtedly be beneficial, but most of it comes down to working with, and more especially *playing with*, your child.

My suggestion that you plow ahead without benefit of expert opinion probably sounds like heresy, but I think that feeling is a sign of our times. In this age we've been taught we need experts for every little thing. We don't dare do a sit-up without a personal trainer, and will soon be at the place where making potato salad will probably require an expertly written book called *Potato Salad for Morons*. Please.

There are many successful adults with Asperger Syndrome who will tell you they owe their progress to loving parents who just worked with them. If those parents didn't always know the best, most perfect, most technical and efficient way of doing things, they got the job done anyway, as best they could. I suggest that today's parents need to think like this. Rather than wait for an expert to come in and work on these issues for 30 minutes every other week (or more tragically, to wait months even to get that service in place), there's a lot to be said for just getting on with it – taking your child to the park every day, or letting him work or play alongside you and encouraging him in any way that seems to need encouraging.

As for equipment, high tech equipment is nice but remember we are building a first aid kit, not a hospital. We can do a lot with simple items and activities to target different skills. Many of these ideas I got by combing therapy catalogs and therapy websites and a few I dreamed up myself or have heard about from other parents. Anyway, even buying a couple of bigger ticket items such as a trampoline or hammock chair is cheaper than private therapy. Janet G. from Minnesota found this out when she got the bill (after insurance) from 11 weeks of occupational therapy. 'Just think how well I could outfit my living room with $950 worth of equipment!'

Some ideas to improve fine motor skills

Play with chopsticks, clothespins, tweezers, tongs, stickers, Colorforms, magnet games, felt boards, refrigerator magnets, peg boards, sewing cards, dressing dolls, pop beads, jigsaw puzzles, stringing raw pasta, finger puppets, shadow puppets, sorting coins, art work of all types, squiggle writers, wind-up toys, loading Pez candy dispensers, rolling jacks, knuckle bones or dice, sorting cards, simple electronics kits, planting seeds, sprinkling decorations on cookies, using cake decorator icing tubes, sand art kits, snap-together model kits, bake-in-the-oven 'stained glass' ornaments, glitter pictures, pipe cleaner art, beadwork, decorating foam balls for Christmas ornaments, scissor work, easy magic tricks, certain kids' games like Mr. Potato, Operation, Etch A Sketch, Lite Brite, Pick-up Sticks, or Jack straws, and of course, building or construction toys such as Lego, K'nex, and simple erector sets.

For finger strength, try craft dough, putty, squeeze balls, action toys that require squeezing a bulb, staplers, staple removers, tongs, tweezers, pop beads, scissors, spray bottles, atomizers, fingernail clippers, paper punchers, squeeze bottles, spray bottles, squirt guns, play bow and arrow, buttoning, video game controls, kneading bread.

Some ideas for large motor activity

Running, jumping, individual sports (bowling, swimming, karate), canoeing, bicycling, skating, scooters, jungle gyms, obstacle courses, gymnastics, trampoline, friendly wrestling, carpentry (sawing, hammering), gardening (digging, mowing, weeding), exercises and using exercise machines, hiking, house painting, car washing, playing Twister, crab walking, crawling, indoor or outdoor rock climbing. Team sports (basketball, football, soccer) are also good for large motor activity but may be difficult for a child with Asperger Syndrome.

Some ideas to improve using two hands at once

Marble maze, building toys, dressing dolls, playing dress-up, jump rope, either pretend or real housekeeping (mopping, sweeping, vacuuming, doing dishes), using a rolling pin, folding clothes, hanging clothes onto hangers, wringing out a face cloth, tying knots, building forts out of furniture, shoveling, digging, raking, playing on swings with two hands, pushing someone on a swing, pushing a baby pram, swinging a baseball or cricket bat, rowing or paddling a boat or canoe, carrying things like a few books or a laundry basket, climbing ladders or a rope, exercises like jumping jacks, 'wheel barrows,' clapping rhythm, hand play to accompany songs.

Ideas to improve sensory integration

The cause of our children's discomfort – sensory input – also seems to be the cure. You do not want to assault your child with troublesome sensory input but you do want to gradually increase your child's tolerance to various sounds, smells, etc. I think the key is to take things in small doses, allow the child some control over the issue, offer many opportunities, and make it as appealing as possible.

Smell sensitivity

Flowers, scented craft dough, kitchen spices (both my kids used to be crazy about playing in my spice drawer), potpourri, scented candles, cologne, various extracts, essential oils, scented pens, 'scratch and sniff' books. You can make a scent guessing game using little bottles or film canisters, by inserting cotton balls scented with various extracts. Your child can guess the scent, find matching scents, or just enjoy them.

Oral sensitivity and oral motor

Children's whistles, noise makers, duck calls, bird calls, pitch pipes, harmonicas, kazoos, those roll-out paper party favors, blowing bubbles, penny whistles, recorders, drink straws, pin wheels, any blow-action toy, fun toothbrushes, battery operated toothbrushes, baby chew toys, lollipops with battery-operated holders to spin them.

Tactile sensitivity

For hands, try collages, finger painting, sponge painting, glue work, papier mâché, clay or craft dough, working with cookie dough, mixing meat loaf, doing crayon rubbings using large paper on various rough surfaces. Make a grab bag and put different things in it for your child to detect by feel only. For very young children, make a sensory book where each page has a different material (or a set of blocks with different material on each side). Some of these materials might be burlap (hessian), plastic, wood, feathers, fur, sandpaper, carpet, satin, velvet, corduroy, wool, felt, rope, leather, vinyl, or metal. Play in ball pits, a sand or water table, dig for 'fossils' in a box of rice or dried beans. *For feet*, encourage going barefoot, walking in sand or soft dirt, walking on the grass, or on smooth concrete. Try finger painting but with feet dipped in paint, make footprints in mud, plaster casts, stomp on bubble wrap, put plastic bags on the feet and slide on carpet. Try foot massages or footbaths. *For face*, apply 'war paint' or make-up, do face painting, soapsuds beards, whipped cream beards. *For all-over sensitivity*, play dress up or roll your child up in various types of fabric, mats, sheets, bubble wrap, cardboard, etc. Enjoy dramatic scarves and boas, roll in the grass or sand, apply body lotion or sun lotion. Play with Silly String, Fun Foam. Enjoy massage, tickling, and vigorous rubdowns with towels.

Auditory issues

Try some of these: books with sound effects, taped stories, rattles, jingle bells, rhythm instruments, musical instruments, wind chimes, rain sticks, a CD or tape or computer download with various sound effects, music records of all types, making tunes out of glasses filled to various heights with water, squeak toys, talking toys, computer games with sound, rhyming books, Dr. Seuss, silly poems and songs. Play with tape recorders, talking toys, and radios. Expose child to loud noises gradually and with warning, in small doses, and let the child decide if he's had enough – trains, airplanes, roller coasters, movie theatres, sports arenas. Perhaps have earplugs along to put in when needed or be prepared to leave.

Need for deep pressure

Good firm hugs, rolling a big ball over the child, rolling him up in mats or blankets, sleeping bags, tucking the child tightly into bed, back rubs, draping oneself carefully on the child's back, using a weighted blanket, covering child with sofa cushions. Be careful with all of the above actions, so that you do not injure the child or obstruct breathing in any way.

Knowing where one's body is in space

Trampoline, swings, spinning seat toy, hammocks, hammock chairs, crawling through tight places, playing leapfrog, carrying heavy things (backpacks), hauling heavy things. I have heard that weighted vests are helpful for some kids. You can order them from specialty companies, or make your own from a simple vest pattern, or just remove the sleeves from a shirt. Then, sew flat weights (washers or drapery weights would work fine, or even raw rice) into the hem, shoulder seams, and into the pockets. Just a little added weight can make your child feel more grounded.

Balance issues

Try using a very low balance beam, walking along a sidewalk crack, following a painted design on the playground, sitting or lying on a huge ball, using a scooter, skateboard, scooter board, bicycle, or tricycle. Walk along a curb, follow stepping stones, follow a rocky path, or try roller skates, in-line skates, ballet, gymnastics, or karate.

Ideas to improve social skills

Work on social skills using the list in Appendix 3 as a start. Organize your own social skills club or start a neighborhood kids' club with organized activities. Join a babysitting co-op to increase the number of kids who come into your house. Use puppets or dolls to work through social situations. Create social stories for your child (see Chapter 10). Read the Berenstain Bears books to your kids. They are humorous primary-school level books that deal with many of the social situations kids find themselves in. Among the topics covered are bullies, teasing, bad habits, homework, getting into fights, and so forth. I'm sure there are other great kids' books. Discussing TV shows can have great benefits. Some of our favorite family shows have been *The Waltons, Little House on the Prairie, The Wonder Years,* the *Mary Tyler Moore Show,* the *Andy Griffith Show,* and just about any TV show in black and white. Board games are terrific for lessons of turn-taking, and learning to win and lose. Eating at the dinner table enforces table manners and learning from adult conversation. Include your child on errands, and discuss and practice situations. Make a game out of 'what would you do if?

Ideas to improve facial recognition, facial expressions and body gestures

Look to cartoons and comic books or children's TV programs, for exaggerated facial expressions. Play Guess Who? The Mystery Face Game or Guesstures. Cut up old photos in two or three pieces and have your child reassemble them; look at old photo albums to see family members at varying ages; play charades as a family; or look at magazine photos of people and talk about their expressions.

Auditory discrimination

Put different things into each of several small containers (margarine tubs, film canisters, empty pill bottles), and ask your child to guess what is in there. Use rice, sand, marbles, thumbtacks, nails, popcorn kernels, dried beans, or coins, for example. Or blindfold your child and let him follow you around the house by listening to a little sound – you could whistle, snap your fingers, or use a small squeaky toy. Tongue-twisters help kids hear beginning sounds. For hearing the middle or ending sounds of words, have fun with silly sentences like 'Sue blew up two new balloons for her poodle Booboo.' Ask your child to count on his fingers all the 'oo' sounds he hears. To work on ending sounds, give your child a buzzer or bell and have him to listen for a particular sound at the end of each word ('t,' for instance). Call out words and when he hears a word that ends in a 't' he can push the buzzer. Play a game by stringing words together using the last sound of one word to prompt the first sound in another. Have your child close his eyes and listen for sounds – a dog barking outside, birds tweeting, a distant radio, traffic noises, the fan or refrigerator, etc.

Visual perception

Have fun with marble mazes, puzzles, tangrams, card games, books like *Where's Waldo* (UK: *Where's Wally*), activity sheets where you have to find the hidden pictures, or spot the differences between two pictures. Try different tinted glasses, and looking through colored acetate over schoolwork. Look at optical illusions and 3D art. Play 'I spy' with things you see around the room. For example, you might say 'I spy a yellow flower' and then see if your child can find where in room there is a yellow flower. It might be on your T-shirt, the calendar, or other tricky spot. Look through kaleidoscopes, binoculars, microscope, telescope or toy periscope.

It's boring where we live. How can I find good field trips and activities?

Parents sometimes feel that if they don't live in the middle of New York City, they won't find things to do that are interesting and educational. Here is a list to whet your appetite. Not all of them will be available in your area, but this list should keep anyone from being bored!

Excursions

Try museums, planetarium, botanical gardens, concerts, plays, library lectures, bookstore readings, TV stations, and factory tours. Ask for a tour in the back of the bowling alley, the butcher's or baker's. Call your chamber of commerce or tourist bureau and ask for a visitor's package, or visit the lobbies of a few hotels and pick up brochures. The local police, fire stations and city offices (mayor or city council) may give regular tours and talks. Local art galleries and even places like a football stadium sometimes conduct tours. Don't forget local parks, nature walks, lighthouses and forest ranger stations, dams and utilities, the historical society, or the post office. Just ask.

Volunteerism

John learned a great deal helping me do volunteer work for the blind. All I did was stuff some envelopes (which he helped with), but we got lots of information on eye diseases, eye safety, Braille (got a sample chart with all the bumps), and info on various projects in other countries. He learned a lot. You could volunteer (together perhaps) for any charitable organization and not only learn about the cause, but also get exposure to office work, retail work, conducting tours (docent), recycling, cooking or other. Historical societies and libraries like volunteers, and the city may need people to plant trees, build a nature trail, etc.

Clubs and classes

A local homeschooling club is the obvious and may offer things for older teens. Ours had a study group for the National Geography Bee, and a team entered in the city (Denver) mock stock market game sponsored by the city newspaper. The club also had a science group and ran a little newsletter. You might also look at other area clubs – chess club, astronomy club (I *loved* this club, lots of late night forays into fields looking at cool stuff!), gem/rock/lapidary club (learn a lot about geology), and so forth. Don't forget scouting. Some areas have a Boys' and Girls' Club.

Try some classes: sports courses, first aid and safety courses, crafts, hobbies, etc.

Daily living

Don't forget everyday sorts of activities: daily journal, cooking, laundry, home safety, comparison shopping, learning to order from menus and conduct business over the phone. Give your child opportunities for real life experiences such as writing a letter of complaint, opening a savings account, or reading a bank statement. John learned how to alphabetize at the video store, putting movies back on the shelves.

Chapter 8

Medication

An old joke is that the two happiest days in a boat-owner's life are the day he acquires his boat and the day he gets rid of it. I think many parents have the same feeling about their child's medication. I count myself among those who leaped onto the medication rescue boat hopeful that the proper medication would make life better for my son, and thankful when it did, only to jump away from it later with the uneasy feeling that medication was not the answer for us.

Because I am not a doctor, I cannot recommend for or against medication, and frankly our personal experience was minimal. I can, however, give you some personal observations, and leave you with some things to think about, questions for you to ask, and reference points for doing your own research. In the end, the right answer is going to be up to you. You will need to discuss the issue with your doctor and go from there.

There is no medication for Asperger Syndrome

That is perhaps the one point on which all experts agree. If you were by chance hoping for a pill to counteract Asperger Syndrome as a whole or 'make it go away,' that isn't going to happen, since the syndrome is a collection of many characteristics. From a philosophical standpoint, since the syndrome brings some gifts along with the deficits there are many people (including myself) who would not choose to eradicate Asperger Syndrome even if such a magic pill were invented.

What is more useful is to talk about medication's potential to relieve some of the baggage that often saddles people with Asperger Syndrome. If your child is experiencing intense anxiety, rage, or attention problems, medications exist to help with those issues and you may wish to consider them. There are also medications for some of the conditions that frequently coexist with Asperger Syndrome, including Attention Deficit Disorder, Tourette Syndrome, depression, or obsessive-compulsive tendencies.

In our case, John was prescribed Ritalin to help him deal with issues having to do with attention, focus, coping with transitions, and concentration. I don't know if Ritalin is the most common medication among those prescribed to Asperger patients, but based on conversations with other parents, it is certainly prevalent. Many folks feel that ADD is a natural subset of Asperger Syndrome anyway.

Our experience with Ritalin

John was prescribed Ritalin by a pediatric neurologist in 1988, when he was four years old. When we first gave it to him, we didn't really notice that much of a difference in his behavior or mood at home. The home environment is not the best test, however. The real trial was school.

We held our breath that first school day waiting for information on how he was doing. The report was good! The teachers found that Ritalin made John more settled at school, more willing to sit, work, and cooperate, and more organized in his thinking. The difference was apparent right from the first few days and teachers were so exuberant about the positive changes that I half expected them to send thank you notes home in his backpack. Really, Ritalin made a big difference. Even John, whom I asked much later about Ritalin's effect on him, said it always made him feel 'smarter.' I interpret that to mean that he felt more organized in his thinking and more able to follow his school lessons. So why did we ever take John off of it?

We had been aware from the beginning that Ritalin (or its generic equivalent) may cause some side-effects, including lack of appetite, possible slowing in weight gain, and sleep problems. John was in the nintieth percentile for height and weight for his age and we felt a bit of insomnia was an acceptable price to pay.

We were also warned that there might be a relationship between use of Ritalin and the appearance of motor tics. Thirteen years later, it appears that experts are still going back and forth on this. Of course, according to my reading back then, the experts didn't say that this drug *causes* motor tics, but that it may 'exacerbate' the situation. My understanding is that this means it may lower the tic threshold, bringing to the surface an underlying condition that was there all along but had heretofore been unexpressed or untriggered.

I could never figure this out. Is this akin to saying that such-and-such medication does not cause weight gain, it simply lowers your metabolism and allows your regular calorie intake to express itself better? The bottom line is, your pants still won't zip up! Getting back to the subject, whether my son would have had motor tics anyway and Ritalin hastened their emergence, or just *what*, all I can tell you is that we didn't see motor tics before he started Ritalin, and we did see them after he'd been on Ritalin a short while. Make of that what you will.

Another feature of his medication was that John didn't come off each dose very well. We were not completely happy with giving John a small dose in the morning and a small dose at noon because of this up and down effect and because the school's varying daily schedule meant that some days he got his pill earlier or later than he should have. It's easy to start blaming everything, good or bad, on the time of day. I think this can lead to parents excusing or ignoring things.

Things improved with a longer-lasting time-released pill, but we still had the downward spiral each afternoon. The hour before dinner has been jokingly called 'arsenic hour,' when kids are hungry and parents are exhausted, but for John, this time of day was worse. He had frequent headaches and spent many afternoons on the couch feeling wrung out. He was also an emotional mess, so that the smallest things defeated him and tears sprang over seemingly nothing. I hated seeing him like this and it was difficult to live with.

John hated it too. In spite of his admitting that Ritalin made him feel 'smarter,' he was aware that it also made him feel unwell. He didn't want to take it, complained about it, and some mornings would hide it under the rim of his cereal bowl. To underline the effect that tiny pill had, however, let me say that the teachers always knew which mornings those were!

It was because it was so effective that he did take it for three years. I have to credit Ritalin with saving our sanity and the teachers' sanity, and in helping John cope in the classroom. I do understand parents who sing its praises because when it works, it works. I'm sure the same can be said for many other medications that make daily living easier.

In some other ways though, I wonder if it prolonged things. It helped him and us endure things, but maybe we shouldn't have been *enduring* them but rather changing them. Maybe if we hadn't had Ritalin easing the chaos, we might have had to face other harder decisions sooner, like taking John out of the school system altogether and lessening his stresses. Do we just want to cope with problems year after year, pushing them under the surface? Or do we want to solve the problem?

I recognize that there may be different origins for the various issues for which Ritalin and similar medications are prescribed, so my child's situation may not apply to your child, but in our son's case I liken the situation to an allergy attack and choosing the remedy for it. When you're in the grips of sneezes, stuffed nose and runny eyes, you will naturally want to use an antihistamine pill to get you through any acute short-term discomfort. It only makes sense and the benefits are immediate and a great relief. But what if the allergy affects you most or all of the time? Taking a pill every few hours ad infinitum might keep you on your feet, but at some point it makes sense to investigate what is provoking the problem if at all possible. In the case of airborne allergies, these actions would likely include getting an air filter, perhaps pulling up carpets, or making even harder decisions – perhaps you need to get rid of the family cat or move out of hay fever country. Only you can decide if such actions are a good trade-off.

Of course, I realize that Attention Deficit Disorder is not an allergy, so you can argue that this point I'm trying to make is tenuous. Fine. My argument may indeed break down for many kids who truly need Ritalin or other similar medication and can't function without it no matter what lifestyle changes are made. If that is the case, you rightly turn to the medication that works and know that you are doing the best thing for your child. I am not against needed medication at all. I can only tell you of our own experiences, and that we were able to discontinue our child's medication when we stopped helping him just *cope* with being overwhelmed and started looking at and eliminating the *causes* of his being overwhelmed.

On the other hand, although I said that Ritalin may possibly have delayed our own exploration, it could be that it actually speeded it up. Maybe it gave us the respite we needed to collect our energy and thoughts, so that we could do our research and reach answers faster. If you are constantly putting out fires, you don't have time to go off and study how those fires get started, do you? So I honestly don't know how to evaluate the experience. I guess the bottom line is that for us, it was truly an effective coping mechanism, which we desperately needed at the time, and for which I am truly grateful, but it was not our final answer. Homeschooling, dietary changes, vitamins, and social skills training have proven to be more positive long-term choices for us.

Some worrying trends and general observation

I don't want to be branded as anti-medication, but I will admit that I am last-resort medication. Many families affected by Asperger Syndrome have discovered that one medication or another has allowed them to get through each day with less turmoil, more peace, and general and undeniable improvement in their family's quality of life. How can anyone be against that? If a medication can lift depression or allay rage, curb impulsivity or increase focus, then it is a tool not to be sneered at. Even though no medication exactly tends to Asperger Syndrome as a whole, by eliminating at least a few of the troublesome side issues, the child is often in a better position to absorb the education and therapy that more directly address the challenges of the syndrome – communication and social skills for instance.

On the other hand, the subject of medication for people with Asperger Syndrome does cause me some worries because of some trends that I see. These trends from my layman's perspective are as follows.

First, medication is taken too lightly by many, or at least not with the gravity that is warranted. In this instant fast-moving society, people seem to want a quick fix and all too often go in search of a pill that offers the promise (if not the delivery) of an immediate solution. Frankly, we've been trained by doctors and drug companies to think that whatever the medical problem, the best solution is to throw a pill at it, and the stronger and more expensive the pill, the better. Well, maybe I've overstated this, but I do think it's common for people to expect too much of medicine and for doctors to oblige. I'm not just pointing fingers at other people here. When we were in the most turmoil with our John, I admit that we wanted a pill *now,* if not sooner, and if the doctor hadn't handed us a prescription, no doubt we would have asked about it.

Second, even families who are very uncomfortable with the idea of medication are sometimes pressured into it. A *USA Today* news story from August 2000 outlined cases of public schools pressuring or criticizing (even threatening) families who resist giving their children medication such as Ritalin. Since when are schools competent to make such judgments?

Ruth from Michigan has felt this sort of pressure to medicate:

> We were going to put my daughter (fifteen) back in school, but the principal basically told us that in order to come back to school she would have to start taking her meds again. Since she was able to quit taking her medication when I homeschooled her last year, I think I'll just keep her home with me!

Third, psychiatric drugs are being prescribed to younger and younger patients, even to toddlers. Dr. Coyle of Harvard Medical School's psychiatry department calls it troubling,

> given that there is no empirical evidence to support psychotropic drug treatment in very young children and that there are valid concerns that such treatment could have deleterious effects on the developing brain. (*USA Today* August 8 2000)

I was recently dismayed to discover that although my son was prescribed Ritalin at age four, Ritalin has been studied for prescribing only to children six and older. I know children on anti-depressants such as Remeron or Paxil for which, according to the US Food and Drugs Administration (FDA), 'safety and effectiveness for the pediatric population have not been established.' Seroquel and Zyprexa are anti-psychotics with the same sort of unknowns for anyone under age eighteen, but six- and nine-year olds are on them. These drugs or others routinely prescribed to children (see list below) may work well, but adverse reactions span from the annoying to the terrifying. Among the side-effects from some of the drugs listed below are tremendous weight gains, insomnia, mania, and reactions so severe as to need hospitalization. These are only the visible acute things that parents can see and react to, but there are less visible or immediate side-effects – increased chance for cataracts, kidney and liver problems, and more.

Fourth, many kids are prescribed several medications at once. If our knowledge of the effects of single medications on children is inadequate, our understanding of interactions among several together has got to be worse. I know of many young children on multiple medications, for example a preschooler on three medications, *none* of which has been studied in kids under twelve, let alone in combination. Two of those drugs have not been studied in anyone under eighteen and carry warnings of possible long term and irreversible tardive dyskinesia (involuntary movements) among other possible effects. Am I crazy to be concerned? Some of the scariest episodes I know of kids being admitted into the hospital are kids who have been on several medications. Certainly there were behaviors that led to medication in the first place, but sometimes medications feed the problem. This letter from Deeanna in Texas is one vivid example:

> Things have been much better here the last two weeks! Jeffrey is doing so much better that it is almost scary!!! I believe that this is in part to the structure of restarting a school schedule, even if it is home school for now. I think it really helps him just to have so much more to do every day. He doesn't get overwhelmed by a lot of things to accomplish as long as there is an order to them and he is not rushed. He gets overwhelmed by too much time and too little to do – or a lack of highly structured activities. [Author's note: Jeffrey had had to be removed from school because of escalating behavior problems. After several days of vacation, his mother started homeschooling.]
>
> I also believe that his improvement is due, at least somewhat, to a decision we made with regard to his medication. ****NOTE**** I am NOT suggesting this is the right answer for everyone. Believe me, it was a last resort for us, and one we VERY carefully monitored!!!!! OK, having said that... We, over the last two weeks weaned Jeffrey off of all three of the medications he was on. We did this after consulting with the psychiatrist who saw Jeffrey in the hospital last fall. She told us how to do this and what to watch for as he was coming off the medications. We saw none of the possible side effects and

none of the psychotic symptoms we were afraid might escalate. In fact, the psychotic symptoms improved, leading me to believe that Jeffrey had in fact…had a toxic reaction to his Zoloft or Adderall. After looking back through my journal, I noticed that we had to hospitalize Jeffrey, after his symptoms grew worse last fall, only a week and a half after his Adderall was increased and Zoloft introduced. We were assured at the time that neither of those medications could have caused the regression. Well, now I don't believe that. Jeffrey is on no medication whatsoever and he has completely stopped soiling himself and his room. He is doing beautifully on his home schoolwork. He is attentive and really seeking approval. He is still exhibiting the learning disabilities, lack of social skills, focus, etc., the baby talk, vocabulary deficits, is either nonverbal/withdrawn or talking incessantly and inappropriately. In other words, he is still looking very AS, but the depressive symptoms, the delusions, hallucinations, suicidal and homicidal ideations, making himself vomit, banging his head into the walls and furniture – these have ALL disappeared!

We have an appointment with a new doctor next Friday to have him further evaluated. I told her on the phone day before yesterday what we had done. She said that she would have done the same thing as soon as we came in for a visit. That made me feel a bit more comfortable about the decision as well.

She also mentioned diet. I told her what we'd done with regard to the elimination diet process and what we'd discovered so far. She said that would have been our first assignment!

Deeanna's letter hardly requires comment over the nightmare that was caused by her son's reaction to medication. The good news is that Jeffrey benefited when Deeanna refused to continue along paths (school and medication) that were no longer working. It's heartening to see that there are doctors out there who are open to looking at things like elimination diets.

Unfortunately I've heard comments from more than one parent expressing concern that their doctor tries to fix every Asperger characteristic by adding a new medication or upping a dosage. It is up to the parent to say 'enough' but many parents do not have confidence to argue with their doctor. Some are bullied by threats that the doctors will drop them as a patient if they do say no to the medication. In that case, it might be time to shop for a new doctor.

Fifth, Asperger children may be particularly vulnerable to certain drugs and dosages. They may benefit on smaller doses of some medications, and find that larger doses actually cause greater problems, and sometimes cause a paradoxical reaction – that is, the opposite way one would expect (Grandin 1995, p.119). Dr. Attwood is similarly cautious with respect to anti-psychotics. He writes:

> Medication can be used as an option to treat anger. The availability of a quick acting sedative can be appealing. As a matter of expediency for a particularly stressful period, medication can be appropriate. However, it is only a temporary measure and children and adults with autism and Asperger Syndrome are particularly vulnerable to the long-term side effects of medication prescribed as a sedative, especially the antipsychotics. Medication can be valuable but must be prescribed to treat specific signs, be reviewed regularly, and be of short duration. (Attwood 1998, p.164)

Another problem is the sheer number of drugs in the arsenal. This is a double-edged sword of course. If one medication causes a bad reaction, it's nice to know there's another one to try. That is also the bad news, however, because it can cause a child to be on a long merry-go-round ride, trying one medication after another in varying combinations and in varying doses. I too think that an 'office water cooler mentality' begins to develop after awhile. That is, one's idea of 'normal' begins to be defined by the handful of people you talk with most often (the expression comes from office buddies chatting by the water cooler). For example, in Colorado a water cooler mentality might convince you that going into debt to own a four-wheel-drive vehicle is normal because 'everybody does it.' Someone in Los Angeles might think road rage is normal. And I think if you hang around mostly in autism or Asperger Syndrome circles (although the emotional support can be wonderful) you may also soon get on a first-name basis with a long list of medications. Those medications that once seemed foreign and scary start to sound as common as a peanut butter sandwich. I chose that analogy on purpose because one bite of a peanut butter sandwich could kill me (severe allergies), but my point is that we shouldn't ever get complacent about medications. Our kids are so varied in their needs and also in the way they react to drugs, whether you hear about a drug once or a dozen times, it does not tell you how your child will react to it.

Obviously, knowledge is key. Temple Grandin benefits from medication and has a chapter in her book that is titled 'Believer in Biochemistry' but she also laments that many doctors do not know how to prescribe medication for autistic people properly and tells of the many horror stories she has heard of bad drug reactions among the autistic population. At the end of her chapter, she says, 'My message for parents is simple, and it's advice that a good doctor gave my mother over forty years ago: trust your instincts about doctors, about medications, about yourself, and, most important, about your child' (Grandin 1995, p.130). What excellent advice.

The last problem I want to mention is that when you are treating with medication, your child may not be learning his own coping skills, and you may depend on medication to replace education. If he is on a drug to reduce anger, is learning anger management techniques going to get done? If impulse control is mediated through medication, will there be an emphasis on learning to control one's own impulses?

I recognize that this point is arguable, because some parents will maintain that a particular medication has done nothing but good – it has allowed the child to think in a more organized fashion, get more out of lessons, preserve self-esteem because of better behavior, and so forth. That's great and I do believe in figuring out whatever makes a child successful. Medication *may* be the best answer for your situation. I'm just offering things to think about.

Actually if you are mentally giving me an argument on every single point that I have made on the subject of medication, that's OK by me. If you can come up with arguments to poke holes in my observations, it means you have thought about the issue and whether it applies to you. That's all I ask. Hey, I'm just a mom and I sure don't know the answers. I just have questions, that's all.

I do apologize to parents who may be insulted by my bluntness, but I have had contact with many parents over the years and a few have such a cavalier regard for medication that they would use it to solve such problems as a one-week bout of insomnia, a child's habit of chewing on a shirt collar, or fear over swimming lessons. This is insane, don't you think? Not that you couldn't find a medication to fix these things, you probably could, but it is shooting gnats with cannons. These parents (they are in the minority, thank heaven) are concerned and caring, but they've somehow gotten the message that drugs solve everything and that if one medication is good, more must be better. What they need to do is start parenting.

Drugs used

Here is a partial list of various drugs I have noted to have been prescribed for children with Asperger Syndrome, divided according to sub-issue or commonly co-morbid condition. It's provided in order to help parents do their own research and ask more informed questions of their doctors.

The length of this list does not imply that most people with Asperger Syndrome are on several medications. Many people are on no medications whatsoever, having been able to cope with anxiety, mood swings or other problems through other means, notably reduced stress triggers, education, and/or diet and nutrition.

Now, here is the list. Read as generic product (brand name) and the minimum age that has been studied for effectiveness and safety. Where [NBE] is listed, my research found statements that effectiveness and safety have not been established for pediatric patients. This may be equivalent to [18+]. Note – some studies conflict and professionals disagree. Your own research results may vary!

Attention or hyperactivity issues

Amphetamine salts (Adderall) [3+]

Methylphenidate (Ritalin) [6+]

Methylphenidate (Concerta) [6+] (extended release)

Dextroamphetamine sulfate (Dexedrine) [3+]

Pemoline (Cylert) [6+]

Guanfacine (Tenex) [12+]

Depression issues

Buproprion (Wellbutrin) [18+]

Imipramine (Tofranil) [NBE]

Desipramine (Norpramin) [NBE]

Fluoxetine (Prozac) [NBE]

Amitriptyline (Elavil) [12+]

Mirtazapine (Remeron) [NBE]

Trazadone (Desyrel) [NBE]

Paroxetine (Paxil) [NBE]

Serzone (Nefazodone) [18+]

Obsessive-compulsive issues
    Clomipramine (Anafranil) [10+]
    Fluvoxamine (Luvox) [8+]
    Sertraline (Zoloft) [6+]

Bi-polar disorder
    Thioridazine (Mellaril) [2+]

Tourette Syndrome
    Pimozide (Orap) [12+]
    Clonidine (Clonidine) [12+]

Anti-psychotic, violence, outbursts
    Risperidone (Risperdal) [NBE]
    Quetiapine (Seroquel) [NBE]
    Olanzapine (Zyprexa) [NBE]

Anxiety or panic disorder
    Venlafaxine (Effexor) [NBE]
    Diazepam (Valium) [6 months+]
    Alprazolam (Xanax) [18+]
    Lorazepam (Ativan) [12+]
    Buspirone (Buspar) [18+]

Seizures or epilepsy
    Lamotrigene (Lamictal) [16+]
    Valproic acid (Depakote) [16+]
    Gabapentin (Neurontin) [18+]

Topiramate (Topamax) [NBE]

Clonazepam (Klonopin) [NBE]

Some notes

- In the above list, the medications may be used for other things than are listed. For example, Prozac is used for both depression and obsessive-compulsive disorder.

- Many of these drugs cannot be removed quickly but rather must be withdrawn gradually and under a doctor's care.

- A drug may interact with other prescription medicine, over-the-counter medicines, and also herbal supplements such as gingko. Be sure to tell your doctor about anything else you are taking, even vitamins.

- Some of the above drugs are meant for short-term use only, and may lose their effectiveness in a matter of a few weeks, and/or have not been tested for long periods.

- Not all medications are available in all countries. Some go by different names or are approved for different uses.

Some practical matters

The following items are miscellaneous notes that I have learned about the daily grind of using medications. Should your child require medication, you might find these items of information useful.

Telling the school

Should you tell the school about new medications? My gut feeling is that you should not. Let the school make its observations based on what they notice for themselves, without you prejudicing them either way. The one exception might be if you suspect your child could suffer a sudden adverse reaction. If your child is prone to epileptic seizures and is starting a medication that may possibly lower the seizure threshold, for example, it is only fair to give them warning.

Keep good records

This tip came from a San Diego parent Alisha Goya, who suggests you record any and all medications your child has taken in the past, even if they didn't work for him. Says Alisha:

> I always figured that if it didn't work, all I needed was the name of the medication. Wrong! The reason for keeping the records is, if you change doctors the new doctor will want to know how much and for how long. That way he can determine if the dosage was enough and if your child was on it long enough to get a true trial of the medication.

Controlled substances

If your child is prescribed a drug that is a controlled substance (Ritalin is in that class), you will have a few added hassles. We found that our overall prescription had to be initiated by a specialist, not our family doctor, so that meant a yearly visit to a specialist and all that goes with it – referrals, insurance grief, waiting for an appointment, and a trip to a hospital (scary for John). Throughout the year the specialist's prescription was meted out a month at a time by the family doctor, but he could not call it in to the pharmacy. Now we were logging in twelve more trips per year to the doctor just to physically pick up the piece of paper and hand-carry it to the pharmacy. OK, now I'm sounding petty. This is indeed the very minor downside to medication, but petty or not, it's practical information parents might like to know.

Generic equivalent

Sometimes you will be given a generic equivalent rather than a brand name of a given drug. This may be OK and can save you money, but we found that the generic version did not always do as well as the brand name. If it makes a difference, ask your doctor to specify brand name.

New medications

Sometimes the newest medications are not available to you. This is because insurance often requires that older and cheaper medications are tried first.

School nurse

Check out the school nurse situation at your child's school, if medication needs to be given during the day. School nurses are overworked and in short supply in many parts of the US. A survey of 482 schools revealed that over 60 per cent had more than 750 students per nurse, and for a nurse to attend to 60–85 students daily is not unusual. The trend toward mainstreaming of children with serious health issues is credited with causing the increased workload (Tucker 1998).

No wonder it is sometimes left up to teachers or aides to round up kids for medication or sometimes even give it to them. In some instances, parents have reported that their *own children* are expected to watch the clock and decide when to go to the nurse for medication. Maybe I'm overprotective, but it seems ludicrous to me that children who are being medicated for distractibility and inattention are nonetheless put in charge of monitoring their own medication schedule of a controlled substance.

Where to find information about specific drugs

To be as informed as possible about the medications, here are some resources for further drug information such as uses, dosage, side-effects, etc.

- Physician's Desk Reference: your doctor and also your pharmacist will have a copy of this book, since it is the primary one-stop look-up source for all FDA-approved drugs.

- Your pharmacist: he or she is often the most knowledgeable about drug interactions, and pharmacists will generally be more accessible than your doctor if you have a question.

- The following websites have look-up tools for drug information:

  - http://www.rxlist.com/
  - http://promini.medscape.com/drugdb/search.asp (you may need to register)
  - http://www.mentalhealth.com/ (Canadian sources of information)
  - http://www.fda.gov/search.html
  - http://www.psych.org

Chapter 9

Diet

Before we discovered the influence of diet (up to around age eight), I had noticed that Chris had good days and bad days. I don't just mean that on some days he behaved better than others, although that was certainly true. I mean that physically *he* seemed to change from one day to the next. Some days he would be focused and we could have conversations in which he was obviously engaged. Other days he would be 'disengaged.' He would have more typically autistic traits. He would spend greater amounts of time off to himself, wagging his stick in front of his eyes, or bouncing off the walls without regard to whom he ran over in the process.

On those days, whether or not he had a behavior problem or was simply zoned out, there was a disturbing disconnectedness about him. He couldn't seem to hear us. He laughed at things that weren't funny. He felt no pain. He was more echolalic (repeating our words back to us), or answered questions with bizarre heaven-knows-what. He made less sense on those days and was giddy. Even his eyes looked different. They had a glassy appearance that seemed out-of-focus.

I remember one day when he was particularly bizarre and unmanageable. We finally had enough and Bill put him up in his room, sitting him in a chair facing the wall until he would calm down. I remember hearing John sitting up there in the gathering dusk, all alone in his room, laughing and laughing. As much as I had been trying to blame my husband and myself for his problems and assuming that we just hadn't figured out parenting, that night I had no such illusions. It was not parenting. This child was having serious troubles. I remember Bill and I had a very somber discussion that night, wondering out loud what the future held for us all and for our sweet boy. It was the night that all of our worries finally got said aloud to each other. This wasn't normal. Was it going to get worse? Was it ever going to get better? The discussion led to no answers, only disquieting questions.

My own mother and father belong to a rare breed of parents. They do not interfere. So I took particular notice when they called after having just been to see us for a visit. My folks of course knew that John was in special education and I suppose they knew how hard we were all struggling, although I don't remember that we'd discussed it during the visit or had had any particular upsets. During the phone call, however, Mom mentioned that she'd seen an interesting book on food allergies and behavior, and asked if she could send it to me. I said, 'Sure.' Dad interrupted on the extension to remind her to 'MYOB' (mind your own business), so Mom quickly added, 'Well, never mind. This book may not be anything. Still, I may as well go ahead and send it to you.'

The book she sent was *Is This your Child?* by Doris Rapp (1991). Rapp is a pediatric environmental allergist. She concerns herself with substances (foods, inhalants, etc.) that may cause adverse reactions in children. I'm not referring to traditional allergy, where the reaction takes the usual form of hives, runny nose, rash or asthma sort of reaction. Rapp looks at more subtle responses, perhaps better referred to as an intolerances rather than allergies. Effects might be physical, such as red ears, body temperature changes, complexion, constipation, stomachache or headache. Or, effects can be more behavioral – mood swings, hyperactivity, tantrums, zoning out, or other.

One paragraph described some children in the grip of food-related allergy episodes in which they would 'develop glazed eyes and appear spaced out.' Rapp wrote:

You scream but...your words do not even register. This can be due to allergies affecting the brain. Sometimes these children really don't hear until they look, act, and feel normal again. (Rapp 1991, p.68–69)

This sounded much like John! But what was causing the problem?

I read the book with both interest and frustration. I loved that it made me feel less alone reading about other families with these mystery kids, and it also held promise that maybe we could figure out some of John's issues. It was fascinating to read about all the things that could cause a reaction. However, it seemed like darned near *anything* could cause a reaction in someone – any food, chemicals from carpets or paint, dyes, cleaners, and so forth. The answer to some of our troubles just might be contained in that huge book, but where? It seemed a very large haystack. But then I found a needle.

More than 350 pages later, I read a description of a boy named Bruce. The boy had several food issues (so did John, as we later learned), but the part that put two and two together for me was reading that after drinking milk, Bruce had become unmanageable and *his eyes became glassy*. Maybe John's problem was milk (Rapp 1991, pp.426–428).

I did nothing with this information for a while. We were soon to begin homeschooling, and I decided to wait until I had John home full time before fiddling with diet. I bided my time reading other books on allergy and intolerance. It seemed that there were two definite camps. Most traditional allergists were strict in their definition of allergy and tended to discount the more behavioral symptoms. The other camp, environmental allergists, took a broader look, but their information seemed so all encompassing with possible allergens and possible reactions I soon became overwhelmed. Also, many of the tests described seemed strange and unfamiliar and I worried that this might be a field that attracted not only respected professionals but also fringe fanatics. The more I read, the less I knew. But still, that passage in Rapp's book kept popping into my mind. John drank milk for breakfast, lunch and dinner. Yogurt and cheese slices were common snacks. We all ate a lot of ice cream. What if?

After we pulled John out of school and began homeschooling, we were ready to experiment. I took John off milk and all obvious dairy products. Within 24 hours, we had our first breakthrough, which I wasn't expecting. He didn't wet the bed. With the rare exception, bed-wetting had been a *nightly* occurrence up until this point, age eight. Even one dry night was cause for celebration. But suddenly, bed-wetting was a thing of the past, and sheets remained dry night after night. The wetting stopped completely, except for one lone accident a few weeks after that.

Other effects were less dramatic, but there. John still had behavioral meltdowns and still fussed or flew off the handle, so it was easy to think, 'this milk thing isn't making any difference'. But actually, it was making a difference. John might still have lots of issues, but he was gradually becoming more reachable. His eyes were in focus more and more, he was not talking as bizarrely, and he behaved more like a normal child would. He still had issues and he still had Asperger Syndrome (the actual label coming years later), but if you sent him to his room, he would at least be upset about it, not sit in the dark and laugh. It was progress.

The progress we saw from taking him off dairy gave us strength to do more experiments. I remember trying to test him for chicken and also corn, two other common allergens. From the reading I did, the way to test a suspected food was to eliminate it from the diet completely for several days and then do a 'challenge' by giving that food in a reasonably large amount. Sometimes this can be a somewhat difficult adventure. Some foods, such as corn, are difficult to eliminate in all their forms, so I probably never did this one correctly. But also, if your child is reacting to several foods and you only eliminate one, you may not be able to tell a difference because the others are still causing a reaction. All you can do is try, by removing foods you suspect and adding them back in gradually. I kept a food journal in which I recorded what he ate and noted behavior throughout the day.

I started to suspect John's favorite sweet things – candy, flavored drinks (including the orange-flavored breakfast drink he had every morning), and frozen ice treats. I didn't know if it could be the sugar in these items or artificial colors, but by this time in my search for answers, I came across an old book by Dr. Benjamin Feingold (1975) at the library. He wrote of the possible relationship between certain foods and kids' hyperactivity, specifically mentioning artificial colors, flavors, and preservatives, and to a lesser extent some other natural foods (those that contain high levels of natural salicylates, especially certain fruits and vegetables. More research revealed that this has long been a controversial theory – some parts of the scientific community remain skeptical. Still, taking my son off these suspect foods didn't cost anything except patience and I had nothing to lose.

For two weeks, I eliminated sweets and then planned a 'challenge' day, which I was sure he would enjoy. As it happened, on the challenge day, I not only gave John two packets of highly-colored candy on an empty stomach, he also escaped up the street with his little brother and begged a couple more pieces of candy from a neighbor, eating not only his but his brother's.

I was *not* prepared for what happened next. As luck would have it, a former co-worker I hadn't seen in years dropped in. He thought he would surprise me but I'm pretty sure he got the bigger surprise. John was wild, like nothing before. We both watched stunned as he flung open the door, ran full-tilt toward us shouting and laughing, in what to my untrained eye seemed like a sort of mania. I finally dragged him up to his room and told him to calm down (yeah, right). At this point he burst into tears, flung himself at the wall and screamed over and over that he wanted to die. I'd never heard anything like this before and my poor visitor was shocked. He mumbled, 'Uh, maybe I should go. You seem to have a situation here.' With apologies that 'things aren't usually like this,' I let him. I could only imagine the picture we'd presented to him, but that was of less importance than the discovery we made that day. John definitely reacted to this stuff!

Over subsequent months, besides the artificial colors and flavors (especially vanillin), we also isolated oranges as being troublesome, and grapes, raisins, apples, and cherries to a lesser degree. John wouldn't eat eggs, so I suspected a problem with those too, but I didn't force any on him. The food journal and careful observation taught us many things and John's behavior began to improve.

By the time we moved to England we felt we had a pretty good handle on things. We still had slip-ups, though. John once, on an empty stomach, ate two pieces of vanilla birthday cake with vanilla icing and vanilla ice cream (all artificially flavored), and washed it all down with soda. That episode lasted four days (one day of mania, one day of sobbing and depression, and two days of feeling bad with chills, pale complexion, headache, and upset stomach). Usually it took quite a lot to bring on a full multi-day episode (we had a similar four-day episode after Easter sometime later), but even the rare trip to McDonald's or other fast food place would set him off in smaller ways. By this time, I had learned to spot the physical reaction – the red ears, eye circles, dilated pupils, and pale complexion – before the behavioral spiral started. Just being able to anticipate the emotional roller-coaster before it started helped us cope better. For one thing, seeing the physical signs reminded us that it was a physical problem. We didn't take our son's rages personally but rather took them for what they were – physical reactions. It's amazing to me that these body signs had probably always been there, but only keeping a food journal had started us consciously looking. I shudder to think of the parenting mistakes (not to mention the self-blame) that occurred in the pre-food journal days, when we assumed poor behavior meant either a bratty kid or putrid parenting or both.

I need to explain something, since I mentioned occasional in-dulgence in fast food. For my son, a *small* food indiscretion did not usually trigger a response, unlike some unlucky children I have read about for whom even one bite of a forbidden food can set off a full reaction. Our situation is closer to how someone might interact with alcohol. Let's say that a woman who is a social drinker can tolerate a single glass of wine after dinner every night with no problem and no visible effects. The same woman, if given two or three glasses of wine before dinner, however, might get drunk. Even just her usual single glass of wine could cause drunkenness on certain days when she is tired, ill, or perhaps also taking a cold medicine. We can understand that the same wine that triggers no visible reaction one day can cause very visible problems the next. I make this point because often parents will say that they don't think a certain food could possibly be a culprit because their child eats it every day but doesn't have a major reaction every day. That may be because the child is a little like that woman and her glass of wine. The child can perhaps cope with certain amounts, but once in awhile the internal glass gets too full and spills over into a reaction. Rapp uses an analogy of a barrel. When the child's body cannot keep up with processing all the culprit foods he is ingesting, the barrel eventually overflows and you see a reaction (Rapp 1991, p.62).

Our path crosses with research

Some of you may consider most of our discoveries to be old news today, but back then we were nearly working in a vacuum. It was not until our second year of the homespun diet and after we reached the UK that we began to learn of research that might be connected. A British organization called Allergy-induced Autism (AiA) had recently formed to unite families who believed there might be a connection between diet and their child's autism. This was real news and we joined immediately. Through it and subsequent connections with people on Internet, we were able to participate in two studies.

The opioid theory

Karl Reichelt in Norway and later Paul Shattock at Sunderland University's Autism Research Unit have produced research to indicate that incomplete digestion of dairy protein (casein) and/or grain protein (gluten) is occurring in a subset of autistic people and the faulty mechanism seems to result in an opioid effect on the brain. That is, when these proteins are incompletely digested, instead of being broken down and excreted as they should be, they linger in the body as peptide chains. These peptide chains mimic substances called endorphins, which are morphine-like in their effects and occur naturally in the brain. Everybody apparently has some of these chains as a brief interim stage in digestion, but these opiate-like substances persist for too long and in abnormally high levels in some autistic individuals. Additionally, researchers postulate that these peptide chains manage to cross through the gut wall (intestines) into the bloodstream and across the blood brain barrier into the brain. For those affected, the problem may be casein, gluten, or both. We decided to have John tested for this phenomenon.

John had always eaten grains but by the time I learned of the opioid study John had been off milk for two years because of our own dietary findings. After discussion with Paul Shattock I loaded John up again and gave him chocolate milk, yogurt and ice cream for testing purposes. John was happy for the chance to eat foods that had become only fond memories at this point, but after he'd had his fill the poor kid then spent the next few hours with a wastebasket next to him, feeling like he was going to lose it all. He kept it all down though and we got a urine sample off to Sunderland University.

The test result from Shattock's group was not as clearcut as I had hoped. The gluten portion was a definite negative – no surprise. The casein results were in the 'ambiguous' category, not a definite yes or no. This may have been because John is less severely affected than some autistic people, or it might have been because he'd had little or no dairy for so long before that one load. Perhaps his gut wall had been more permeable when younger but had improved over the years. Perhaps the vitamins we'd been giving him (see separate section below) had aided in more complete digestion than had occurred when he was younger. It remains a mystery. I suppose I would have liked to see a more definitive 'yes' to that test, but a 'could be' was sufficient. How much proof did I really need anyway? We'd seen firsthand the opiate-like effects from dairy when he was younger, and during a few isolated instances since that time, and we knew he did better without it.

The sulfotransferase theory

At about the same time I was adding 'gluten,' 'casein,' and 'opioid' to my vocabulary, we had the chance to learn about yet another possible slipped gear in the body machinery. Dr. Rosemary Waring at the University of Birmingham was tracking what appeared to be a problem in sulfation in people on the autistic spectrum. Sulfate is a substance that attaches itself to certain toxins to help them leave the body. If sulfation (detoxification using sulfate ions) doesn't occur at a sufficient level, the toxins may pile up and cause problems in the brain. Certain substances seem adversely to affect this process, including citrus, highly colored foods (whether naturally colored or due to artificial colors) and paracetamol (Tylenol). To have John's sulfation tested, I was asked to give him a dose of paracetamol and send a sample of the urine collected over the next eight hours.

One sidelight of the test was that several parents were reporting that it often took nearly the entire eight hours to collect any urine at all. That was the case with John too. I find that intriguing and feel like it must mean something, but I have not uncovered any research that mentions it.

The test showed that John, like others on the autistic spectrum who were tested, has a sulfation deficiency and should continue to keep the amounts of problem foods low or avoid them altogether. Once again, something we had discovered by ourselves via food journal and observation was later at least partially explained through a research study. (Note: both the opioid and sulfate issues are discussed on AiA's website. See Appendix 7.)

Other food intolerance testing

We also tried one other test worthy of mention. It's called the ELISA test, which stands for Enzyme-Linked Immunosorbent Assay. It is a test for food sensitivities, as revealed by the presence of a certain type of antibody (IgG) in the blood. (For the record, traditional allergy testing looks at IgE antibody via a different method.)

The ELISA test required a small sample of blood, which was sent to a lab and tested against a panel of dozens of foods. Our family doctor was skeptical of this process and only begrudgingly ordered the blood draw for us. She felt we were wasting our money and encouraged me to write down all foods I suspected of causing troubles but not to show this to the lab. I did so. I wrote down 'milk, egg, orange, and vanillin' as the most suspect foods and then I also chose green pepper. I hadn't noticed any problems with green pepper but chose it because it is high in salicylates. The results came back with a match on milk, egg, and orange. The lab had no test for vanillin, and green pepper turned out to be negative. Out of 85 foods tested, the matches were very close. I was impressed and became a believer. The lab also discovered that John reacted to peach, which I hadn't thought about, because he hadn't eaten peach since he was a little kid (and had broken out in a rash). The test remains somewhat controversial among traditional allergists, but we found it worthwhile. While it is completely unrelated to the gluten/casein testing or the sulfation testing, it nonetheless shows foods that can cause problems in other ways. For us, milk and orange showed up as culprits in more than one test.

Vitamins

From reading Chapter 1, you may remember that John became increasingly anxious and depressed by the middle of sixth grade (his first year in the regular school system), and our attempt to get him professional help through a psychiatrist had led to a dead end. The only things the psychiatrist had done were to make me feel foolish and to advise me that John just needed some friends and all would be solved. It was humiliating. After she washed her hands of us, though, at least I still had what I had tried to bring to her attention – some interesting reports on vitamins and how they might be used to alleviate some of the problems associated with autism.

The reports came from the Autism Research Institute, which is headed by Dr. Bernard Rimland. Dr. Rimland's reports touched on many vitamins and minerals, but the centerpiece of his findings seemed to be that large doses of B6 in combination with magnesium were found to have clear benefits for nearly half the people with autism tested. Benefits might vary but could include such gains as better eye contact, less self-stimulatory behavior, more interest, fewer tantrums, more speech (Rimland 1987). He also coordinated with a laboratory (Kirkman Labs) to develop a custom mix of vitamins and minerals that he felt would be optimal for people with autism. The stuff was, and is, called Super Nu-Thera®. With the vague feeling that I might be throwing money away (family doctors love telling patients that taking extra vitamins just makes expensive urine), I ordered some. I figured that something had to be done for John's depression and this was something at least to try. (See Appendix 7 for details.)

John started on it over Christmas vacation. As directed, I started him at a low dose at first, with the intention of ramping him up to full dose gradually. A week later, still on the small dosage, he returned to school. Later that week he mentioned his English teacher and said, 'She asked me if I switched personalities with Mark over Christmas.'

'Who's Mark?' I asked. John explained that he was a kid who was always talking and joking in class. That piqued my interest. *John* was talking and joking in class? I went in to talk to this teacher and she confirmed her comment and asked if John were on medication, because he seemed like a totally different person. She said he was more involved in class, participated more, and seemed happier.

I was astounded. At home I hadn't really noticed any big personality change. He was always rather talkative at home anyway, and although his 'Why was I born?' talk had mercifully ceased, I hadn't known whether to attribute that to the vitamins or being distracted by a nice Christmas and time off from school. But this objective view from his teacher was news. I decided to survey all of John's teachers. One teacher (the crabbiest one with whom we'd always had problems) reported 'no change' to all my questions, but all the rest of his teachers agreed that John was more talkative and 'tuned in' than the previous semester. One teacher added that he thought John seemed a bit more nervous.

All in all, I was thrilled. If one week of vitamins could bring about an actual change in someone's outlook and demeanor, observable by people who hadn't a clue about the vitamins, I was a believer.

The good news kept getting better. John was no longer hitting himself over every frustration. In fact, he seemed less frustrated in general. Some weeks later, I realized that John hadn't complained about a headache in a long time, whereas he used to get two or three in a week. Also (I realize this sounds strange), John's sweat smelled better. His body odor had always seemed somehow 'different' from most body odor. It was not worse, only different – there was a mustiness to it akin to a damp basement. But after the vitamin changes, the musty odor disappeared.

Vitamins may have helped in another way too. The 'new John' wasn't putting up with bullying. The entire first semester, John had meekly endured busted lunch boxes, blown-out umbrellas, being poked and tripped, having books dumped on the floor and so forth. But a few days into the second semester, one of the more bothersome bullies poked him. John told him to stop. The kid did it again. In the time it takes to slam a book closed, John grabbed the boy's hand and pinned it behind him. Both boys got into a bit of trouble with the teacher (Why? I now ask myself) but when I went in to school to discuss what had happened, the counselor smiled and quietly confided that while the school couldn't condone it, John had probably made a few points for himself in the eyes of the other kids. I hated that my son was involved in anything even remotely violent, but it's hard to argue with success. That bully never again bothered John.

Was it the vitamins? No proof, but I believe they were a major contributor. John was not off in a dream world as much, and was more 'in the moment' and able to take care of himself. I was concerned it might make him more impulsive in general, but that didn't occur. His more outgoing personality did result in him trying harder to be popular. That was the semester he took on the persona of Ace Ventura. I could live with that and he did earn a certain amount of positive attention from the other kids.

At the time we ran out of our first bottle of megavitamins, we were in the midst of moving back to the US so I just bought over-the-counter B6, B-complex, magnesium and then a one-a-day type of multi-vitamin. I gave him less B6 this time. Even though I'd been thrilled with the results from Super Nu-Thera® and the studies showed it to be very safe, the unusually high doses of B6 still made me uncomfortable. I'd already been made to feel like a lunatic by the psychiatrist and some of the teachers for putting stock in vitamins, and in my 'mind's ear' I could hear people exclaiming, 'you're giving him *how* much?' Besides, since his autistic traits were mild compared with many of the people who had been in the studies, I reasoned that a lesser dosage might be more appropriate anyway, and it has continued to work well for him five years later.

Throughout that last year in England, I'd become acquainted via Internet with Bonnie Grimaldi, a mom whose son had long been in the grips of Tourette Syndrome and who had tried many prescription drugs for it, all with side-effects and none with success. After her day job in a medical technology lab (she has a Bachelor of Science in Medical Technology and graduate coursework in a biochemistry degree), she spent her nights doing vast amounts of research on the role of vitamins and minerals in mitigating Tourettic tics.

John had had some tics (our pediatric neurologist had mentioned Tourette in his report), so it was perhaps inevitable and certainly providential that Bonnie and I tripped across each other out there in the Internet ether. We chatted back and forth with the passion of two moms with a mission. I have no medical background, but helped her dig up research reports as best I could, emailing them to her under the motto, 'I find 'em, you explain 'em.' She did the infinitely harder part of making sense of them and developing a cohesive theory. Occasionally I found a nugget to speed her research along, or a puzzle piece she'd been looking for. I am still proud of the tiny part I got to play in her research.

The fruit of Bonnie's work was to fine tune a vitamin regimen that has offered immense relief to her son and also aids hundreds of other people. She has graciously allowed me to reprint it here. As always, any modification to your diet should be discussed with your physician. She continually updates her regimen, so please refer to her web page for the latest version[1], as well as a comprehensive discussion of her diet and vitamin regimen and for a link to her theory. Her web site is at http://www.BonnieGr.com In the morning, her son takes:

1.   1200 mg lecithin granules or gel cap

2.   Antioxidants:

[1]   As we go to press, I have received exciting news that her vitamin regimen will soon be available as an all-in-one supplement. Please refer to website for further information.

- Beta Carotene 10,000 IU (optional)
- Vitamin E 400 I.U. [200 IU for children 6–10]
- Vitamin C 500 mg
- Zinc 30 mg.
- Selenium 15 mcg (optional)
- Coenzyme Q10 30 mg (optional)
- Glutathione (reduced) 25 mg

3. Vitamin B complex capsule (B50 – 11 B factors)
    [Children 6–10 should use a tablet form and cut it in half
    for half the dose.]

- Vitamin B1 (thiamine) 50 mg
- Vitamin B2 (riboflavin) 50 mg
- Vitamin B6 (pyridoxine HCl) 50 mg
- Vitamin B12 (Cyanocobalamin) 50 mcg
- Biotin 100 mcg
- Pantothenic Acid 50 mg
- Folic Acid 50 to 400 mcg
- Niacinimide 50 mg
- Inositol 50 mg
- PABA 50 mg
- Choline 50 mg

4. *No-flush* niacin (inositol nicotinate) – 250 mg (divide a
    500 mg capsule or tablet in half). [Children 6–10 should
    get only ¼ tablet or 125 mg.]

5. Solary Grapenol Grapeseed Extract (1 mg per pound
    body weight per day)

6. DHA 500 mg

In the afternoon:

1. 50 mg of niacin tablets (regular, since no-flush variety doesn't come in 50 mg doses). [Children 6 to 10 should cut this tablet in half for 25 mg.] This may be taken three times during the day as needed for tics – decrease dose if flushing occurs. Flushing feels like sunburn and may itch or it may be a mild rash. This lasts only 15 minutes and is not an allergic reaction and is not harmful.

Note: do not exceed 500 mg/day [or 250 mg/day for children 6 to 10] of total niacin (no-flush niacin, niacinamide in B-complex and regular niacin). More can be taken with a doctor's strict supervision.

Just before bed:

1. Amino Acid Chelated Calcium-Magnesium tablets:

   - 780 mg Calcium
   - 468 mg magnesium

   Note: six tablets of Schiff brand provide this. Some people prefer to take two tablets in the morning and four in the evening.

2. Vitamin B complex capsule or tablet – follow same directions as above

3. Taurine 500 mg

Further notes: the B-complex is important. A deficiency can occur if only one B vitamin is given in isolation.

Foods to avoid: foods with tyramine (chocolate in large quantities, aged cheese, red wine, soy sauce, raisins, canned fish, cured meats); any food you know you are allergic or react to; aspartame; food dyes and vanillin; caffeine; and pseudephedrine (Sudafed) containing decongestants and antihistamines. In addition, limit foods that are high in sugar.

OK, that was Bonnie's regimen for her son. The vitamin regimen for John right now is somewhat similar, and may be summarized as follows.

In the morning John takes a B-complex (similar to above), a B–6 capsule (50 mg), an antioxidant tablet (similar to above, with vitamins A, C, E, plus zinc and many other trace elements), and a 1200 mg lecithin gel cap.

At bedtime, John takes a calcium tablet balanced with magnesium.

You can see that there are similarities between what I give to John and what Bonnie gives to her son. The main differences are that I stress B6 more because of Rimland's studies of the benefits of B6 in autism, and Bonnie stresses the forms of B3 (niacin and niacinimide) more because of her research emphasis on Tourette. Bonnie also gives grape seed extract (primarily for antihistamine and antioxidant properties) and DHA (an Omega–3 Essential Fatty Acid beyond what is modestly provided in the lecithin).

As in Bonnie's diet recommendations, John avoids aspartame, food dyes, vanillin, raisins and cured meats. Because of his individual food issues, he also avoids milk, yogurt, oranges, and eggs. He limits use of paracetamol (Tylenol) and eats chocolate and other sweets only in moderation.

What John eats

His breakfast is usually rice, pasta, popcorn cakes (similar to ricecakes), or dry cereal. Lunch is frequently salad with homemade dressing, pasta, peanut butter sandwich, chicken sandwich or reheated dinner leftovers if he is near a microwave. Fruit choices are usually pear, banana, or melon chunks and he often has carrot or cucumber sticks.

For dinner, I cook soups, stews, meat-and-potato dinners, tacos, pizza, chili, casseroles, hamburgers, fried rice, etc. It is typical dinner fare, however most everything is cooked from scratch. I do not use canned soups in casseroles, and never use mixes or commercially frozen dinners. I leave the cheese off

John's pizza and off one end of the casserole. If I make a dish such as chicken tetrazini that uses bacon and cheese, I will save out some sautéed chicken, vegetables, and noodles for John before finishing the casserole.

Things get a little looser in the snack department. His favorite snacks are usually real food such as a bowl of pasta, rice, or leftover soup, but he also enjoys pistachio nuts, peanut butter sandwich, popcorn cakes, tortilla chips or popcorn. Best drink choices for him are water, carbonated water, and tea (either iced or hot). He is not a saint however, and drinks soda as most teens do. He also has the occasional small chocolate bar or fast food burger. Where these used to bother him a lot as a youngster, now as a teen of seventeen, he is better able to tolerate moderate indiscretions. He makes most of his own food choices these days.

Some miscellaneous questions

Q. Do you worry that he isn't getting enough calcium since he doesn't drink milk?

No. He takes a calcium supplement nightly, combined with magnesium for better absorption. This has the added benefit of helping him get to sleep. There are many non-dairy foods that provide calcium, including broccoli, cabbage, tofu, nuts and seeds, cooked dried beans, corn tortillas, and leafy greens such as kale and spinach.

Q. Should I put my child on John's vitamin regimen?

I am not a trained medical person and cannot tell you what supplements you should give your child. I can only tell you what has been helpful for mine. Research is always adding new knowledge. Your child will have different needs and tolerances. I suggest you use the regimen (as well as Bonnie's and that of Kirkman Labs – see Appendix 7) as a starting place only for your own research. A good book on nutrition will give you a background against which to set your research. As always, discuss any dietary changes with your physician.

Q. How do I do an elimination diet?

Nearly every allergy book contains an elimination diet. They all differ slightly, but the basic premise is to remove temporarily (four days to two weeks depending on which book you read) any foods from your child's diet that you suspect may be causing problems. Stick to this pared down diet for several days. If food intolerance/allergy is an issue, you should see an improvement in your child, although behavior may worsen briefly. Then, add the foods back in one at a time and note any changes, every couple of days, so that you don't get confused over which foods may be causing a reaction. Any food reintroduced should be given on an empty stomach and in a fairly unadulterated form. For more guidance, any library should have allergy books that contain elimination diets. As always, you should consult your doctor before undertaking any diet.

Note: be *careful* about any foods that you suspect are true allergies (producing hives, swelling, rashes, asthma or the like). Those should not be added back in at all and you should consult an allergist. This is especially true for peanut allergy, which can be quite severe or even fatal.

Q. I'd heard that gluten-free and casein-free diets are very difficult and expensive. Where do I begin?

You can begin at the high end or the low end of this question. If you have access to a lab and your budget allows, you can pay for lab tests and get some definitive answers. See Appendix 7 for testing facilities. Then if the test results are positive, you will know what kind of a diet your child needs. At that point, you can research how to do the very best diet. There are websites, books, food outlets, newsletters, and entire organizations to provide support.

Or, you can begin at the low end, like we did. Do an elimination diet, using a food journal, starting with the casein issue first (since it is an easier diet than the gluten-free one). Feed your child only basic (scratch cooking) non-dairy foods. If dairy is causing problems, you should begin to see some effects in a few days. (Sometimes there is a worsening of behavior first for a few days before it gets better.) If you can see your child improving on the no-dairy diet, you do not need to have formal testing done because you already have your answer. For long-term and stringent adherence to a casein-free diet, you will want to do further research. There are often dairy products hidden in foods you might not suspect, such as hot dogs and bread. The right support will tell you which brands are OK and which are not. For what it's worth, I never worried about the tiny amounts that might be hidden here and there. Most of my cooking was from scratch so I knew most everything that was in what John ate. Consequently, I never needed to buy special brands of anything nor had to visit health stores. John made major improvements in this manner. Some people find that the diet needs to be as close to a hundred per cent dairy-free as humanly possible and I have no reason to doubt parents who tell me this. For their children, that is probably true. I can only tell you that my somewhat less stringent method (maybe 95 per cent compliance) worked for us. Therefore, even if you have no money for lab tests, or have no access to expensive specialty foods, I can attest that a casein-free diet is still doable and worth trying.

Going without wheat and most other grains (gluten-free) is tougher. It takes a longer time on the diet to see results. Because of the difficulty, you may want to pay for the test rather than following a rather challenging diet for several months only to discover that it is not an issue after all. However, again, if you do not have access or money for a test, you can still do the diet. Finding gluten-free bread and pasta is usually a priority, so locating a satisfactory source of those items will make things easier. Again, connecting with good support will furnish you with recipes, food outlets, and so forth, to make this more of an adventure and less of an ordeal.

Q. I've heard of other lab tests to do. Which are beneficial?

There is an organization called Defeat Autism Now (DAN), which has developed a protocol for testing. The organization also provides a list of doctors (located throughout the United States and also other countries) who will follow this protocol and will work with you to get all the testing done. Besides the gluten and casein issues, many other issues are looked at (vitamin and mineral levels, and so forth). I do not have personal experience with it, however.

Throughout all of your explorations, keep in mind that the diet and vitamin issues appear to be relevant for only one subset of the autistic population. Some families have spent a lot of money on lab tests only to find out that their answers did not lie in that direction at all. If I had the money and access to do all the testing, I probably would. If I couldn't go that route, I would not let that stop me from seeing how far I could get with a food journal, home cooking, and some basic vitamins. If these things don't work, then you haven't lost anything and have saved yourself the expense of a lot of tests that would have been negative. If they do work, you will have some good answers.

Chapter 10
Final Thoughts

There are just a few more topics that didn't get covered elsewhere in the book.

Costs, in case you are curious

For some reason, people find it politically incorrect to discuss money when it comes to their kids' needs. I think it is important to discuss it. We have a finite amount of the stuff and when we're out, we're out. At this very moment, I know parents too broke to pick up their kids' medications or pay the physical therapist. It's important for planning purposes too, so you can figure out how to get the most benefit out of your dollar; and I think it's important because the number one cause of divorce is money and the divorce rate in families with special needs kids is very high. Maybe there's a connection. People can only take so much stress.

(These figures are in US dollars, rounded, and may vary across the country, and of course in other countries.)

- Physical therapy – $100–175 per one hour private session

- Psychologist – $115 / 50 minutes

- Social skills group – $240 for 8 sessions, 90 minutes each

- Autism evaluation from specialist – $800–1200

- Full autism clinic evaluation – $2000–4000

- Special needs summer camp – $400–1000 / week

- Special education lawyer – $150 / hour
- Alphasmart Keyboard – $200
- Medication for ADD – $80 / month
- Private tutor – $20 / hour
- Weighted blanket – $200
- Mega-vitamins – $49 / 3-month supply
- ELISA food screen – $200–350 / 93 foods tested
- Gluten/casein peptide test – $99
- Expert witness for court (doctor) – $1000
- Retainer for appeal hearing – $750

Some behavioral ideas that have been helpful

The list below represents some of the many techniques I've used over the years. Each worked, in its own way (at least once!). Seriously, many folks have found these techniques helpful. Notice that not one of them involves punishing:

1. Keep stress low and avoid letting your child feel overwhelmed.

2. Work on the behavior (the *what*) rather than obsessing on the emotional side (the *why*). We parents seem to want our kids to 'just know' what they should and shouldn't do, but we need to get over this. We can't wish intuition into existence: we can set the rules and educate. When good things follow (i.e. our kids get compliments or rewards for their improved behavior), I think they may start to internalize the *why* of it.

3. Focus on the good. I pass out compliments and tell my kids what I'm proud of.

4. Distract. Rather than focusing on bad behavior, which I think John tends to obsess on if I focus on it, I get him

involved in other things. If he starts to bug his brother, I call him out to the kitchen to have him taste the spaghetti sauce or I give him a job to do.

5.   I give space and time to chill out. When John was little, the room he shared with his brother was always in chaos. When he got his own room, I left most of the toys in his brother's room (John didn't play with many of them anyway) and I presented him with a fairly sparse, clean room and told him it was *his* to make the way he liked it. He declined my offer to decorate, and I discovered that what he liked was order. He lined up shoes, books, etc. and keeps his room barracks neat. He also keeps it dark with a blanket over the window. I know this is not exactly a behavior topic, but I wonder how many years he felt overwhelmed living in a messy room with someone else. Giving him control over his environment has been important to his mood.

6.   Occasionally I draw a line in the sand. When we were homeschooling and my son went through a period at age eight of refusing to do even a small amount of work, I set a timer and told him I expected ten minutes of solid work on a certain thing. When he fussed, I said fine, but when you're done fussing, I will reset the timer and expect ten minutes of good work. We did this only a few (very hard!) times before he did his ten minutes. I think you have to be careful to make sure you're asking for something you *know* your child can do (avoid Swahili-syndrome – see p.20), but I think it's OK to reinforce the idea that sometimes we have to do things we don't want to, and plowing through is the best way to get it done.

7.   Pre-plan to avoid problems. One day before a visit to a friend's for coffee, I told my son, 'Mrs. C. really likes you. She doesn't like it when *some* kids come over and run all

over the place and chase the cat and grab cookies or toys without asking, but she is pretty sure that when *you* come you will play quietly and ask nicely for things and pet the cat nicely.' Now, Mrs. C. really did like John, but the rest of the story was conjecture. We had never been to her house before. And I was worried John would be too stimulated and act up, but he maintained good behavior that time and every time we visited her house.

At the time, I thought the success came from him having the pleasure of being rewarded with kind words, but now I believe that I had accidentally fallen into the power of using a social story. A simple, short and positive story gave him important clues and perhaps eased his anxiety about what the trip would be like (there will be toys, a snack, a cat, and he knew what the expectations were). The term 'social story' has come to mean a special sort of story that follows a set of guidelines and is very instructive and non-threatening to the child. Carol Gray originated them as a special technique. You can read more about them and see an example at

http://www.autism.org/stories.html

8.   Try a behavior chart. This was helpful to get John through his morning routine when he was little. Charts don't always work for kids with Asperger Syndrome because our kids can obsess about the chart or get overanxious, or even meltdown over the anxiety of reaching the goal or not. If it works for your child, though, that's great. I do think the pictorial value is good.

9.   In recent years I have learned of the power of visual cues (pictures and symbols, etc.). A personal friend has been homeschooling for a couple of years and wrote me the other day that she'd been to a workshop that talked about visual cues. She came home and applied it to her homeschooling efforts. She drew pictures as she talked

and her daughter became *so* excited and involved she couldn't believe it. She then drew a picture for each activity she planned for the day and her daughter was more compliant than she had ever seen her. It has revolutionalized her approach.

10. Use other people to illustrate good and bad behavior. This is less confrontative than talking about the child's own behavior. By simply pointing out a screaming child who won't come out of the ball pit at McDonald's, for example, my son could see for himself what poor behavior looked like.

11. Change one's way of looking at outings. I used to expect John to endure several errands with the promise of a treat for good behavior at the end. It was a typical mom thing to do but with kids with Asperger Syndrome, it rarely works. One day, I reversed things. Instead of telling him we were picking up groceries and maybe a treat if he were good, I told him we were going to the grocery store to get him a treat. And that was our focus of the trip, however I also had time to get whatever I needed and he was happy and compliant the whole time. I'm not sure why this worked. Was it because he didn't have to wonder if he would get a treat or not? Was it because he felt comfortable having my attention and more in control? I don't know, but it worked.

12. Start small and build up. It seemed for a while that every trip to the grocery store ended in a meltdown so I determined that we needed to break this cycle. I concentrated on taking John to the grocery store and staying a couple of minutes. Then I praised how he had made it through the store without a single problem. I wanted him to know that he could do it as a confidence builder, and also to break the thought pattern in his head that shopping trip = meltdown.

13. Use your words. I have learned to express my own anger or annoyance using words instead of expecting John to read my face.

14. Do use 'do' language. Telling my son what to do rather than what not to do is much more positive and much more informative.

15. Rehearse. At home we have rehearsed things like walking through a door without banging it on someone, shaking hands, eating at the table, reacting to a bully, etc.

16. Do not assume that your child is manipulating. Assume that he doesn't understand, or can't control himself due to being too stimulated or frustrated.

17. Schedule it. Even distasteful activities are better tolerated when they are on a calendar or schedule. That makes them visual, scheduled and able to be anticipated (no surprise), and it feels like a rule.

18. Encourage your kids to stretch and grow, but don't push them over the edge. If they tell you something is too much, try again some other day.

Some pertinent quotes

You've heard me talk long enough, so I will close with some quotes that I hope you will find as empowering as I do.

> It does not matter how slowly you go, so long as you do not stop. (Confucius)

> Genius is one per cent inspiration and ninety-nine per cent perspiration. (Thomas Edison)

> Opportunity is missed by most people because it is dressed in overalls and looks like work. (Thomas Edison)

Sometimes a scream is better than a thesis. (Ralph Waldo Emerson)

Well done is better than well said. (Benjamin Franklin)

The only way round is through. (Robert Frost)

Never mistake motion for action. (Ernest Hemingway)

A committee is a thing which takes a week to do what one good man can do in an hour. (Elbert Hubbard)

Men have become tools of their tools. (Henry David Thoreau)

Conclusion

By now you should see that Asperger Syndrome has its difficulties and challenges but also its gifts. There is much that can be done to help the child with Asperger Syndrome to feel better living in his own skin and to cope better in society, even as he retains his lifelong unique way of looking at the world.

Of those things that parents can do to help their kids, I've talked about the ones that we used and a few that worked for other people. Coincidentally, they are techniques that can be done anywhere, and that take little or no money. That is not to say they are free. Love, time and effort are required, the most precious things we can give to any child.

John is nearly grown to adulthood and about to take on the world. He is a wonderful young man ready and able to continue on his own path now. It's been an amazing journey for both of us, and I wouldn't have missed it for the world.

As for you, the reader, I hope my tale has helped to empower you and to convince you that parents can trust their instincts. You know your child, so just start where your child is. He will lead the way. Help your child succeed and then build on each success. The hitchhiker's journey has no short cuts but it's a great trip, full of surprises and new vistas. Fear not, just put one foot in front of the other. Don't let the sun go down today without taking some steps – play with your child, ask him what he's thinking, share a story or a joke, talk about the big important issues and the little ones, or just spend some time working quietly side by side. Your child does not need pills or classes or fancy programs nearly as much as he needs you.

Diagnostic Criteria

The most commonly used diagnostics criteria should be able to be found at your doctor's office or the local library. Pertinent excerpts are also sometimes found on the web. You might try www.mentalhealth.com or http://autism.about.com/cs/diagnostics/index.htm

DSM-IV

Diagnosis and Statistical Manual for Mental Disorders, Forth Edition.

Published in 1994 by the American Psychiatric Association American Psychiatric Press. ISBN 0 89042 062 9

ICD-10 (World Health Organisation, 1993)

International Statistical Classification of Diseases and Related Health Problems, tenth revision.

Vol 1: ISBN 9 24154 419 8
Vol 2: ISBN 9 24154 420 1
Vol 3: ISBN 9 24154 421

In addition, Tony Attwood's excelent book *Asperger Syndrome: A Guide for Parents andProfessionals* contains diagnostics criteria from the above sources, as well as critera by Gillberg and Gillberg, and also the criteria from Szatmari, Bremner and Nagy. See reference section for further information on this book.

Dr Attwood is also co-author of the Australian Scale for Asperger Syndrome and has given me permission to reprint it below.

A. Social and emotional abilities

1. Does the child lack an understanding of how to play with other children? For example, unaware of the unwritten rules of social play.

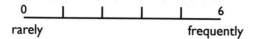

0   6
rarely   frequently

2. When free to play with other children such as school lunchtime, does the child avoid social contact with them? For example, finds a secluded place or goes to the library.

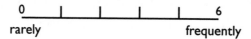

0   6
rarely   frequently

3. Does the child appear unaware of social conventions or codes of conduct and make inappropriate actions and comments? For example, making a personal comment to someone but the child seems unaware how the comment could offend.

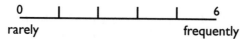

0   6
rarely   frequently

4. Does the child lack empathy, i.e. the intuitive understanding of another person's feelings? For example, not realizing an apology would help the other person feel better.

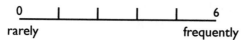

0   6
rarely   frequently

5. Does the child seem to expect other people to know their thoughts, experiences and opinions? For example, not realizing you could not know about something because you were not with the child at the time.

0   6
rarely   frequently

6. Does the child need an excessive amount of reassurance, especially if things are changed or go wrong?

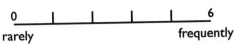

7. Does the child lack subtlety in their expression of emotion? For example, the child shows distress or affection out of proportion to the situation.

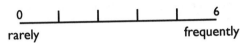

8. Does the child lack precision in their expression of emotion? For example, not understanding the levels of emotional expression appropriate for different people.

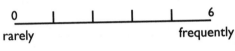

9. Is the child not interested in participating in competitive sports, games and activities?

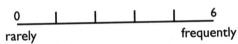

10. Is the child indifferent to peer pressure? For example, does not follow the latest craze in toys or clothes.

B. Communication skills

11. Does the child take a literal interpretation of comments? For example, is confused by phrases such as 'pull your socks up', 'looks can kill' or 'hop on the scales'.

12. Does the child have an unusual tone of voice? For example, the child seems to have a 'foreign' accent or monotone that lacks emphasis on key words.

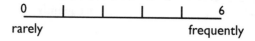

0   6
rarely   frequently

13. When talking to the child does he or she appear uninterested in your side of the conversation? For example, not asking about or commenting on your thoughts or opinions on the topic.

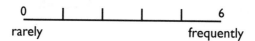

0   6
rarely   frequently

14. When in a conversation, does the child tend to use less eye contact than you would expect?

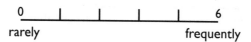

0   6
rarely   frequently

15. Is the child's speech over-precise or pedantic? For example, talks in a formal way or like a walking dictionary.

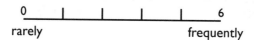

0   6
rarely   frequently

16. Does the child have problems repairing a conversation? For example, when the child is confused, he or she does not ask for clarification but simply switches to a familiar topic, or takes ages to think of a reply.

0   6
rarely   frequently

C. Cognitive skills

17. Does the child read books primarily for information, not seeming to be interested in fictional works? For example, being an avid reader of encyclopedias and science books but not keen on adventure stories.

18. Does the child have an exceptional long-term memory for events and facts? For example, remembering the neighbor's car registration of several years ago, or clearly recalling scenes that happened many years ago.

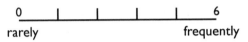

19. Does the child lack social imaginative play? For example, other children are not included in the child's imaginary games or the child is confused by the pretend games of other children.

D. Specific interests

20. Is the child fascinated by a particular topic and avidly collects information or statistics on that interest? For example, the child becomes a walking encyclopedia of knowledge on vehicles, maps or league tables.

21. Does the child become unduly upset by changes in routine or expectation? For example, is distressed by going to school by a different route?

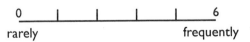

22. Does the child develop elaborate routines or rituals that must be completed? For example, lining up toys before going to bed.

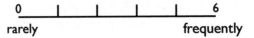

0 | | | | 6

rarely   frequently

E. Movement Skills

23. Does the child have poor motor coordination? For example, is not skilled at catching a ball.

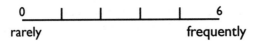

0 | | | | 6

rarely   frequently

24. Does the child have an odd gait when running?

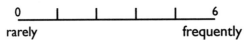

0 | | | | 6

rarely   frequently

F. Other characteristics

For this section, tick whether the child has shown any of the following characteristics:

(a) Unusual fear or distress due to:

- ordinary sounds, e.g. electrical appliances
- light touch on skin or scalp
- wearing particular items of clothing
- unexpected noises
- seeing certain objects
- noisy, crowded places, e.g. supermarkets

(b) A tendency to flap or rock when excited or distressed

(c) A lack of sensitivity to low levels of pain

(d) Late in acquiring speech

(e) Unusual facial grimaces or tics

If the answer is yes to the majority of the questions in the scale, and the rating was between two and six (i.e. conspicuously above the normal range), it does not automatically imply the child has Asperger Syndrome. However, it is a possibility and a referral for a diagnostic assessment is warranted (Attwood 1998, pp. 17–19).

Asperger Syndrome Resources

United States
General info

Autism Society of America (ASA)
7910 Woodmont Avenue, Suite 300
Bethesda, MD 20814–3015, USA
Tel: 800 3AUTISM or 301 657 0881
http://www.autism-society.org

On-Line Asperger Information and Support (OASIS)
http://www.udel.edu/bkirby/asperger/

Asperger Syndrome Coalition of the US (ASC-US)
ASC-US, Inc.
PO Box 49267
Jacksonville Beach, FL 32240–9267, USA
Email: info@asc-us.org
http://www.asperger.org/

National Information Center for Children and Youth
with Disabilities (NICHCY)
Box 1492
Washington, DC 20013–1492, USA
Tel: 800 659 0285
http://www.nichcy.org/index.html

Advocacy and Legal

Individuals with Disabilities Education Act (IDEA) 1997
To obtain a hard copy, contact your state's Department
of Education or see
http://home1.gte.net/insource/IDEA97.htm

Council of Parent Attorneys and Advocates (COPAA)
PO Box 81 – 7327, Hollywood, FL 33081–0327, USA
Tel: 954 966 4489
Email: copaa@copaa.net
http://www.copaa.net

Wrightslaw
http://www.wrightslaw.com
Email: webmaster@wrightslaw.com
Note: this site, while commercial, provides useful articles on special
education law.

Amicus for Children, Inc.
1023 Old Swede Road
Douglassville, PA 19518, USA
Tel: 610 689 4226
Email: amicusforchildren@att.net
http://www.amicusforchildren.org/
This is a non-profit charity to help parents advocate.

Respite

National Respite Locator Service
ARCH National Respite Network and Resource Center
Chapel Hill Training-Outreach Project
800 Eastowne Drive, Suite 105
Chapel Hill, NC 27514, USA
http://www.chtop.com/locator.htm

IEP guidance

Individualized Education Program (IEP) Guide
ED Pubs
Editorial Publications Center
US Department of Education
PO Box 1398
Jessup, MD 20794–1398, USA
Tel: 877 4 ED PUBS
http://www.ed.gov/offices/OSERS/OSEP/IEP_Guide/

United Kingdom

General Info

National Autistic Society (NAS)
393 City Road
London EC1V 1NG, UK
Autism HelpLine 0870 600 8585
Tel: 020 7833 2299
Email: nas@nas.org.uk
http://www.oneworld.org/autism_uk

Respite

National Autistic Society's Befriending Scheme
Volunteers Manager UK
NAS Volunteering Network
4th Floor Castle Heights
72 Maid Marian Way
Nottingham NG1 6BJ, UK
Tel: 0115 911 3369
Email: crintoul@nas.org.uk
http://www.oneworld.org/autism_uk/help/befriend.html

Advocacy and Legal

Advocacy Service Manager
National Autistic Society
393 City Road
London EC1V 1NG, UK
Education Advocacy Line: 0800 358 8667
Tribunal Support Scheme: 0800 358 8668
Email: advocacy@nas.org.uk

Action ASD
Assessments and Special Educational Needs (SEN) Statements Info
Tel: 01706 222657
Email: info@actionasd.org.uk
http://www/actionasd.org.uk/Education.html
This is a local Lancashire support group with helpful articles.

For a free parents' booklet on SENs from the UK Department for
Education and Employment (DfEE)
Tel: 0845 6022260
Download the SEN guide at:
http://www.dfee.gov.uk/sen/senguide.htm
Download the Tribunal guide at:
http://www.dfee.gov.uk/sen/sentrib.htm

Independent Panel for Special Educational Advice (IPSEA)
6 Carlow Mews
Woodbridge
Suffolk IP12 1DH, UK
Tel: helpline 0800 0184016 or 01394 382814
Tel: general enquiries 01394 380518
http://www.ipsea.org.uk

Canada

General Info

Child and Family Canada
http://www.cfc-efc.ca/
Has an online library of 1300 documents on various
child development issues.

Autism Society of Ontario
1 Greensboro Drive, Suite 306
Etobicoke, Ontario M9W 1C8, Canada
Tel: 416 246 9592
Email: mail@autismsociety.on.ca
http://www.autismsociety.on.ca/

Autism Society Manitoba
825 Sherbrook Street
Winnipeg
Manitoba
R3A 1M5, Canada
Tel: 204 783 9563
Email: asm@escape.ca
http://www.enable.mb.ca/enable/asm/

Advocacy and Legal

Canadian Association for Community Living
Kinsmen Building
York University
4700 Keele Street
Toronto, Ontario M3J 1P3, Canada
Tel: 416 661 9611
Email: info@cacl.ca
http://www.cacl.ca/english/index.html

B.C. Self-Advocacy Foundation
3rd Floor, 30 East Sixth Avenue
Vancouver, BC V5T 4P4, Canada
Tel: 604 875 1119
Email: gschiller@bacl.org
http://www.vcn.bc.ca/bacl/bcsaf.htm

Australia

General Info

Autism Victoria
PO Box 235
Ashburton
Victoria 3147, Australia
Tel: 03 9885 0533
Email: autismav@vicnet.net.au
http://home.vicnet.net.au/~autism/

Autism Association Queensland, Inc.
PO Box 363 Sunnybank
Queensland 4109, Australia
Tel: 07 3273 0000
Email: mailbox@autismqld.asn.au
http://www.uq.net.au/~zzacook/aaq/

Autism Association of South Australia
PO Box 339
Fullerton, SA 5063, Australia
Tel: 08 8379 6976
Email: aasa@adelaide.on.net
http://www.span.com.au/autism/

Respite

> Respite Centre
> 3 Constellation Way
> Wynnum, Queensland, Australia
> Tel: 07 3348 2960
>
> Also see DIAL and DIRC listings below.

Advocacy and Legal

> Queensland Disability Information and Awareness Line (DIAL)
> 3rd Floor 75 Williams Street
> Brisbane, Queensland, Australia
> Tel: 07 3224 8444 or 1800 177 120
> Email: dial@disability.qld.gov.au
>
> Disability Information and Resource Centre (DIRC) South Australia
> 195 Gilles Street
> Adelaide, South Australia 5000, Australia
> Tel: 08 8223 7522
> Email: dirc@dircsa.org.au
> http://www.dircsa.org.au/pub/docs/links.htm#Index
> An excellent resource with links to agencies throughout Australia.

Social Skills

Children with Asperger Syndrome learn social skills intellectually rather than intuitively. Conscious and helpful teaching is key.

The items below are some topics to consider. As for how to use them, consider these ways:

1. Homeschooling.

2. Regular school: give to teachers' conferences or use it as a memory jog to insert concrete goals into school contracts.

3. With specialists: a speech therapist might be asked to work with your child but have no prior experience with Asperger Syndrome.

4. To boost parenting: let the list of social skills remind you of the challenges your child faces. It may help improve your patience and maintain a positive rather than punitive mindset.

5. In the community: use it to guide a social skills 'club'.

One final note: It's easy (but a trap!) to turn social skill goals into a negative checklist of behaviors to be corrected. Don't fall for this. The idea is NOT to make life easier for the parent. The idea is to make life easier for the child. Try to make it fun using games, charades, jokes, cartoons, movies, storybooks, field trips, etc.

1. What is a friend?

Do they give things to you? Share with you? Do they take turns with you? Offer to help you? Walk with you?

2. What is *not* a friend?

Do they make fun of you? Hurt you? Do they try to make you do bad things? Do they take things from you?

3. Making a friend

Making a friendly face – what does it look like? How do we sit if we want to make friends?

4. Making friendly conversation

What topics might be good or not so good? How do we tell if someone wants to be friends? What are some nice greetings? What are some nice topics? What happens if the other person doesn't like our topic? What is a nice way to end a conversation? Eye contact – why do we look at people? Conversational turn-taking (note: passing around a conversational ball or talking stick is useful to show taking turns).

5. Being in a group

Teamwork – what is a team? Can everybody be in charge? What can you do if everyone has a different idea on what to do? What should we do if we want to join into a group? Should we try to lead the group right away? Playing fair, playing by rules, making up new rules, taking turns, playing board games, working cooperatively. Building something together, making sure everyone participates.

6. Winning and losing

Learning to lose – learning to say 'Good game!' and 'Better luck next time.' Learning to win – learning to say 'You played well' and 'Thanks for the great game.' Shaking hands, thumbs up, patting someone on the back.

7. Ownership and respecting people's things

Who owns it? If you find it, is it yours? Asking to borrow something. How long do you keep it? Returning something you borrowed. Asking someone else to bring something back.

8. Voices

Indoor voices and outdoor voices. How to whisper. When to whisper.

9. Body space

Hugs – too tight? Should you ask first? Whom may you hug? The mailman? A stranger? How long do we hug? Who might hug you? What are some occasions you might hug or be hugged? Will you be warned?

10. Emotions

What does happy look like? Angry? Surprised? Afraid? Confused? Embarrassed? Excited? Worried? Sad? Proud? Startled? Make each of those faces. See someone make a face and guess the emotion. Identify magazine pictures.

11. Lying

What is lying? Fact versus opinion. If someone says the cookie tastes good, and you taste it and it doesn't, was that person lying? If someone makes up a silly ghost story, is that lying? Pretend play – fantasy versus real.

12. Things that upset us

Changing situations. Weather – it might rain on our picnic. Plans – we wanted to go see a special movie, but the theatre isn't showing it anymore.

13. Waiting

Waiting in line – where might we have to wait in line (grocery store, movies, amusement parks)? Will getting upset help? What *will* help us to wait?

14. Handling upset

Anger – what does it look and feel like? Using words instead of actions. What words? Expressing anger, asking for help. Calming techniques – slow breathing; counting to ten; taking a walk; going someplace quiet.

15. Being lost or losing things

How can we keep from getting lost? What should we do if we do become lost? What are some things that we might lose? What are things we can do to prevent it?

16. Money

How do we know what something costs? What do we do if we don't have enough money for something? Should we give people money if they ask for it?

17. Clothes

Dressing for the weather. Why do we change clothes every day?

18. Fire and smoke

Fire alarm rings? What does it sound like? What does it mean? When will it stop? What should we do?

19. Smoke alarm?

Same as above.

20. Being on the bus

Do we sit or stand? Talk to driver? Open windows? Throw things out? What happens if the bus doesn't turn on the road we think he should? Why does a bus just sit there and wait sometimes?

21. Public bathrooms

What might be different from your home bathroom? Why is it extra noisy? Why so many toilets? Why hand dryers? Why does it smell different? Especially good or bad?

22. Ordering food

So many choices! Small, medium, large, what might be asked. What if they do not have what you order? What if you want a burger but it's still breakfast time?

23. Making choices

There is no wrong answer (flavors of ice-cream, which dessert). A choice means any answer is good. If we choose one, we can't have the other – but next time we can change our choice. What if we don't like what we choose?

24. Special places

- ○ Movies (cinema): what if the movie is too long or too scary or too loud? Toilets. Treats. Sitting still. Whispering.
- ○ Bowling: rules, safety, noises, smell, different shoes.
- ○ Swimming: changing clothes, sun lotion. Obeying the lifeguard, safety.
- ○ Shopping: carts (trolleys), holding hands, what you can touch.
- ○ Museums: staying behind ropes. Look, don't touch.
- ○ Library: whisper, walk, so many choices! How to find a particular book, what if they don't have it?
- ○ Park: safety, trying new things, taking turns, being brave; taking a rest.
- ○ Fences, gates, boundaries: what they are for.
- ○ A friend's house: ringing the doorbell and waiting, what rooms are OK, asking for drinks, opening cupboards, trying out toys, etc.

25. Hygiene

- ○ Nose blowing – how to do it? Practice.
- ○ Sneezing/coughing – cover the mouth.

- ○ Washing – proper way to wash. Why we wash.

26. Phone skills
- ○ Calling someone – greeting, identifying oneself, asking for someone, thanking them. Leaving a message.
- ○ Answering the phone – only if mom or dad wants us to, how to answer, how to take down a message.

27. Empathy/Theory of Mind
What are some clues to how someone feels? What does that other person know? Did they see the same film you did? When you started talking about 'him', did you tell the other person who that 'him' was? Tell who, where, what, when, etc.

28. Understanding expressions
See Idioms (Appendix 4).

29. Food issues
Table manners. Serving ourselves. How much is OK? Can you ask for seconds? Putting more than one thing on a plate at a time. Keeping things on the plate. Using the napkin. Practice with fork, knife, and spoon. Cutting things or asking for help. Playing with food. How do you let people know that you are full or do not want any more or don't like something? Saying nice things about dinner. What can we do at the table? (Sing? Crawl under it? Throw things? Talk? Tell jokes?)

30. Cars
Seatbelts. Parking lot (car park) safety. Crossing the street, traffic lights, noisy trucks, car horns. Sounds and smells.

31. Dealing with special people
Babies – should we pick them up? Give them things? Throw them a ball? Push the pram? Old people – should we jump on them? Tell them they look old? What kinds of things are good to do around older people?

32. Dealing with animals
Will they bite? Do you tease them? Take their things? Feed them? How to treat them.

33. Elevators (lifts), escalators

Is it safe? How long is the ride? Which buttons? Will the doors squish us? Getting on and off. Will it speed up?

34. Special occasions

Birthdays – someone else's? Our own? Christmas or other holidays – special events, noise, what to expect.

35. Body movements

Going through a door politely without slamming it on someone. Shaking hands. Pointing a finger. When is it OK? Following a pointing finger with your eyes.

36. Mistakes

Is it OK to make mistakes? Should we laugh at someone's mistake? What if someone laughs at our mistake? What if it really *is* funny? Is it OK to not be good at something? Is it OK to try something we never did before? Is it OK to ask how to do something, or to say 'I don't know how'?

In some ways, everything seems like a social skill, so it's easy for this list to swell. Still, I hope it's been helpful for you to see what one parent thinks of in the area of social skills. Best of luck as you devise your own list.

Idioms

All bark and no bite
All eyes up front
Are you up for it?
At my wit's end
At the end of my rope
Back to square one
Bad apple
Bad seed
Birds of a feather
Burning the candle at both ends
Buy a clue
Call someone on the carpet
Carry on
Champing at the bit
Cheeky
Chill out
Chuck a wobbly (Aus)
Combing through my notes
Cop out
Couch potato
Crocodile tears
Cry wolf
Cut someone a break
Dark cloud on the horizon
Dark look
Dirty look
Don't count your chickens
Don't push it
Don't push my buttons
Don't put words in my mouth
Don't rock the boat
Don't yank my chain
Double-edged sword

Drop your eyes
Dropping a hint
Eagle-eye
Eat your heart out
Elbow-grease
Fast-burner
First cab off the rank (Aus)
Fix your gaze
Flu shot (Aus) / flu jab (UK)
Frog in your throat
Gag order
Get a grip
Get one's nose out of joint
Get your kicks
Give her a hand
Give in
Give out
Give them a big hand!
Give up
Glass is half empty
Glass jaw
Glued to the TV
Gobsmacked (UK)
Gun shy
Have a try (US) / have a go (Aus)
Have your cake and eat it too
Head in the sand
He can't carry it off
He's green
Hit the nail on the head
Hop to it
In a funk
I've got your number

John Doe
John Q. Public
Johnny-come-lately
Jump right on it
Keep your eyeballs peeled
Keep your shirt on
Kick someone out
Kick the bucket
Lend me a hand
Lend me your ear
Let the cat out of the bag
Lift your spirits
Like a chicken with your head cut off
Like a cut snake (Aus)
Like water off a duck
Loan shark
Lost in thought
Lower your voice
Lucky stiff
Mary Sunshine
May I have your name?
Mutton dressed as lamb (UK, Aus)
Nose up in the air
Off-base
On the wrong side of the bed
Paint yourself into a corner
Pot luck (US) / plate dinner (Aus)
Pull any punches
Pull your leg
Put a sock in it
Put on your thinking cap
Put some wellie into it (UK)
Raise a question
Raise your voice
Rat on someone
Read between the lines
Read someone's face
Read the fine print
Roll with the punches
Rub someone the wrong way
Scream your head off

Seven ways to Sunday
Shattered
She won't stand for it
Silver lining
Sink your teeth into it
Sit down
Sit up
Skin and bones
Sleep on it
Smell a rat
Smell trouble
Smoko (Aus)
Sour grapes
Splitting hairs
Spot something
Standing order
Stay on your toes
Stick to it
Stick together
Stop on a dime (US)
Take a powder
Take a stab at
Take for granted
That takes guts
The cat's got your tongue
Thick-skinned or thin-skinned
Throw a fit
Throw someone a look
Tie one on
Turn the other cheek
Uncle Sam
Under his thumb
Under the table
Up a creek without a paddle
Up a tree
Wear your heart on your sleeve
Wet behind the ears
What are you trying to pull?
What does it stand for?
Wrap it up
You have a lot on your plate

Fifty-five Ways to Save Money

1. Sell your most expensive car. Buy second-hand or do without a second car.
2. Pay cash for everything or pay off credit cards in full each month.
3. Clip credit cards if you are tempted to spend too much.
4. Pay all bills on time. Pay off more than the minimum amount required.
5. Cancel magazine subscriptions and book or record clubs.
6. Cancel premium cable channels (or cable TV in general).
7. Cancel appointments for luxury items – getting nails done, massages.
8. Give up those daily frills – that latte, donut, candy bar or newspaper.
9. Don't use cellular phones. Cancel phone options on your regular phone.
10. Shop around for insurance, telephone companies, and Internet service providers.
11. Don't buy from door-to-door salespeople or over the phone.
12. Revise family vacations. Go on day trips or camping trips instead.
13. Drive past fast food outlets.
14. Make some of the gifts you give.
15. Write letters or use email rather than long distance telephone.
16. Throw out catalogs unread.
17. Shop at yard sales and thrift shops.
18. Buy ahead (this winter for next winter).
19. Drink more water and less soda. Cut down on junk food.
20. Make a garden. Trade vegetables with neighbors.
21. Shop for groceries using a list.
22. Have kids buy treats with their own money. This cures the 'I wants.'
23. Learn to make convenience items from scratch – pizzas, sauces, etc.
24. Buy staples in bulk.
25. Identify cheapest family dinner favorites and serve more often.

26. Find cheap hobbies that require minimal equipment.

27. Play board games instead of going to the movies.

28. Wear extra layers and turn down the thermostat.

29. Check your house insulation.

30. Turn off lights. Charge your kids a fee every time you find a light left on.

31. Get a fan and turn off the air conditioning.

32. Make everything you own last longer, and be organized so you know where it is.

33. Cancel health club and country club fees. Exercise at home or on walks.

34. Find free entertainment around town – concerts, lectures, etc.

35. Repair clothing promptly. Work on clothing stains promptly.

36. Buy in season, buy on sale, and stock the freezer and pantry.

37. Save water. Wash only full loads and bathe only dirty people.

38. Trade games, puzzles, and videotapes with the neighbors.

39. Borrow or rent things you need only once (chain saw, post hole digger).

40. Read frugality books (e.g. *Your Money or Your Life* or *Tightwad Gazette*).

41. Haunt frugal-living websites: http://stretcher.com is a favorite.

42. Cut down on gift-giving. A card is often enough.

43. Make your own Christmas cards or send Christmas postcards or email.

44. Cut the kids' hair yourself. Cut your own hair or your spouse's.

45. Try home remedies.

46. Carpool to work or look into using the bus.

47. Bring lunch to work. Avoid vending machines and business lunches.

48. Get friendly with humble foods – rice, oatmeal, the lowly dried bean.

49. Trade babysitting services or join/start a babysitting co-op.

50. Use the library for book, video, and tape rentals.

51. Bike or walk instead of using the car.

52. Combine errands.

53. Keep tires at proper pressure for best mileage.

54. Quit smoking.

55. Quit drinking.

Homeschooling Resources

General info on curricula, unit studies, and lesson plans

http://www.thegateway.org/
http://homeschooling.about.com/education/homeschooling/

Educators Publishing Services
31 Smith Place
Cambridge, MA 02138–1089, USA
Tel: 800 435 7728 or 617 547 6706
Email: epsbooks@epsbooks.com
http://www.epsbooks.com/

John Holt Book Store
2380 Massachusetts Avenue Suite 104
Cambridge, MA 02140–1226, USA
Tel: 888 925 9298 or 617 864 3100
Email: info@HoltGWS.com
http://www.holtgws.com/index.htm

Common Sense Press
8786 Highway 21
Melrose, FL 32666, USA
Tel: 352 475 5757
Email: info@commonsensepress.com
http://www.commonsensepress.com

United States

http://www.home-ed-magazine.com/HSRSC/hsrsc_lws.rgs.html
This site is a state-by-state look-up of legal information.

National Home Education Network (NHEN)
PO Box 41067
Long Beach, CA 90853, USA
Fax: 413 581 1463
Email: info@nhen.org
http://www.nhen.org/

For word processing the Alphasmart keyboard is available from:
Alphasmart Inc.
20400 Stevens Creek Blvd., Suite 300
Cupertino, CA 95014, USA
Tel 888 274 0680 (toll-free)
Email: info@alphasmart.com
Website: http://www.alphasmart.com

Canada

Canadian Home Based Learning Resource Page
http://www.flora.org/homeschool-ca/
The site lists provincial information, support organizations, chat rooms,
among other things.

Association of Canadian Home-Based Education (ACHBE)
C/O J. Campbell
PO Box 34148, RPO Fort Richmond
Winnipeg, Manitoba R3T 5T5, Canada
(Please include SASE or $1.00 if you require a written response.)
Email: homeschool-ca-admin@flora.org
http://www.flora.org/homeschool-ca/achbe/

United Kingdom

Education Otherwise
PO Box 7420
London N9 9SG, UK
Helpline: 0870 730 0074
http://www.education-otherwise.org/
This national charity offers local and national contact for home
educating families.
The website provides access to legal, curriculum and other information.

Home Education Advisory Service
PO Box 98
Welwyn Garden City
Herts
AL8 6AN, UK
Tel: 01707 371854
Email: admin@heas.org.uk
http://www.heas.org.uk

The Learning Store
Unit 2 Zephyr House
Calleva Park
Aldermaston
Berks RG7 8JN, UK
Tel: 0118 970 8704
Email: ingo@learningstore.co.uk
http://www.learningstore.co.uk/

Australia

Australia Homeschooling: A to Z Home's Cool
http://www.gomilpitas.com/homeschooling/regional/australia.htm
This site lists many support groups, legal information, supplies,
curriculum and more.

Homeschooling Supplies
PO Box 688
Werribee, Vic 3030, Australia
Tel: 03 9742 7524
Email: office@homeschooling.com.au
http://www.homeschooling.com.au/

Home Education Research and Legal Information (HERLIN)
Melinda Waddy
54 Pilbara Crescent
Jane Brook WA 6056, Australia
http://www.3dproductions.com.au/legal/index.html

New Zealand

New Zealand Homeschooling: A to Z Home's Cool
http://www.gomilpitas.com/homeschooling/regional/
NewZealand.htm

Homeschooling Federation of New Zealand
P.O Box 41226
St Lukes, Auckland, New Zealand
http://www.homeschooling.org.nz/

New Zealand Home Education
Paula Marriner
PO Box 14
Stratford, New Zealand
Tel: 021 215 9660
http://www.home.school.nz

Dietary Resources

United States

Publications

Rapp, D. (1991) *Is This Your Child? Discovering and Treating Unrecognized Allergies in Children and Adults.* New York, NY: William Morrow.

Biomedical Assessment Options for Children With Autism and Related Problems, (or DAN! Clinical Manual). This is a 40-page manual available from Autism Research Institute (see address below).

Organizations

Autism Research Institute
4182 Adams Avenue, San Diego, CA 92116, USA
Fax: 619 563 6840
http://www.autism.com/ari/danlist.html
This website has lots of interesting reading on possible biochemical connections to autism.

Feingold Association – US (FAUS)
127 East Main Street, No. 106, Riverhead, NY 11901, USA
Or PO Box 6550, Alexandria, VA 22306, USA
http://www.feingold.org/

Vitamin and supplement resources

Kirkman Laboratories
PO Box 1009
Wilsonville, OR 97070, USA
Tel (outside Oregon): 800 245 8282
Tel (Oregon): 503 694 1600
Fax: 503 682 0838
http://www.kirkmanlab.com

Testing resources

The Great Plains Lab (Peptides test for gluten/casein)
9335 West 75th Street
Overland Park, KS 66204, USA
Tel: 913 341 8949
Fax: 913 341 8949
Email: gpl4u@aol.com
http://www.greatplainslaboratory.com

York Nutritional Laboratories, Inc. (IgG ELISA food allergy test)
2700 North 29th Avenue
Hollywood, FL 33020, USA
Tel: 954 920 6577
Fax: 954 927 2332
Email: info@yorkallergyusa.com
www.yorkallergyusa.com

DAN!

This is a group of doctors willing to pursue biochemical issues in
autism. For a listing of their names and locations, consult Autism
Research Institute (contact info above).

Other Information

Bonnie's Vitamin and Diet Regimen
http://www.BonnieGr.com

United Kingdom

Publications

Brostoff, J. and Gamlin, L. (1992) *The Complete Guide to Food Allergy and
Intolerance.* London: Bloomsbury.

Shattock, P. (undated) 'Back to the Future: An Assessment of Some of the
Unorthodox Forms of Biomedical Intervention Currently being Applied to
Autism.'
http://osiris.sunderland.ac.uk/autism/durham95.html

Associations

Allergy-induced Autism (AiA)
AiA New, 8 Hollie Lucas Road
King's Heath
Birmingham B13 0QL, UK
Fax: 01733 331771
http://www.autismmedical.com/

Hyperactive Children's Support Group (HACSG)
71 Whyke Lane
Chichester
West Sussex, PO19 2LD, UK

Testing resources

Dr. Paul Shattock/Paul Whitely (peptide testing for gluten/casein)
University of Sunderland
School of Health Sciences
Sunderland SR2 7EE, UK
Tel: 0191 510 8922
Fax: 0191 567 0420
Email: aru@sunderland.ac.uk
http://osiris.sunderland.ac.uk/autism/index.html

York Nutritional Laboratory (IgG ELISA food allergy test)
Osbaldwick
York YO19 5US, UK
Tel: 01904 410410
Fax: 01904 422200
Email: info@allergy.co.uk
http://www.allergy-testing.com

Australia

Publications

Dengate, S. (1998) *Fed Up: Understanding How Food Affects your Child and What You Can Do About It.* Milsons Point, NSW: Random House Australia.

Royal Prince Alfred Hospital Allergy Unit
Allergy Service, Suite 210, 100 Carillon Avenue
Newtown, NSW 2042, Australia
This unit produces the following publications (or they may be obtained from your dietician):

The Simplified Elimination Diet

Salicylates, Amines and MSG

Friendly Food: the Complete Guide to Avoiding Allergies, Additives and Problem Chemicals

Organizations or associations

FAILSAFE
Produces a newsletter, list of additives to avoid, dieticians/elimination diet help: http://www.ozemail.com.au/~sdengate
This website provides a newsletter, food additives list, and other helps for implementing a low-chemical elimination diet for food intolerance.

Kirkmans Super Nu-Thera®Caplets
These vitamins include a megadose of Vitamin B6 along with Dr. Rimland's recommended amounts of magnesium and several other important vitamins and minerals. Here is what is in an average dose recommended for a child 60–90 pounds in weight:

Vitamin A	*5000 IU*
Vitamin D	*200 IU*
Vitamin C	*500 mg*
Vitamin B1	*15 mg*
Vitamin B2	*15 mg*
Vitamin B6	*500 mg*

Niacinamide	*30 mg*
Vitamin B12	*10 mcg*
Pantothenic Acid	*50 mg*
Vitamin E	*30 IU*
Folic Acid	*400 mcg*
Biotin	*100 mcg*
Magnesium	*250 mg*
Zinc	*10 mg*
Manganese	*1500 mcg*
Calcium	*250 mg*
PABA	*30 mg*
Inositol	*100 mg*
Choline Bitartrate	*100 mg*
Selenium	*50 mcg*

References

American Psychiatric Association (APA) (1994) *Diagnostic and Statistical Manual for Mental Disorder* (DSM-IV). Washington, DC: APA.

Attwood, T. (1998) *Asperger Syndrome: A Guide for Parents and Professionals.* London: Jessica Kingsley Publishers.

Ayres, J. (undated) Sensory Integration International, The Ayres Clinic, Answers to Frequently Asked Questions. http://www.sensoryint.com/faq.html

Beechik, R. (1988) *Easy Start in Arithmetic: Grades K-3.* Arrow Press.

Beechik, R. (1988) *Strong Start in Language: Grades K–3.* Arrow Press.

Beechik, R. (1991) *The Three R's.* Arrow Press.

Beechik, R. (1992) *You Can Teach Your Child Successfully: Grades 4–8.* Arrow Press.

Beechik, R. (1998) *Dr Beechik's Homeschool Answer Book.* Arrow Press.

Brown, C. (ed.) (1998) 'Managed Care Can't Stop Us, Says Sacks.' *Psychiatric News 33*, 7, 3.

Bykowski, M. (1999) 'Typical Pediatrician has 1,500 Patients, Study Finds.' *Pediatric News 33* 3, 8.

Cohen, C. (2000) *And What about College? How Homeschooling Leads to Adnissions to the Best Colleges and Universities,* 2nd end. Cambridge, MA: Holt.

Council for Exceptional Children (2000) 'Conditions for Special Education Teaching.' A recap of the report is available at: http://www.specialednews.com/story%20archive/1000/conditions1031.html

Dacyczyn, A. (1999) '*The Complete Tightwad Gazette: Promoting Thrift as a Viable Alternative Lifestyle.*' New York: Random House.

Dominguez, J. and Robin, V. (1992) *Your Money or Your Life.* New York: Penguin Books.

Enos, G. (ed) (1997) 'Primary Care Physicians have Trouble Accessing MH Services, Study Finds.' *Mental Health Weekly 7*, 40.

Feingold, B. (1975) *Why Your Child is Hyperactive.* New York: Random House.

Flesch, R. (1955) *Why Johnny Can't Read – And What You Can Do About it.* New York: Harper.

Flesch, R. (1981) *Why Jonny Still Can't Read: A New Look at the Scandal of our Schools.* New York: Harper and Row.

Garnett, M.S. and Attwood, A.J. (1995) 'The Australian Scale for Asperger's Syndrome.' Paper presented at the 1995 Australian National Autism Conference, Brisbane, Australia.

Grandin, T. (1995) *Thinking in Pictures.* New York: Random House.

Grossman, J.B., Klin, A., Carter, A.S. and Volkmar, F.R. (2000) 'Verbal Bias in Recognition of Facial Emotions in Children with Asperger Syndrome.' *Journal of Child Psychology and Psychiatry 41,* 3, 369–379.

Healy, J. (1990) *Endangered Minds.* New York: Touchstone.

Hirsch, E.D. (ed) (1989) *A First Dictionary of Cultural Literacy: What Our Children Need to Know.* Boston: Houghton Miffin.

Hirsch, E.D. (ed) (1997) *What Your First Grader Needs to Know.* New York: Doubleday.

Holt, J. (1982) *How Children Fail.* New York: Dell.

Kilgore, C. (1999) 'Child Development: Parents Know Best.' *Pediatric News 33,* 8, 1, 5.

Maguire, E.A., Gadian, D.G., Johnsrude, I.S., Ashburner, J., Frackowiak, R.S. and Frith, C.D. (2000) 'Navigation-related Structural Change in the Hippocampi of Taxi Drivers.' *Proceedings of the National Academy of Science of the United States of America 97,* 8, 4398–4403.

Nowicki, S. and Duke, M. (1992) *Helping the Child Who Doesn't Fit In.* Atlanta, GA: Peachtree.

Picard, M. and Boudreau, C. (1999) 'Characteristics of the Noise Found in Day-care Centers.' *Journal of the Acoustical Society of America 105,* 2, 1127.

Rapp, D. (1991) *Is This your Child?* New York: William Morrow.

Rimland, B. (1987) 'Vitamin B6 (and magnesium) in the Treatment of Autism.' *Autism Research Review International 1,* 4.

Tucker, M. (1998) 'School Nurses Overworked and in Short Supply.' *Pediatric News 32,* 11, 40.

World Health Organization (WHO) (1993) *International Staistical Classification of Diseases and Related Health Problems* (ICD-10). Geneva: WHO.

Zwillich, T. (1999) 'Most Doctors Had Treatment Denials by HMOs.' *Pediatric News 33,* 10, 64.

Index